Seasons of Life
Encouragement for Walking in Faith

Carol A. Wert

Cover Design and Editing by
Stefanie Henne

Author Photography by
Kristin Frantz

© 2021

Thank you to God the Father
for the wonderful gift
He has given me,
putting words into my heart
and allowing me to share them with others.

Thank you to my husband, Michael,
and the rest of my family
for their constant love and support.

Thank you, Stefanie, for your friendship,
your design talent,
and your patient editing.

Thank you, Kristin, for being willing
to trudge through muddy ground
to take photos of me and
for making me look so good!

My heart overflows with gratitude and love
for those already mentioned and
for those who shaped my life,
inspired my steps, and
encouraged my faith -
Daddy, who is still with me,
and Momma, now in Heaven.

This is for all of you and for the glory of God.

*"Now to our God and Father be glory forever and ever.
Amen."*
(Philippians 4:20)

Introduction

We all travel this earth experiencing the seasons of life. Just as in nature, each season is designed with its brilliant colors, diverse paths, storm clouds of different degrees, and sunshine and moonlight to show the paths we trod.

No one season is like another, and no one path is the same as the next. Each experience is woven into the fabric of our stories no matter the depth, width, height, or breadth of the emotions we feel, the thoughts that permeate our minds, or the steps we take. In the end, all things will come together to show the beauty that is born of the joy as well as the ashes and the encouragement that can be found in the journey traveled and the destination reached.

There is an incomparable splendor that shines in a life gracefully journeyed and abundantly lived. Everyone has something to share in the living of their lives that is beneficial to others. Whether the encouragement is that of mountains climbed and rapids crossed or the simple acts of kindness, compassion, and integrity carried out unobtrusively, these acts are meant to be passed to others at different places in their journey. After all, we were not created to be alone but to be in community.

As I compiled the writings for this book, that need for community became even more apparent in our world. Many of these writings were composed in 2018, 2019, and the beginning of 2020. The rest have been written since the world and our country changed so drastically with the spread of Covid-19 and shortly after the calendar turned to 2021. You probably will be able to tell which ones are which as you read them. The sense of community that has always been needed in the world is needed even more desperately now. There are so many who feel isolated and forgotten in these past months. There are so many divisions that need healing.

Another thing you will notice is that seasons in life tend to overlap just as seasons in nature do. The lines are blurred between lessons, grace, thanksgiving, and the like. I believe this is just another of God's perfect tools in orchestrating our lives for our good and His purpose and glory.

I pray that you will find encouragement in these pages. I pray that you will learn that joy resides even in the midst of struggles. I pray that you will find laughter, comfort, and friendship as these writings are shared with you. And then I pray that you will pass them to someone who can find the same in them.

Love and blessings!

Carol

The Season of Lessons to be Learned

Why a Season of Lessons?

The first thing we must accept in life is that there is always something to learn. Not only is there always something to learn, but there is always an experience to be had before learning. It's a vicious circle. We fall into something, (hopefully) learn from it, and move forward only to fall into the next something. It's called growth and maturity. Without it, we would remain just as we are - never changing and never becoming what we were born to be. How disappointing! How sad to know in our hearts we are made for a purpose, but the purpose is never fulfilled because we don't grow. I can only think that would leave a dark abyss in our hearts that can only be lighted and bridged by Divine intervention.

Accept the experiences, the lessons, and the cycle. Look back on your life with each new graduation into the next thing. You'll see the perfect metamorphosis God is working in your life. You will smile and be encouraged to move on in His will to the next step.

We must all remember: The Season of Lessons is unending as long as we travel this earth.

"The LORD foils the plans of the nations; he thwarts the purposes of the peoples. But the plans of the LORD stand firm forever, the purposes of his heart through all generations. Blessed is the nation whose God is the LORD, the people he chose for his inheritance." **(Psalm 33:10-12 NIV)**

A Seasonal Perspective

The weeping cherry tree in our backyard has looked dreary and brown ever since losing the lush green foliage of summer. It's been kind of depressing to look at, and so I've been avoiding turning my eyes in that direction when I leave the house.

That is until yesterday when I had to take the dogs out in the late afternoon. The sun was just beginning to set, and the remaining rays touched the bare twigs and branches of the tree with color. I couldn't help but grab my phone and take a photo. That beautiful color seemed to wind its way through my eyes, around my bones and muscles, and deep into my soul.

The sunlight had turned the indiscriminate greys and browns into pinks. As I looked at the photograph, I noticed the camera saw something that my eyes didn't. The rays hadn't just turned the branches pink - they had made it seem almost as if that pink was dusted with gold. Just to witness this transformation was warming, even breathtaking. Just as the falling of the foliage a month ago indicated the impending change of season to the cold, bleak, and seemingly lifeless winter months, last evening's sunset portrayed the promise of the birth and inevitable full bloom of spring that will have its way at chasing away winter's reign in just a few short months.

The truth is our beloved weeping cherry is not grey and lifeless at all; it is just resting. In its current bleak state, it is preparing for the warmth and beauty it

10

will create on exactly the right springtime day. Were it to constantly portray the gorgeous pink blossoms and lush green foliage, it would eventually spend its energy and truly die. And so, it rests in this season and performs in another.

This is just another in the long line of lessons nature has to teach. Oh, that we were attentive to the teaching! We too have our seasons. There are times our energy overflows and is meant to be spent on the purposes set before us. During those times, the beauty of our spirit committing the task at hand presents itself in beautiful colors of love and kindness. Our hands reach out to touch others with compassion and generosity. Yet were we to try to continue beyond the scope of our energy, we would begin to stumble and perhaps even fail at the task. The beauty of spirit would wither and begin to die; it would be usurped by exhaustion, frustration, and impatience.

We must, like the cherry tree, learn to embrace the down time of the cold seasons in our lives. We must use those seasons to rest, restore, refresh, regain our strength, and realize our purpose. While we long to be all we can be, we must admit that we are human. We have limits to our abilities and energy. They are not unable to be exhausted but must be rebuilt through quiet reflection.

In the times of rest and reflection, it's important to remember that we are not lifeless. The colors of our springtime still shine inside if we take a moment to look deeply within. As rays of light fall upon our tired souls, we will see the tones of pink and gold that promise the beauty of full blossom at exactly the right moment - just like the weeping cherry.

"To everything there is a season, a time for every purpose under heaven: a time to be born and a time to die; a time to plant and a time to pluck what is planted; a time to kill and a time to heal; a time to break down and a time to build up; a time to weep and a time to laugh; a time to mourn and a time to dance; a time to cast away stones and a time to gather stones; a time to embrace and a time to refrain from embracing; a time to gain and a time to lose; a time to keep and a time to throw away; a time to tear and a time to sew; a time to keep silence and a time to speak; a time to love and a time to hate; a time of war and a time of peace."
(Ecclesiastes 3:1-8 NKJV)

Bling!

Sometimes a little sparkle is all it takes. A grey day turned bright, a dark mood turned light, and a drab moment turned into something special are all possible by adding a little bling to your attitude.

Even the coldest of days can be warmed by the shimmer of sunlight on the ice crystals forming on new fallen snow, or glittering flakes coating the bare branches of the trees. If a simple thing like a single ray from the sun can do that, imagine what you can do just by letting your interior sparkle shine outward!

Everyone loves a little bling. No, I'm not talking about diamonds, rubies, or sapphires; I'm talking about that spark that has the capacity to turn an entire day around. We all have it within us. Many times it may go unnoticed because we're concentrating so heavily on what is going wrong as opposed to the everyday things that are going right.

Here's the thing: it costs you nothing! Yes, you might have to put forth a bit of effort. Your attitude didn't end up in the pits all by itself, and your spark won't come forth by itself either. It's a matter of changing your feelings, which are fleeting and inconsistent anyway, by transforming your mind. Once you consciously decide to smile everything changes. Once you determine not to be dark and dreary your inner light becomes more evident.

Don't be ruled by how you feel in the moment; let what you know rule you. "This too shall pass," as they say. Your circumstances don't define you, but how you continue to react to them could have the effect of defining how others will see you. That could have the effect of defining how their day is going to unfold.

Invest in a little bling. Let the sparkle in your deepest recesses come out to erase the wearisome mood you've adopted. Let it reach your eyes and your heart, and then give it to others. You'll be surprised just how quickly those temporary circumstances melt in the sparkling light of your spirit.

Just as the sun's rays bring the beauty of sparkling ice crystals to delight your sight, so your sparkle has the power to delight someone else. Delighting someone else has the power to bring the sparkle back to you. It's a wonderful, circular giving of light. It lifts everyone involved to new and incredible heights.

Take note of the bling in your days and be thankful. Transform your mind from the drudgery of momentary happenings to the constant state of living in light. You have the power to banish the darkness. Be generous with your sparkle!

"Here's another way to put it: You're here to be light, bringing out the God-colors in the world." **(Matthew 5:14 The Message)**

Time for Family

The importance of family can never be overstated. Those with whom you were raised, those you have raised, and those you have chosen that may not be blood but have become family shape the person you are and the life you live. Family is, indeed, everything. Cultivating love of family takes time and effort. There are many who would say, "Well, they're family. You have to love them." I prefer to say that you've been blessed with family, and you need to purposefully set your mind and heart on loving them in a way that honors and encourages them.

Loving someone is easy when things are going well. It's a simple fact that when we agree or when times aren't tough, love can abound without much effort. It's when disagreements occur and when situations arise that are difficult or more than difficult that love becomes difficult as well. Don't get me wrong, it's not that we stop loving when tough times come into our lives or the lives of our family. However, we must be more aware of the needs of those we love during these times, and that takes effort. That takes time.

Life is full of things that take up our time. Work, personal needs, even "play" take up time that is precious in any increment. Time, as much as we'd like it to be, is not infinite. The key is to realize that those we love need our time too. And here's the bad news - we must realize that there will be those instances when we

15

must give up what we want or even need to be there for those we love when they're facing a crisis. I say "bad news" because we seldom, for any reason, truly want to give up things we are trying to gain. Society teaches us on a daily basis that we should have a "me first" attitude. To a degree that's true. You must be able to take care of yourself - spiritually, mentally, and physically - before you are equipped to take care of another. However, you must also be willing to give up certain things to give care to someone you love when they need it. It's a balance that is important and quite possible to achieve. And here's the good news - giving up things for ourselves to help those we love carries a lifetime of blessing.

To me there is nothing more important than seeing those I love healthy and happy - seeing them have joy and purpose in their days. You can give that joy and purpose to someone. It's not really difficult once you set your mind on taking the time, making the effort, and putting someone else first. Think on all the times that someone did the same for you. Think about the joy brought into your life because someone simply took the time to care for you. Isn't that something you want to afford to others, something you want to be able to give back to those you love most?

Love is not just a thing. It's an action and a reaction. It's a purposeful effort to bring joy, purpose, and blessing into someone else's life. It's particularly important when times are hard and there seems no end

16

to a circumstance. And as important as it is, it's so simple to give. Bless others by living out the love you feel for them. Honor the place they have in your life, no matter the circumstances surrounding them and you. Give it generously, without limit or regret. It's what you were born to do. It's nothing less than they deserve.

"Love is patient and kind. Love is not jealous, it does not brag, and it is not proud. Love is not rude, is not selfish, and does not get upset with others. Love does not count up wrongs that have been done. Love takes no pleasure in evil but rejoices over the truth. Love patiently accepts all things. It always trusts, always hopes, and always endures. Love never ends. There are gifts of prophecy, but they will be ended. There are gifts of speaking in different languages, but those gifts will stop. There is the gift of knowledge, but it will come to an end. The reason is that our knowledge and our ability to prophesy are not perfect. But when perfection comes, the things that are not perfect will end. When I was a child, I talked like a child, I thought like a child, I reasoned like a child. When I became a man, I stopped those childish ways. It is the same with us. Now we see a dim reflection, as if we were looking into a mirror, but then we shall see clearly. Now I know only a part, but then I will know fully, as God has known me. So these three things continue forever: faith, hope, and love. And the greatest of these is love."
(1 Corinthians 13:4-13 NCV)

Toxic or Treasure, Let It Go

We all tend to hold onto things too tightly. Whether the toxic things like anger, betrayal, hardened opinions, and bitterness, or the good things that come in waves of blessing, we keep a tightfisted grasp and refuse to let go.

Here's the thing: whether what is in our grasp is good or bad, our hands and hearts begin to hurt from the effort. Our focus on life wavers, and we suffer from tunnel vision. Sleep eludes us. Day to day tasks are difficult because we just cannot let go. Why do we put ourselves through this?

The determined holding of the bad doesn't make the issues go away. We're not imprisoning them; we're simply keeping them in our sights like some form of mutated justice. Truly, that is misguided. It doesn't bring new solutions to old problems. It simply damages our abilities to see, think, and act clearly. Trying to keep the good on a leash so as not to lose it only tarnishes what we think we have. It doesn't stay shiny and new, and our hands are full of things that keep us from reaching for the new things we should be receiving.

We were not created to be holding tanks for life's experiences, whether those experiences were joyous or heart rending. We are meant to live with open hands, hearts, and minds, allowing all of life to flow over and through us. We need to disperse the bad things into the air after learning from them, much as a child blows on a dandelion gone to seed, watching them fly on the breeze as they are taken from us. Life's joys

18

and blessings are not meant to be hoarded or put on shelves solely for our enjoyment, but instead are meant to be scattered in love and kindness as we move through our days so that others can benefit from the same things that have benefited us.

We were not born to harbor ill will but to give grace. We were not born to be selfish but selfless. We are not here for our own contentment but for the contentment of all we meet.

This is not to say we cannot allow ourselves to feel emotion. We just need to learn that emotions are fleeting. We cannot build a wall around them to hold them and still live a life that is filled with peace. Peace comes in letting go of the bad and generously sharing the good.

So blow the seeds of sadness, bitterness, anger, and the like away from you. Release your grasp on feelings of betrayal and resentment as you let grace flow freely. In the same way, open your hands to spread the blessings you have been gifted. Gift others with love, joy, compassion, mercy, provision, and kindness. It's what we're meant to do. It's how we are made.

"Be angry, but don't sin; don't let the sun go down on you while you're angry, and don't leave any loophole for the devil."
(Ephesians 4:26-27 New Testament for Everyone)

"In everything we do, we show that we are true ministers of God. We patiently endure troubles and hardships and calamities of every kind. We have been beaten, been put in prison, faced angry mobs, worked to

exhaustion, endured sleepless nights, and gone without food. We prove ourselves by our purity, our understanding, our patience, our kindness, by the Holy Spirit within us, and by our sincere love. We faithfully preach the truth. God's power is working in us. We use the weapons of righteousness in the right hand for attack and the left hand for defense. We serve God whether people honor us or despise us, whether they slander us or praise us. We are honest, but they call us impostors. We are ignored, even though we are well known. We live close to death, but we are still alive. We have been beaten, but we have not been killed. Our hearts ache, but we always have joy. We are poor, but we give spiritual riches to others. We own nothing, and yet we have everything.
(2 Corinthians 6:4-10 NLT)

Monsters Under the Bed

Sometimes words escape me. I've been rolling around a concept for the last few weeks, but it refuses to take shape in my mind. It seems just out of reach in some darkened corner. I can "see" its shadow lurking, but I just can't grasp it to get it from the recesses through to my fingertips and onto the keyboard. It's frustrating.

In that frustration, however, came some realization. Perhaps, just perhaps, on some level I am resisting grasping the concept out of an underlying fear. After all, it is currently residing in some darkened corner of my mind. Maybe it harbors some deep, dark secret that I don't want to come into the light for some reason.

That may sound silly based on the shallow surface of those words. Yet we all have those places we just don't want to go in our lives. The problem is that things purposefully left in the dark tend to grow larger and scarier as time goes forward.

Much like a child with monsters under the bed or in the closet, we desperately try to ignore them. Also, much like that same child, we cannot ignore them for very long and instead end up dwelling on them until they consume us, with the result being that we have zero rest in our hearts. Sleeplessness of spirit results just like the child who cannot sleep for fear of what lurks just beneath.

Shedding light doesn't take much effort and truly is not that scary. Think of a candle brought to flame. The flame doesn't fear the darkness that surrounds it but embraces it, shedding its light to the farthest corners of the room in which it sits. It should be that way with the darkness we collect in our lives. After all, we cannot light the way for others who are in much darker places if we don't banish our own murky waters to let the crystal seas shine.

Whatever your darkness is, step into the bright sunshine to reveal it. In all probability, it will turn out not to be a monster at all but a harmless dust bunny - much more harmless in the light than it seems in the dark. Lead by example in releasing yourself from that silly little thing that causes you to fear. There is really no fear in the sun's rays because it cannot breed in the light. Instead, there is realization, peace, and rest. There is joy.

I think I'll light a candle to brighten the corners and go see if I can grab that dust bunny in my mind. There just may be another book in the making in there!

"Let your light so shine before men, that they may see your good works, and glorify your Father who is in Heaven."
(Matthew 5:16, 21st Century KJV)

Plenty to Spare

We all live in relative comfort. We have roofs over our heads, food on our tables, and clothes on our backs. We have what we need and often more than we need. We have luxuries galore - new or newer vehicles for commuting and pleasure travel, multiple televisions with multiple channels, square footage of living space that is most likely more than enough for its occupants, closets filled with clothes and linens, and refrigerators and freezers filled with enough food for months. Our bank accounts (for the most part) leave a balance after the bills are paid. Add to that our retirement accounts that carry a balance and earn a return each month. We dine out, and we go on vacations. We hit the pillows at night without really worrying where our provisions will come from the next day. We plan, we save, and we hoard.

There comes a time when enough is enough. I think we all get that tugging in our inmost being that says we should be doing more with what we have than we are. Instead of listening to that inner voice, we push it away and continue on our merry way. We avert our eyes when we see something unpleasant, like the evidence of need among people in our neighborhoods, our community, and our world. If we don't see it or pretend we don't, it can't exist, right?

Wrong.

There are millions worldwide that go to bed hungry and thirsty each night. (And when I say "bed," I mean wherever they find to lay their heads and not necessarily a mattress and pillow.) Many do not wake up the next morning. There is an overabundance of people who have no solid roofs over their heads if they have any roof at all. Many more have no more than one or two sets of clothing, no vehicles, and have never dined out or even gone on a weekend getaway. They cannot pay their monthly bills even without the luxuries of television and spacious accommodations.

Have you ever considered there's a reason we have been blessed as we are, a reason we have our needs met with enough to spare?

I am a firm believer that we are to take care of each other in this world. We have been placed here for the purpose of helping others and not just ourselves. If someone is hungry, we need to feed them. If someone is wearing tattered material that no longer provides warmth or cover, we need to clothe them. If someone is cold because they've fallen on hard times, we need to help with their heating cost. If they're sick, we need to help get them the care they need. The list goes on and on, but you get the idea.

We absolutely have to give for the good of this world. What we give will differ from time to time. Sometimes it will be funding. At others it will be material items. At still others it will be a helping hand in an area that we have expertise. All times it will be a matter of giving love, encouragement, and hope.

We cannot turn a blind eye to others in need when we have more than we need. It is, in my mind, simply inhumane. It is also a betrayal of the love, grace, and merciful provision we have been given.

*"'For I was hungry, and you gave
Me something to eat; I was thirsty, and you gave
Me something to drink; I was a stranger, and you invited
Me in; naked, and you clothed Me; I was sick, and
you visited Me; I was in prison, and you came to
Me.' Then the righteous will answer Him, 'Lord, when
did we see You hungry, and feed You, or thirsty, and give
You something to drink? And when did we see You as a
stranger, and invite You in, or naked, and clothe
You? And when did we see You sick, or in prison, and
come to You?' And the King will answer and say to
them, 'Truly I say to you, to the extent that you did it for
one of the least of these brothers or sisters of Mine, you
did it for Me.'"*
(Matthew 25:35-40 NASB)

Look Up!

We don't know where all this is headed. We don't always know where we're going during these chaotic days. So much has changed, yet there are some things that have not.

The mornings are still chilly, but I've taken to my rocking chair on the patio the last several mornings with my tea anyway. There's something so calming in listening to the birdsong, looking at the changing landscape as it adapts to spring and just soaking in the quiet of the dawn hours. This morning I watched as a pair of red winged blackbirds walked the yard, sometimes flitting up to the garden fence posts or the mimosa branches, doing their springtime courting dance. I witnessed the crows trying to invade the sunflower feeder and the tiny purple finches chase them away in spite of their lesser physical stature - small but mighty.

The sun rose as it always does, even if only glimpses of it became evident as the clouds gathered. But oh, the deep blue of the sky before that happened! The same sun will travel across our skies until sunset this evening, whether the cloud cover allows us to see it or not. At that point the moon will rise, and the stars will be called into service for the night. In between the sunrise and sunset we will accomplish our tasks, prepare and eat our meals, and allow our thoughts to wander to things that dart through our minds moment by moment. And hopefully, we will remember that there is something much bigger than the current crisis that threatens.

If we keep looking at the ground, we will miss the beauty of the skies overhead, just as we will miss the blessings of today if we keep focusing on any given situation at hand. We are not big enough to control what's happening. Actually, we are quite small. Yet we are mighty. We are mighty because in our ineptitude and weakness, there is a strength that transcends it all. Just one look up to the skies and all that goes on there, sometimes beyond our vision, will tell us that.

God is bigger than we think. So often we tend to put Him in a box that fits the size of our vision. The truth is, there is no box big enough to hold Him. There is no situation tough enough to thwart Him. There is no weakness - even ours - that is weak enough to negate His strength.

And so, as we blindly stumble along the path today deafened by the noise of our crisis, we must do two things. Look up, and listen! The skies will declare His mastery and majesty and the birds will sing His praise. Those things will tell us the secret the finches already know. Small is mighty; weak is strong. We may be experiencing blindness as we try to walk through each day, but God is not blind. He sees all things. He uses all things. The current situation will pass, but He never will. He will remain as he always has and always will.

"I will lead the blind by ways they have not known, along unfamiliar paths I will guide them; I will turn the darkness into light before them and make the rough places smooth. These are the things I will do; I will not forsake them."
(Isaiah 42:16 NIV)

Responding Without Extremes

In this early spring of 2020, we are all facing a new normal, so to speak. We wake each day knowing the news will be different than the day before and wondering when all of this will end. Businesses and schools have closed, and we are being asked to make physical contact with as few people as possible. Some of us have voluntarily taken leave from our jobs to protect at-risk family members, which is what I did. Others have been put out of work by business closures. Still others continue working in critical and essential businesses while taking any precaution humanly possible to reduce their own risk. It seems a never-ending crisis.

Reactions to this health emergency range from one extreme to the other. Some are going on with life (seemingly) completely unconcerned, while others are panicking to the point of clearing store shelves and fighting over needed items. Regardless of which category any of us falls into, this is the new normal.

In talking to different people, the community of believers in all denominations seems to have extremes as well. Many have suspended services and meetings and gone to online streaming, if they have the capability. Some have continued business as usual but with extra precautions taken. There are a few that have taken an attitude that they will continue doing what they do without extra precaution and regardless of risk because they believe God is in control and will protect them.

I am a member of the community of believers. I do believe that God is in control. I do believe we will weather this storm with His guidance and grace. I do not believe in extremes, whether that be going on with my days completely unconcerned or hoarding items I will never use while leaving others in need.

When it comes to how to live through this crisis, I believe that we, as a community of believers, need to do our part. Yes, God is in control as He always has been. Scripture abounds with evidence of that. However, scripture also abounds with evidence that those whose stories are recorded there did their part as well.

God protects. He protected the Israelites from the Egyptians and David from Goliath. Yet the Israelites had to do their part in being willing to walk through the Red Sea as God held back the waters on either side. David had to do his part in picking up the stones and the sling (Exodus 14 and 1 Samuel 17).

God provides. The widow was almost out of food. She had only a little bit of flour and olive oil left. Elijah, on the Lord's instruction, asked her for a piece of bread. When she told him what little she had left, he asked her to make the bread and give it to him anyway. After that, she had flour and oil enough until such time as the rain fell and nurtured the crops (1 Kings 17).

God heals. Naaman had leprosy. Elisha told him to wash himself in the Jordan River seven times. Naaman thought this was too simple of an answer and argued for something more complicated. When he stopped arguing and followed the instructions, he was healed (2 Kings 5).

God does not leave us. There are more scripture references than I can count that tell us God is always with us, always leading, always surrounding, always loving. Psalm 139 is my favorite reference to His constant presence and foreknowledge.

What my heart and my study tell me is that, while this is a critical time, we must mitigate our response and do our part.

We must promote God's protection by protecting ourselves and others in listening to the medical community's guidelines for reducing interaction.

We must help God's provision by not hoarding but only taking what we need and helping supply the needs of others. With many out of work, those of us with some means should be willing to help provide for them.

We must enable God's healing through following the guidelines of those who have more experience and training, as well as by being kind, compassionate, and prayerful. Physical healing is not the only type of healing necessary right now, although that is the type at the forefront of our minds.

Above all, we must remember and remind others that God has not left us and He never will.

"'For the mountains may move and the hills disappear, but even then my faithful love for you will remain. My covenant of blessing will never be broken,' says the LORD, who has mercy on you."
(Isaiah 54:10 NLT)

Lessons in Crisis

There are lessons to be learned, especially during these difficult days. We simply cannot walk through life on a whim thinking only of ourselves and be able to survive a crisis. There comes a time, if it hasn't come already, when we must realize that we are dependent on each other.

The current crisis of Covid-19 will pass. However, we will not come out unscathed. Even for those of us who may not contract the virus or not show symptoms if we do, there will be scars and changes. It is up to us to determine the magnitude of the impact, both for good and bad.

I suppose the real question is this: do we learn the lessons that need to be learned and minimize the detrimental impacts while maximizing the good, or do we skip along our merry way waiting for the despairing avalanche to crush us?

The fact is that, in this or any other crisis, skipping along our merry way isn't the wise decision. There are others who depend on us. There are others who look to us as an example. Do we really want to cause them to stumble? Do we really want to skip headlong into a pit from which we can't extricate ourselves?

I think one of the first lessons to be learned currently is that of respect and appreciation. Suddenly we are dependent on essential workers that we've never given true consideration before. How many of us can honestly say that we've given thought to the stock employees or cashiers at the local grocer? How many have thought about the plight of the truck driver that delivers our needs from warehouse to store? How many have considered how hard it is to work as a chef, line cook, server, or delivery person at our favorite eatery? Many of these lower-paying positions are now at the forefront of this pandemic. They are not in the business of saving lives like medical personnel, but they are in the business of sustaining lives every single day.

Yes, unlike those of us who are non-essential and cannot work from home or are unable to due to the nature of our duties, they have jobs. They are also exposed every moment of every day to the danger of becoming sick or carrying something home to their families and making them sick. I'm quite sure they are grateful to have a steady income. That then begs the question: are *we* grateful they are willing to work through this to have that steady income?

Another lesson of respect and appreciation comes in the form of our medical experts and leaders. No matter which side of the political aisle we sit on, are we thankful they are there trying to do the best they can at making beneficial decisions for us? This illness isn't red, blue, green, or independent of those colors. It's nondiscriminatory. Are we grateful for the knowledge of the medical experts or angry that they're asking us to make sacrifices?

Do we take a moment (at least) to consider their day-to-day stress, which is most likely insurmountable, and pray for their wisdom? Do we consider their time away from family and home?

Perhaps the biggest lesson of all is that of control. We cannot control this. Our essential workers and frontline medical staff can't control this. Our experts and leaders can't control this. And here's where my faith comes in - only God is in control. We must simply do our part under His sovereignty.

And that is the final and biggest lesson. We need to do our part and relinquish our flimsy control. What is our part? First of all, our part is to pray. Pray, then listen. The answers for what we should do next will come. Either God will speak to our heart or place the object of our direction in our path. It could be as simple as a text message that leads to a phone call. It could be a little more difficult, such as giving recognition to workers you otherwise wouldn't notice or leaving a larger tip to those who have prepared your takeout. It could be as complicated as picking up a grocery list from someone in need, shopping for them, paying for them if they don't have enough, and delivering back to them. It could seem as unimportant as calling to check in on a friend or loved one, which isn't unimportant at all, or as necessary and important as spending more time seeking the guidance and wisdom of God.

The lessons will vary by individual. Mine won't be the same as yours. However, God is trying to get our attention, and we must learn the lessons. And when this current crisis is over, *we must keep putting them into practice*. The earth is already healing from the lack of human interruption during worldwide shutdowns. I read articles about that almost every day. Now it is time for humankind to begin to heal as well. It all starts by learning the lessons: surrendering selfish and perceived control, listening, noticing, giving, and loving. The verse from Jeremiah below represents a promise from God to the Israelites during their exile to Babylon. In some way, we have been exiled as well. The Israelites needed to learn how important God and obedience to Him was in their lives, and we must too. Just imagine what a new and beautiful world awaits if we all just learn!

"For surely I know the plans I have for you, says the LORD, plans for your welfare and not for harm, to give you a future with hope. Then when you call upon me and come and pray to me, I will hear you. When you search for me, you will find me; if you seek me with all your heart, I will let you find me, says the LORD, and I will restore your fortunes and gather you from all the nations and all the places where I have driven you, says the LORD, and I will bring you back to the place from which I sent you into exile."
(Jeremiah 29:11-14 NRSV)

The Art of Dialogue

As I look at the world today, it occurs to me how little we remember about the art of dialogue, especially disagreement. Almost no one seems to have the capability to converse on any given issue without falling into insults and name-calling. This applies to conversations that have sunken to the level of trading hurtful barbs. It also applies to memes, misinformation, and outright lies (a slim difference between the last two) being posted to help support one's own opinions. It hurts my heart to see such things. There was a time when people could disagree and still remain civil, remain kind, and remain friends. Perhaps it is the phenomena of social media. You're more or less anonymous with those who don't know you, and you're not in the presence of those who do. In essence, we are hiding behind the screens of our desktops and phones. We can say our piece, insults and all, and walk away after closing the app. There is little, if any, consequence to our words. Or is there?

My brother and I grew up with phenomenal parents. No, they weren't perfect - no one is - but they came pretty close when it comes down to the example they set before us. I cannot help but think that Momma is looking down from Heaven in dismay at the things going on in this world, whether it be between strangers, friends, or family. I can almost see her shaking her head as tears well up in her eyes.

One of her favorite bits of wisdom for me was, "Never go to bed angry." It's a simple phrase but one filled with power. It's a biblical statement from one of Paul's letters, which gives it even more power since it is God-inspired. We all hold that power. We can resolve differences before placing our heads on the pillow at night, or we can hold onto the anger and let it fester while it ruins our sleep and our dreams, not to mention our relationships. In doing the first, we wake the next morning refreshed and with a clean slate to start the day. In doing the second, we're probably already awake when the alarm rings and already running words through our minds to continue whatever the disagreement was because we *have* to win.

What made my parents fantastic in their child-rearing was not that they never had an argument. They did disagree on occasion. I remember hearing some of those misunderstandings and differences. What made them such wonderful examples of love and caring is the fact that even in the heat of a disagreement, their words never sank to a level of hurtful insult or name-calling. The other thing I remember is that as far as I could ever tell, Momma took her own advice and so did Daddy. Resolution, whether it was one agreeing with the other or the agreement to disagree, was reached before climbing those stairs for bedtime.

Their marriage, which lasted 66 years, 16 days, and a couple of hours until Momma was heaven-bound, was an artful dialogue each and every day. If there was disagreement in the evening, I can promise you that the next morning was pleasant, loving, and always sealed with a kiss as Daddy went out the door to work. I look to this example not only for my marriage but also my friendships and online acquaintances.

I wish I could say I had started out my own marriage following Momma's advice. The truth is I did not. Marrying young, it took some time for me to realize the value and truth of her words. Admittedly, that didn't happen until my mid-thirties. Once the value and truth became apparent to me, my striving was to always obey her wisdom. I still wake up each morning with those words at the forefront and do all that is within my power to lay my head peacefully on my pillow each night.

We don't have to agree with each other on everything. We can have a conversation and present our sides calmly, quietly, and with the tact to allow others to speak as well. The key comes in not only allowing them to speak but listening - really listening - to what they have to say. It comes in not being hardhearted and bullheaded. You never know, you might learn something new.

The next step is agreeing to disagree if you can't see each other's sides. Relationships don't need to be ruined over such things. Most of earthly life is subjective. Constant agreement on everything is rare, if it exists at all. The important part is never to degrade, insult, or discount someone else's opinion or belief. You don't know what has caused them to think that way. Insults and degradation only lead to shattered hearts and bonds. I would walk away before doing that to someone I care about and even someone I barely know. There's no point to that kind of behavior. Besides, it speaks more to the character of the one berating than the one being berated.

The last and most important thing to remember before you speak or post is to ask yourself if it is true. Then ask yourself if it's worth ruining a friendship or family relationship over such a thing. The answer is always the same. No, it's not worth it.

In the end, you won't always be able to avoid the anger. That's when Momma's advice works best. Never ever go to bed angry. Hold onto the power of those words and to the truth behind them. That's what my parents always did. They held onto the truth behind those words - biblical truth. In the end it didn't matter to either of them what their opinions were on any given subject of disagreement. What mattered was the truth. What mattered was something of heavenly consequence. Every example they set before us was measured by God's Word.

I think we all need to take a step or two or three back and relearn the art of dialogue, the art of disagreement, and the art of resolution. Come out from the anonymity of the screen and be real people showing real love and real wisdom, even in the heat of debate. Leave insults and harassment at the curb because it has no place in relationships.

"But that is not the way you learned Christ!— assuming that you have heard about him and were taught in him, as the truth is in Jesus, to put off your old self, which belongs to your former manner of life and is corrupt through deceitful desires, and to be renewed in the spirit of your minds, and to put on the new self, created after the likeness of God in true righteousness and holiness. Therefore, having put away falsehood, let

each one of you speak the truth with his neighbor, for we are members one of another. Be angry and do not sin; do not let the sun go down on your anger, and give no opportunity to the devil...Let no corrupting talk come out of your mouths, but only such as is good for building up, as fits the occasion, that it may give grace to those who hear. And do not grieve the Holy Spirit of God, by whom you were sealed for the day of redemption. Let all bitterness and wrath and anger and clamor and slander be put away from you, along with all malice. Be kind to one another, tenderhearted, forgiving one another, as God in Christ forgave you."
(Ephesians 4:20-27, 29-32 ESV)

Honored Not Disposable Elders

A few weeks ago, I met a man walking along a city street. He was in his mid- to late-70s and pushing a baby stroller, its seat tattered and worn and empty. His steps were slow and deliberate. His coat, while it looked very warm, appeared too heavy for his frail stature.

I pulled my car over to the curb to watch him and see what it was that had him out and about on a cold and windy day. It didn't take long for me to leave my car and cautiously approach him so as not to frighten him. He had stopped just a few feet away on the sidewalk and was beginning to search trash receptacles outside a corner grocer.

My heart broke as the realization hit me that he was looking for something to eat. I asked him, already knowing the answer, if he was hungry. Yes, I asked. I didn't want to insult him in any way by just pushing something into his hands that he may not have need of nor want. There is a delicate balance in helping someone in need based on appearance only. The old adage, "Never judge a book by its cover" is appropriate in all situations, even if your heart tells you your first intuition was the right one.

He answered with a very gruff, "Yes, I could eat something." I stepped over to my car and returned with a bag containing some food and personal supplies. He carefully reached out to accept the bag, placing it into the stroller. His eyes never completely looked into mine.

A few more pieces of my heart shattered as the perception of his embarrassment settled into my comprehension. I tried to sound as normal as possible as I told him what was in the bag and asked him if he needed anything else I had - blankets, another coat, hat, gloves, etc. He again answered in a short, gruff tone, "No, I'm good on that."

I left him with tears of grief in my eyes. I had no words appropriate for the parting and that bothered me. While I can sit at this keyboard and write, words flowing through my mind in seconds, there are many times I cannot vocalize in the moment because of the rush of emotions like hurricane winds through my heart and mind. Again, the realization of his embarrassment at having to sift through trash in search of food left a stinging in my eyes. My mind screamed, "This shouldn't happen!" I wanted to shout it to those who were hurriedly entering and exiting the grocer's shop.

The grief stems from the tragic reality of this man's life. No, I don't know his circumstances. No, I don't think he was homeless in the traditional sense of the word. But he was hungry, and I believe that hunger was emotional as well as physical.

The food I gave him would give him a meal and some snacks over a couple of days. What he truly needs is food for the spirit as well as the body. He needs family. He needs others to recognize that he has much to contribute to this world with his many years of experiences that have given him a wisdom those of us who are younger don't possess.

It saddens me greatly that today's society looks upon the elderly as castoffs. They are left alone in their homes or in nursing facilities. Many are forced into poverty because their fixed incomes do not allow for the constant rising costs of medications, taxes, housing, and food. They are seldom, if ever, asked for their counsel when in fact they have much wise counsel to give.

Our culture in the United States in particular seems to view the aged as disposable. Those who are younger know it all because they've graduated from institutions of higher education and landed high-paying positions. We simply are too busy to care for those who cared for us our entire lives and who blazed the pathways before us to allow us to walk them unimpeded. There is little recognition of the sacrifices they have made and the lives they have enriched. It is we who should be embarrassed at how little care we have, not the man who is forced to look in garbage cans for food. Make no mistake about that!

In ancient times, elders were the hub of civilization. They guided and directed. They taught and disciplined. They mentored. And they blessed. They blessed their children and children's children with favor and protection for long, productive, and successful lives ahead. These blessings were not taken lightly. They could be given or withheld. They were coveted and held dear by those who yearned for and received them, just as the elders themselves were.

The time is long past when our elderly should once again be revered and held close in our hearts. The provision for them should and must be as generous as their provision to us has been. No longer should we see one of our beloved aged shivering on the street or tossing through trash in search of a simple morsel of food. We must learn to rely on their wisdom and direction once again. We must begin to care for them as we care for ourselves. We must respect who they have been and who they are now.

We must be generous with our time, our love, and our treasure so that they may live the remainder of their lives fulfilling the purpose they have been given: to teach us the way we should go from here and to feel the appreciation they deserve so much.

Before any one of us makes the choice to neglect or ignore those who have come before us, let us remember that we will be those who have come before in just a short time. Are we disposable as well?

"What good is it, my brothers and sisters, if someone claims to have faith but has no deeds? Can such faith save them? Suppose a brother or a sister is without clothes and daily food. If one of you says to them, 'Go in peace; keep warm and well fed,' but does nothing about their physical needs, what good is it? In the same way, faith by itself, if it is not accompanied by action, is dead."
(James 2:14-17 NIV)

"Youth may be admired for vigor, but gray hair gives prestige to old age."
(Proverbs 20:29 The Message)

44

Inseparable Pairs

I will give praise for the dark and the light. I will give praise for the tears and the smiles. I will give praise for the valley and the mountaintop. I will give praise for the journey and the destination. I will give praise in all things.

I will surrender my fear and my courage. I will surrender my foolishness and my wisdom. I will surrender my lack and my abundance. I will surrender my bitterness and my delight. I will surrender in all things.

In all of these pairs, we cannot have one without the other. For if we had only one, we wouldn't recognize or attain the other. In the same way, we cannot have praise without surrender. Praise requires a complete giving over of ourselves. It means no longer thinking of me but thinking of the One who created me and all the rest of the "me(s)" in this world.

Our vision is so shortsighted. We are unable to see that which goes beyond our circle of need and influence - not because we can't but because we don't want to many times. We must look beyond. We must look to the betterment of all around us and not just within our circle - especially now.

We will not reach the destination of the mountaintop without the journey through the valley. We must travel through the night and the day. We will not get there without the tears of effort and the smiles of small milestones. And we certainly won't get there without reaching out and giving to others, just as they need to do the same.

Surrender it all. That's the only way to take another step. And as each step appears before you, give praise. For without the One who has created you, there is nothing worth putting one foot in front of the other.

"But this I remember, and so I have hope. It is because of the Lord's loving-kindness that we are not destroyed for His loving-pity never ends. It is new every morning. He is so very faithful. 'The Lord is my share.' says my soul, 'so I have hope in Him.' The Lord is good to those who wait for Him, to the one who looks for Him. It is good that one should be quiet and wait for the saving power of the Lord."
(Lamentations 3:21-26 New Life Version)

Are We Truly Loving Others?

Love can take on many different appearances. I think for most people the word love takes on the common connotation of their feelings for those closest to them - spouses and partners, parents, siblings, other family members, and close friends.

Love is so much more than just that. It is more action than feeling. It is the basic consideration for all living things, even those we don't know or might not like. We really have no idea how to love unconditionally, although most of us will say we do. We really never take a broader look at the world at large and whether we're loving beyond our visible boundaries, extending what we've been given in the way we should. We really never take a deeper look into whether or not we're loving in spite of reason and circumstance.

Love is constituted by selflessness - the kind of caring, compassion, kindness, respect, and consideration that is sacrificial. Love costs us something. Whoa! Wait a minute! Love costs us something?

Yes, there is a cost to loving others as we are supposed to love them.

That cost could be financial, although that is a very small portion of the price of giving love. The larger portion is the willingness to pay the price of losing self-interest, self-preservation, and self-gratification. How many can say we are actually willing to put forth that kind of effort, make that kind of expenditure for others?

Loving might mean the surrender of time, treasure, freedom, and life as we know it. Perhaps we are willing to sacrifice our time. We might even be willing to sacrifice our treasure, but our freedom or life perhaps not so much.

One thing is certain: we cannot live without love - not just the emotion itself but also the acts - giving and receiving all things vital to our existence and to truly abundant life. The truth is we must lay down our life to gain it. We must give up our love to receive it. And we must relinquish our freedom to keep the true freedom we've been given. We must do all of this so that the world and its people are not just surviving but thriving.

This is all something to think about the next time we feel like complaining about doing something we don't wish to do, or giving up something we don't wish to give, whether temporarily or permanently. The bottom line is this: we can hold what we have been given (things, time, freedoms) more dearly than the lives of others who journey this world with us, or we can love beyond borders and personal boundaries, giving all that we have been given so others can feel love and live abundantly along with us.

The former will make our lives worth nothing, but the latter will give our lives inestimable value. For without love, we are nothing.

"If I could speak all the languages of earth and of angels, but didn't love others, I would only be a noisy gong or a clanging cymbal. If I had the gift of prophecy, and if I understood all of God's secret plans and

possessed all knowledge, and if I had such faith that I could move mountains, but didn't love others, I would be nothing. If I gave everything I have to the poor and even sacrificed my body, I could boast about it; but if I didn't love others, I would have gained nothing."
(1 Corinthians 13:1-3 NLT)

Even in Uncharted Territory, You Matter

   While this was written for those graduating in 2020, it applies to all teens everywhere. There will always be questions as they enter the adult world. They will always wonder who they are, if they've accomplished anything of importance, and if their lives matter. Never let them question for long. Teach them that they are treasured.

   Today, I want to honor those who are standing on the starting line of their futures. Our 2020 graduates are entering uncharted territory after already living in a pandemic no-man's land these past several months. They have, in all probability, questioned their importance, their worth, their chosen paths, and their now distanced relationships in the midst of all of this chaos. In my mind, the biggest of those questions are these:

   Do I and all that I've accomplished so far really matter? And what now?

   I would like to address this unprecedented class directly.

   Yes, you and your efforts and accomplishments matter. Your futures are bright and filled with promise, even if it doesn't seem so in this particular moment. You are grieving the loss of the end of your teenage and student years, which seem to be going out with a whimper rather than the bang it should be. However, there is good news!

   I and many, many others are so very proud of you. You have walked through these years with their struggles and achievements, their hopes and disappointments, and their assurances and doubts with a very special kind of willpower and dignity that only you could possess.

Things look bleak right now as you forego proms and commencements. However, this moment in time is anything but bleak. It is *your* shining star that gives the rest of us light. We look at you and know that the future holds great things because of you. It is your accomplishments and contributions to our lives that give us all hope. You matter! You have not worked this hard for nothing! You have brought such insight and joy to those around you. Countless smiles and warmed hearts can be attributed to you.

As far as the answer to, "What now?", I must admit that no one is quite sure of that. Life will certainly look different. What I am sure of is this: you will enter your future with the same willpower and dignity with which you completed your education, and you will do it brilliantly. Yes, there may be uncertainty. Yes, there will be new bends and corners in the path. Face them knowing you are not alone - you were never alone. You have been created for a particular purpose, and that purpose will be fulfilled.

Take with you the lessons from this chaotic time. Remember that you can still love and be loved even if you can't be in the same place for a time. Remember that home is the best place to be at any point in life, wherever home may be. Remember that you can dance with others, but you can also dance when you're alone. You can march to your own drumbeat and still be in step with those you love.

Remember that the most important things are simple and free. Remember that selflessness never goes unnoticed and has great and eternal rewards. Lastly, remember that the greatest lessons learned are not in the classroom but in the living of everyday life. Your classroom education has spurred you on to what your career will be. The way you approach living everyday life will define who you are and allow you to see who you've been created to be.

You are not forgotten. You are not alone. You matter more than you will ever know. You have made us proud. You have given us great joy. We thank God for you and for all of those things. Look forward to your future, knowing we stand behind you and are here if and when you need us and that you are infinitely loved.

"For we are God's masterpiece. He has created us anew in Christ Jesus, so we can do the good things he planned for us long ago."
(Ephesians 2:10 NLT)

Always Shining

Do you recognize the light that fills your days? It's easy to see on a clear morning, but not so much on a day when clouds fill the skies and a cold, constant rain falls from the heavens. Yet the light is there, waiting just beyond the darkness for the perfect moment to break through in all its glorious beauty. We simply cannot appreciate the moments of brightness without the dim moments in between. And we certainly cannot see the light if we don't purposefully look past the dark. Take each day for what it is, clouds and sunshine alike, knowing they all have purpose. Press through the grey to find the wondrous colors of life. The Son is always shining, and He's waiting for you to reflect His brightness to the world just as the sea reflects the rays of the morning sun. We belong to Him, just as the sun and clouds belong to Him. It is up to us to recognize the light even in the midst of darkness. It is up to us to act like the children of hope that we are. It is up to us to be His glory.

"So with deep love, I pray for my disciples. I'm not asking on behalf of the unbelieving world, but for those who belong to you, those you have given me. For all who belong to me now belong to you. And all who belong to you now belong to me as well, and my glory is revealed through their surrendered lives."
(John 17:9-10 The Passion Translation)

Giver or Taker

      Benches filled with people's life belongings were far too common while we were vacationing. There were dozens upon dozens of people without homes, most of them sleeping on benches by the ocean during the night. For Michael and me, the sadness of their plight was overwhelming. We had not seen so many on the streets in one place other than those cold Sunday mornings when The Carpenter's House would travel downtown here at home to serve bagged lunches and provide blankets and clothing, and it seemed there were even more in the city we were visiting. Yes, some we saw last week were simply panhandlers. Others were truly homeless and struggling just to find a morsel to eat for any given meal.

      However, I digress. This is not a story about their situation, although that is what struck our heart chords first. This is a story of giving what you have even when you have nothing.

      This particular bench was right below our third-floor balcony and was the bed of a man named Steve. I'm not sure of his age, but I'd say it was late 40s to 50. While the benches are comfortable to take a respite from walking the beach or boardwalk, I can't imagine sleeping on one every night. His mattress was a dismantled cardboard carton over the bench seat - something that couldn't possibly be comfortable. As the sun would set in the west on the other side of the buildings, he would snuggle down under a blanket with which he also covered his head. The next bench was the

54

sleeping quarters for a man named Christopher. Christopher was about the same age.

During our entire stay, I never saw these men ask anyone for anything. They simply slept on the benches, arose with the sunrise, and sat and watched the ocean or went (as we later found out from a conversation with them) to the local ministry for a meal when meals were available or a quick shower in the facilities the ministry provided.

On Wednesday afternoon, Michael and I were in our usual spot on the balcony reading and watching the waves. I looked up from the pages and saw a young mother walking while pushing a stroller with one hand and holding the leash of what looked like a Labrador pup in the other.

She stopped just next to the benches in what appeared to be a panic. The dog had gone to the bathroom while walking the last few steps. As she searched her pockets, it became apparent that the bag she had carried for just such an instance had fallen out somewhere along the way. She was obviously extremely upset that she couldn't clean up the mess and removed her cell phone from another pocket to call for help while trying to hold onto the leash and rock the stroller a bit. Again, she was visibly upset to anyone who would notice her.

I cannot tell you how many people like you and me passed by without stopping to see if she was okay or what was wrong. As Michael left the room to go to her, Christopher returned from wherever it was he had been. He went to her to see if he could help. Let that sink in for a minute. Most likely dozens of people had passed by without stopping. Yet the person that most would perhaps look upon as a "taker" or "panhandler" and avoid was the one who immediately offered any assistance he was able to give when he came upon her distress.

We watched as he pulled a napkin from his backpack and cleaned the mess. As he was doing that, Steve also returned. After a brief conversation, he left for a few minutes and returned with some poop bags he had found outside a hotel a short distance away. The young mother calmed and thanked them both for their help before continuing on her way.

This doesn't seem like much, does it? It all took place in the space of a few minutes. Yet in those few minutes, the help of these two men was everything to this young mom. Christopher and Steve, who have virtually nothing, gave what they did have when others kept walking. They gave their compassion and their time. They were kind.

That evening, Michael and I went to dinner and then stopped at a pizza place before returning to the hotel. We got a large pizza and went to the benches, introduced ourselves, and offered Christopher and Steve dinner. They took it gratefully. Michael explained that we had seen their act of genuine kindness earlier in the day. Surprised at our gratefulness for their kindness to someone else, they both answered almost in unison. "We just did what we had to do. She needed help." We encouraged them to eat their dinner while it was hot. They said they would but didn't move to do so and instead continued our conversation. We left them with a smile and a good night. They left us with a memory and a lesson.

It has been our experience before and was confirmed again in these two men. Those who seemingly have nothing to give are not shy about giving whatever they have, be it their food to someone else in need, which we have witnessed many times or a helping hand to someone who has much more than they. The young mother learned that in her time of need. We learned it anew in watching the story unfold.

Perhaps it is their very plight that causes their generosity. Perhaps it is simply their need to give something back in the midst of not feeling productive. Perhaps it is that their eyes are opened to so much more than those of us who are so busy trying to acquire more than we already have. I think it is all of that and more.

I don't want to be like the dozens that passed by without noticing or offering to help. I want to be like these two men. I want to give what I have *even if I don't think I have enough.*

"As Jesus looked up, he saw the rich putting their gifts into the temple treasury. He also saw a poor widow put in two very small copper coins. 'Truly I tell you,' he said, 'this poor widow has put in more than all the others. All these people gave their gifts out of their wealth; but she out of her poverty put in all she had to live on.'"
(Luke 21:1-4 NIV)

*"But the L*ORD *said to Samuel, 'Do not look at his appearance or at the height of his stature, because I have rejected him; for God does not see as man sees, since man looks at the outward appearance, but the L*ORD *looks at the heart.'"*
(1 Samuel 16:7 NASB)

Grateful for Sacrifice

Memorial Day - picnics and parades. Unfortunately, many times those are the things we think of on the last Monday of May. Sadly, the fallen are an afterthought for many when it should be all about remembering and honoring those who have given all that they had to their very last breath.

The number of fallen in our country's wars is somewhere around 1,000,000. That means that many families have grieved and remembered and still grieve and remember their loved ones, not just on days such as this but every day. The reason you and I are able to do the things we do, have picnics and parades, speak freely, and live the lives we live is because of the 1,000,000.

What that number doesn't include are those who returned home but for whom a little piece of their spirit dies each day until there is nothing left. It doesn't include those who returned home to no home other than the streets, and whose lives are not lives at all but mere existence and a continued fight for survival. And it doesn't include those who returned home only to take their own lives because they were impossibly broken and left dead inside by their experiences, which left them with the perception that there was no other way. Those deaths average about twenty per day. That's right, per day. I personally know two families for whom that is a reality.

Memorial Day is not a happy day. It is not a day of joyous celebration. It is solemn day to be grateful. It is a day to remember those who gave everything, and that includes the families of the soldiers who are gone. It is a day to honor those who have given everything they had so that we can have what we have. It is a day to think about the cost of going to war for things that, at times, may not be so important as the lives lost. It is a day to yearn for, pray for, and work for peace.

Take more than a moment today to think of those soldiers and their families. Take more than a moment to be thankful for what you have instead of being bitter about what you don't have. Take more than a moment to pray and ask God to bless those who lay down their lives.

I thank all of you who have gone before for your sacrifice. I pray blessings of comfort upon your families. I ask for peace for the world.

"He will give a longing for justice to their judges. He will give great courage to their warriors who stand at the gates."
(Isaiah 28:6 NLT)

Being a Healer

Let's talk about healing. It's something that's definitely needed in this world. Yes, there are the physical ills that require healing, but that's not the healing I mean.

There are many more people suffering from the deepest wounds possible in their hearts, minds, and souls. These wounds have been inflicted by many different sources. Some have been cast by family and friends. Some have been cast by strangers. Some have been cast by circumstances. It doesn't matter how the wound appeared; it simply matters that it did.

All of us carry the scars of past wounds. Here, however, are some questions: what if they weren't scars? What if they hadn't been healed to the point of being scarred and instead hadn't been healed at all? What if they were still raw, bleeding, and causing pain and damage?

Sadly, we live in a society where wounds are allowed to fester. Others are too busy tending their own wounds to notice. Some people simply don't care to take the time to help in the healing process. Still others impede the healing process by picking away and reopening the wounds again and again. Yes, we must care for our injuries in an attempt to become whole. We also must take the time to care for the injuries of others because they deserve the opportunity to become whole as well. We certainly shouldn't be the cause of intentional injury.

There are so many broken people around us. How can we just pass by without stopping to heal? How can we throw callous words in their direction and go on our merry way? How can we look at the hurt and violence in our community and just turn our heads because we think someone else will take care of it? People are hurting. We are hurting. If we don't make a conscious effort to begin the healing process for everyone, we are no better than the hardened criminals we are all too quick to judge. We look at them, and in a single second and breath cast blame and pronounce sentence. We feel better about ourselves because we would never do such a thing. Yet look at the things we do and say or don't do and say every day. Should not blame and sentence be put upon us?

Jesus came to this world and didn't blame, judge, or sentence any one of us. He gathered us to Himself, placed us in the Father's arms, and began our healing process while gently leading us through each step. If we are to proclaim His name and His love, we must do the same. We need to begin to stitch up the wounds from which so many suffer with love, compassion, and grace, not with ignorance or cold judgment. We need to begin healing our world because without making the Christlike effort to heal the wounds of others, we will never be completely healed ourselves. And here's some food for thought: each time we refuse to help heal the wounds of the hurting, is it not like reopening the devastating wounds our Savior suffered on the cross for us? I don't want to hurt Him again. I want to become more like Him. Father, help me to heal others and place them in Your arms. Make me like Jesus.

The following verse is a command for tithing so the physical needs of others can be filled. I think it also applies to emotional and spiritual ones. My belief is simply this: you cannot profess faith and ignore the desperate need of the hurting around you, whether that need is for food, clothing, housing, or physical and emotional healing. Embrace the broken with love, compassion, grace, and mercy. Let the healing - all healing - begin!

"At the end of every third year you should bring the tenth part of that year's grain into your towns. And the Levite who has no share of what is given to you, and the stranger, and the child without parents, and the woman whose husband has died, who are in your towns, may come and eat and be filled. Then the Lord your God will bring good to you in all the work done by your hands."
(Deuteronomy 14:28-29 New Life Version)

Just a Little Nugget for Today

Joy isn't something that depends on your circumstances or the people around you. Joy is what you carry in your heart and spirit that transcends troubles, frustrations, and even loss. It depends simply on the beliefs you carry with you, the acknowledgement that every day is a blessing no matter what it holds, and the knowledge that you are deeply and unconditionally loved. We all have the gift of joy from our heavenly Father. If you feel it's slipped away, catch it and hold on tight. Show it to everyone, even if they think you're crazy. Shout your joy from wherever you are! Be just like the ocean's waves as they jump to the shore and retreat to do it again and again no matter the storms that may be approaching. Each droplet of those waves shines as it rushes in, and so should you!

Each morning when you wake, be purposeful in praising with the joy that is within you.

"I will be glad and rejoice in You; I will sing praise to Your name, O Most High."
(Psalm 9:2 NKJV)

64

Joining the Fight

The first weekend of June is Relay for Life here in our town. In 2018, I was asked to give the closing talk based on the theme for that year. The theme was "Fight Back." The following is the text for that talk. The lesson here is this: we can all join the fight - for loved ones, for the sick, for the oppressed, for the impoverished, for anyone, not just those who suffer from the devastation of cancer. There is always someone worth fighting for on this earth. Choose your weapons. You might be the only God given backup someone has.

June 2, 2018

I never planned on writing a book. I certainly never planned on writing a book in which cancer played a role. However, when my mom was diagnosed in January of 2005, all of that changed. I just didn't realize it at the time.

"Grace - A View From the Mountaintop" came out of the pages of my journals. I kept notes of every test, doctor visit, hospitalization, medication, complication, and conversation from the moment Momma was diagnosed with breast cancer. I noted her emotions, her choices, her setbacks, and her victories. I just knew I was going to need those notes. I needed - we ALL needed - those notes to fight.

Momma's version of fighting was much different from ours. While my dad, brother, and I reacted with devastation and grief (although not in front of her, for her we kept brave faces), Momma reacted with calm and (true to her name) with grace. The first surgeon appointment after her biopsy and diagnosis stands out in my mind to this day. As he explained the procedures that were available - a lumpectomy followed by radiation and possibly chemotherapy or a mastectomy, which would also possibly be followed by chemotherapy should the lymph nodes show signs of disease - she quietly but firmly interrupted him. Her voice was clear, strong, and definitive. "I'll have the mastectomy," she said, almost as if she was ordering coffee and a meal. She graciously listened to the choices once again and then repeated hers. She had chosen her sword and was not going to be swayed.

Let me be clear: she was not unfeeling. I know she felt concern for the future, but she was choosing to fight for the life she wanted from Minute 1. She was having none of this cancer stuff. She was choosing to be completely in control of her disease rather than let it control her. It was at that point that Daddy's and my fears were pushed into the murky depths and the warriors in us emerged.

Cancer was now thrust into the background. This became a story about life. Fighting back *is* living. Fighting back *is* faith. Fighting back takes on many characteristics. It can be acting or it can be reacting. Her first weapon of choice was prayer. There was not a day during her entire year-long battle (or her life for that matter), no matter how she was feeling, that her Bible and prayer did not constitute the start of her day once I had helped her bathe, dress, and eat breakfast. Prayer

66

was an integral part of each and every day for all of us before this mountain trek was placed in front of us, but it became even more plentiful during this year. In our minds, it is the most effective weapon in our arsenal. Then there were the sometimes more worldly weapons…

When Momma knew she was about to lose her hair, she acted. She called my daughter-in-law (who was a hair stylist) and said she wanted a new look for Easter. On Good Friday she emerged from the kitchen smiling and with a buzz-cut. Score one for Momma.

My cousin, Jeannie, joined the battle with her sewing skills. She made countless turbans for Momma with designs for holidays, seasons, and special occasions along with solid colors for more subdued circumstances. And when it became apparent that her hair was not going to grow back, Momma turned those turbans into a fashion statement with any outfit she wore, receiving many compliments on the different patterns she chose. Another fight, another win.

As her taste buds began to betray her and give her only metallic flavors, I opened my arsenal of frozen jalapeño peppers from the previous season's garden and homemade salsa from my canning shelves. You'd be amazed how many recipes you can use those in! Her appetite increased, and her taste changed with the spicier menu. She began eating more and regaining strength when she needed it. Still another point in the win column.

Daddy's weapon of choice was presence. There was not a moment he left Momma's side other than for the necessity of taking care of his personal needs or the obedience to hospital rules when she was hospitalized. He sat and quietly held her hand, helped her eat, and relayed the day's news from the local paper, or he silently watched her and prayed as she slept.

My weapon was advocacy. There were many times during that year when my voice had to be raised, my temper had to be lost, and my tougher side had to be displayed in order to get the results needed for Momma's care. *Advocacy is a must in this or any fight.* You cannot let anything deter you from wielding the stones and sling of constant watchfulness and championing for the best care of your loved ones and yourself. There were times people didn't like me very much or became offended. That was a price I was prepared to pay to see Momma benefit from receiving exactly what she needed at any given time.

The weapons wielded by my husband and brother were of the more practical variety. They ranged from lawnmowers to vacuum cleaners to grilling tools. They picked up the slack left behind by the rest of us while we were caring for Momma's needs.

And lastly, my son's and grandson's weapon was that of pure, unadulterated love for this wonderful woman who loved them so much. They provided smiles with every visit, which bolstered Momma's strength and resolve.

The description of the weapons in the fight aren't really so important; it is the fight itself that resonates. The important fact is that Momma was never a *victim* of cancer. She never allowed herself to be a victim but turned the tables on the disease. She fought back with every ounce of strength she had within her, and when that strength waned, we fought back for her with our entire arsenal to replenish what she was lacking. When we felt we were too weak to go on ourselves, the entire community of family and friends took up the sword. It was a battle hard fought and hard won, but it was a battle well worth the fighting.

Momma passed away 5 months ago today at the age of 87. In the end, the hard-fought battle gave her almost ten years of being cancer-free before having a lumpectomy on the remaining breast, and another three years of life, love, and laughter with her family after that. It was not cancer that prefaced her passing, it was the simple ravages of age on her heart. She left this world the way she lived in this world and in the same way she fought her battles - with faith and, of course, grace. She was indeed a warrior.

None of us here - patients or caregivers - are victims of this disease. We have chosen to be in control. We are here to say that we have fought and are fighting back. We will not give up the fight. We will continue to use whatever we have to take control and put cancer in its place. We will pray, love, support, advocate, act, and react. And we will remember that even when we think we cannot take one more step, there are others out there to take us by the hand, lift us up, and carry us. They will take the steps for us.

For those who have gone before us, we must remember that cancer did not *take* their lives. Those lives were not *lost.* In my eyes and in the faith passed on to me by my mom, they were just more wholly healed in a way we do not yet understand. They fought back, we fought with them, and the battle was won by

Almighty God.

Until the day when cancer no longer exists, battles will be waged and won. And we will always fight back. We will always fight back in faith knowing God's got this.

"Then your light will break forth like the dawn, and your healing will quickly appear; then your righteousness will go before you, and the glory of the LORD will be your rear guard. Then you will call, and the LORD will answer; you will cry for help, and he will say: Here am I."
(Isaiah 58:8-9 NIV)

Dedicated to my friends and their families as well as many in my own family who have fought this battle –

> The Wert, Bowman, Ulle, and Rothenberger families
> Sandy and Tim
> Kyle
> Robin and Jeff
> and warriors everywhere

Dock Sitter or Seeker

We're all waiting for the things we desire most. We sit at the dock of life and patiently - but mostly impatiently - wait for our ship to come in. It doesn't matter what the desire is. It could be a better job, bigger house and yard, vacation home, dream trip, or retirement. The list of the things we want for our lives is endless.

The question is this: how much are we missing by sitting at the dock? There are miracles happening all around us. Some are as simple as our next breath, while others are the big things like healing for a loved one or ourselves. Then there is the myriad of miraculous happenings in between that brings so much beauty to life.

Early this morning, I watched a man standing at the edge of the ocean's waves. He stood quietly and in solitude. I don't think he moved even an inch the entire time I watched, and he had been standing there for some time before I went out on the balcony. The question lies in what had him so still, so intent, and so expectant. Was it the ship far offshore that was slowly approaching? Was it something else? What had him so patiently waiting on this beautiful seaside morning?

Waiting in itself is not the issue. Patiently waiting is a good thing as long as we are also aware of what is going on around us and not just focused in tunnel vision fashion on what we want for indeterminate periods of time, which means remaining stagnant. While we are staring off into the sea waiting for that ship, other smaller and no less important ships are passing by our dock. We're missing out on some beautiful moments intended just for us!

As I watched this man so intently watching the horizon, I realized he was not waiting for the ship to come to shore. He never turned toward it for a second. He was focused on the changing colors of the horizon as the sun rose. He was certainly not about to miss this miracle of beauty that was solely meant for this particular morning. Yes, sunrises come and go every day. Yet no one sunrise is like any other. Perhaps this was the miracle he needed in his life at this appointed time - a gateway miracle of sorts that would encourage him to put one foot in front of the other and press on as other miracles were revealed on the way to his goal.

When the sun had risen in its glorious backdrop of color, he calmly turned and walked away. The morning miracle had come. He did not stand there to wait for it to return, but instead focused on moving purposefully into whatever other miracles the day had in store for him. He wasn't a dock sitter. He was a seeker.

May we all become fervent and movable seekers, not dock sitters committed to one single thing in such a way as to become stagnant. Take the first step. Your day's miracles await!

"He alone stretches out the skies and walks on the waves of the sea. It is God who made the Bear, Orion, and the Pleiades and the groups of stars in the southern sky. He does wonders that cannot be understood; he does so many miracles they cannot be counted."
(Job 9:8-10 NCV)

A Tale of Two Sides

We're halfway through 2020, and the division line in our society is growing by the moment. From cries of "injustice" to cries of "criminal," the chasm grows. What in the world are we teaching our children?

Lives matter. In the current day, protesters are insisting that black lives matter. Indeed, they do. George Floyd matters. Those who were struck down before him matter. Those who will be struck down in the future, though I fervently pray there are none, matter. The other side is shouting that police lives matter. Indeed, they do. Those who selflessly serve surely matter. Both those who have been struck and those who serve matter - equally. The life of the elderly man who lies in a hospital bed with a head injury matters. The lives that are pleading for an end to oppression, inequality, and injustice matter. The lives of those perpetrating acts of violence that increase the chasm matter.

Here is the simple truth: God gave *all* of them life. They *all* matter. Jesus died for *all* of them. They *all* matter.

Our responsibilities in this are many. We have a responsibility to care for the widow and the fatherless. We have a responsibility to stand against oppression and injustice. We have a responsibility to cry out for fairness and equality and against anything that negates those. If we cannot speak out against those things on a sweeping level, then we have a responsibility to remain silent as opposed to speaking with bias. We have a

74

responsibility to do what is right, hold on to what is true, and give the grace that we are given.

We have a responsibility to love. We have a responsibility to pray.

It has been extremely excruciating to see the videos of Mr. Floyd dying with a knee on his neck - a knee that remained there for a full two minutes after he became unresponsive. Just as difficult was seeing a 75-year-old man shoved to the ground as those who shoved him watched his blood pour from his head and ears as they walked by. Equally heartbreaking is watching neighborhoods burned to the ground, businesses looted, hearing about officers injured or killed responding to such things, and then seeing their families grieve their terrible loss. Just as saddening is seeing thousands upon thousands peacefully marching and begging for what should already be - sameness in treatment among all peoples.

I can do nothing else but write and pray. Of the two, praying has been at the forefront because I have been unable to find words to put on paper lately. As soon as I start, my tears fall to the point where I cannot see what I am writing.

And so, I urge you to take to heart the encouragement throughout the Bible. Pray. Seek the Lord and petition Him for wisdom, guidance, understanding, mercy, and healing.

Pray for all of those involved in this - in actuality we need to pray for all people, because we are all involved on some level. When you do, be sure not to be selective in your prayers. As Jesus warns, it is easy to love those who love you. It is easy to pray for those you love. It is easy to give grace to those you love. Anyone can do that. You will not find it so easy to pray for those for whom you don't feel love, for those with whom you don't agree, or for those against whom you harbor anger and, dare I say it, hatred in your heart. Yet you must.

Pray for Mr. Floyd and those like him. Pray for the elderly gentleman who was seriously injured. Pray for the businesses lost. Pray for the police officers injured or killed. Pray for those who are marching for justice and equality even in the face of tear gas, pepper spray, and sometimes violent acts against them in their peaceful assemblies. Pray that all people would see the need to treat all they meet with equal consideration regardless of perceived differences.

Pray for the perpetrators of injustice. Pray for the officers who have committed or are thinking about committing acts of violence inconsistent with the honor of the positions they hold against the world's citizens. Pray for those who are looting and burning in their misguided desperation or selfish desire.

Pray for God's grace to flow into you and out to others. Pray for Him to enable you to love all people and not just those you like.

Pray instead of condemning. After all, Jesus Christ did not condemn us. He died for us. He saved us. It's not really a tale of two sides at all. There is only one side - the side of the love of Christ.

"So, then, this is my very first command: God's people should make petitions, prayers, intercessions and thanksgivings on behalf of all people – on behalf of

*kings, and all who hold high office, so that we may lead
a tranquil and peaceful life, in all godliness and
holiness. This is good; it is acceptable with God our
saviour, who wants all people to be saved and to come
to know the truth."*
(1 Timothy 2:1-4 New Testament for Everyone)

Our Tongue Holds the Power

Sometimes we have to address the more difficult and often overlooked topics. Today, gossip comes to mind.

Gossip runs rampant, especially in today's technological miracle of social media. While its use brings to mind something that carries the connotations of being a plague of the young, particularly the high school years, it also invades most facets of adult life - family interactions, workplaces, the local gym, churches, social gatherings, and the like.

It seems harmless enough to our sometimes busy and worldly, clouded minds. "Did you hear that so-and-so did this?" "Did you hear what he/she said to him/her?" "Do you know that they...?" On some level, we feel we're just passing on information. On a deeper level, we are perpetuating something that could have long-lasting and harmful effects on the lives of other people.

Rumor mills abound, and the result is the ruination of reputations, relationships, and lives. Being in the midst of passing on what seems to us to be necessary information makes us the instruments of destruction - weapons that can be far more catastrophic than any weapon of mass destruction in any war between nations. Why? Because the destruction is not immediate as with a bomb; it is not even noticeable at first. Instead, the disaster that will occur is the slow, tortuous damnation of a person or persons that can, at its worst, be impossible from which to recover and, at best, will cause short-term anxiety and depression as the subject wonders why they are the target of such nonsense.

Gossip is an insidious worm that hides under the guise of concern or the need to set something "right." Truth be told, in the end it ruins the gossiper as well as the gossipee. (Yes, I know that's not a word. Let's just call it artistic license.)

I don't have a solution to gossip on a grand scale. I don't even have a solution to gossip on a small scale. The only solution I have, or any of us have, is on a personal level. We all have the capability of self-control. The answer is as simple as this: just don't do it! Determine within yourself to not "whisper down the line." Even *if* the tidbit *is* true, even *if* you get it from the horse's mouth, and even *if* you get it perfectly right in the relaying, you are not helping anyone, including yourself. The easiest course to take is to just walk away. The truth is it is not your story to tell.

We have the power to encourage or oppress. We have the power to lift up or drag down. We hold the power of thriving relationships or floundering ones in our mouths. Choose to encourage, lift up, and help to thrive.

"In the same way, the tongue is a small thing that makes grand speeches. But a tiny spark can set a great forest on fire. And among all the parts of the body, the tongue is a flame of fire. It is a whole world of wickedness, corrupting your entire body. It can set your whole life on fire, for it is set on fire by hell itself. People can tame all kinds of animals, birds, reptiles, and fish,

but no one can tame the tongue. It is restless and evil, full of deadly poison. And so blessing and cursing come pouring out of the same mouth."
(James 3:5-8, 10 NLT)

The Tough Subject of Responsibility

It's simple human nature. We all hate to look at ourselves and take responsibility for certain things in any given situation. We can't see past the perception that we have been wronged. The driver that cuts us off in traffic, the friend or family member with whom we disagree, the workplace incident that seems to shed a bad light on us, the words that stick like barbs in our souls - things just are not right, there is always plenty of blame, and the blame is never ours.

This is not to say others have not insulted, hurt, and at times even abused us. The human world is certainly a cruel place. This also is not to say that our indignation, anger, and defensive reactions are not (in some way) warranted. Our personal responsibility comes in how we react to these things.

Assuming that we did nothing to cause that driver to swerve around us and cut off our path on the road - we weren't distracted by coffee, phone, radio, etc. - we do not have control over his actions. The same applies to those who insult us, providing the first hurtful words uttered were not our own. And again, the issue at work may have been completely beyond our control, simply catching us in the fallout. While our reaction may be quick, it should remain just that - a response that begins and ends in an appropriate manner and time frame.

Disagreements with a friend or family member fall into a different category. There is always an option during these times. It comes down to a simple heart-mind-mouth connection. There should always be forethought when speaking. Are these words really going to help? Is this just a knee-jerk reaction because I don't like the stand they're taking? Is whatever we're arguing about important enough to have significant impact on our relationship or daily lives? In the end, most disagreements are not greatly impactful to life. If, indeed, we find the subject to be that important to our personal, heartfelt, and lifelong beliefs, then by all means we should state our case. However, we need to be responsible enough to do that with words that are not damaging to the other person; we certainly need to know when it's time to stop talking, agree to disagree, and walk away before permanent damage is done.

Abusive situations are a different matter. No one deserves physical, emotional, or mental abuse. These are situations where we must walk away for our own safety. The key to dealing with these issues is in walking away and leaving it alone. We must find someone we trust to work through the resulting emotions and a support system that is willing to be completely honest with us should we seem to be falling into the same type of situation again or perpetuating the situation we have just escaped.

Our initial reactions come from the hurt we have suffered. They are normal. While they may be justified, there is no justification for continuing them over a sustained period. Forgiveness, as difficult as it is to give, is an undeniable requirement in healing. No, the other side may not have admitted to anything or asked to be forgiven; neither have we. No, they may not be deserving of being forgiven; neither are we. No, we might not feel like forgiving them, but we must! Forgiveness heals the wounds our spirits have suffered. It is the first and most important step to becoming whole. For those of my friends who profess faith, where would we be had God not forgiven us?

The next and equally important step is (disclaimer: you're going to have this song in your head all day) to let it go. In today's social media-oriented society, it is quite easy to keep rehashing things. The comments, "likes," and sympathy replies pour in like a river over our wounds. It's a temporary feel-good kind of thing. This only perpetuates the problem in many ways. Yes, it helps to talk things out - with one or two trusted people. Constantly rehashing things in the public arena doesn't accomplish anything good. If we consistently spout the hurts, we cannot heal from them. Instead, we open the wound again and again, requiring healing to begin afresh. The other problem is that the good perception others have of us will begin to be tarnished, which may start the cycle anew. We start to appear bitter, malicious, difficult, and self-centered, particularly if this is all we talk about on any given day. In truth, the bitterness and maliciousness begin to grow in our hearts when we don't forgive, don't let go, and refuse to move forward. No one wants to live in that way.

As hard as it is to admit, particularly to ourselves, we all retain some responsibility - perhaps not for the initial incident (although we do need to examine our hearts when it comes to that, too) but definitely for our continued words and reactions. Where do we begin in solving our problems and healing our hurts? We start in the mirror. We start by taking ownership of our hearts, minds, and mouths. We stand on our own feet and move forward, step by step.

"Then Peter came to him and said, 'Master, how often should I forgive my brother if he sins against me? Seven times?' Jesus said to him, 'I say to you, not seven times, but seventy times seven times.'"
(Matthew 18:21-22 New Matthew Bible)

"Search me, O God, and know my heart; Try me, and know my anxieties; and see if there is any wicked way in me, and lead me in the way everlasting."
(Psalm 139:23-24 NKJV)

Look With Open Eyes

I am reminded on my walks each morning just how indescribably beautiful the world can be. The everyday miracle of the sunrise is a testament to this. I am also constantly reminded on my drives to and from work how cruel it can be. That is quite evident in the numbers of those forced to live on the streets due to circumstances from which recovery is more than difficult.

Being a beautiful, compassionate spirit is a choice. You might not feel like it. You might be having a bad day. Turning that into a good or even great day is quite simple. Choose beauty. Choose compassion. Choose love. Choose to live your life bringing those things to others just as you desire them to be brought to you. You will find that not only are you able to lift the spirits of others from a darkened place but your own as well.

Don't close or avert your eyes to those you see on your daily travels. All of God's children deserve the same care and kindness that you feel you do. A simple bottle of water, snack, or even just a smile and words of encouragement go a long way in prospering His kingdom and your spirit. Love your neighbor!

"One day an expert in religious law stood up to test Jesus by asking him this question: 'Teacher, what should I do to inherit eternal life?' Jesus replied, 'What does the law of Moses say? How do you read it?' The man answered, 'You must love the LORD your God with

all your heart, all your soul, all your strength, and all your mind. And, love your neighbor as yourself.'
'Right!' Jesus told him. 'Do this and you will live!' The man wanted to justify his actions, so he asked Jesus, 'And who is my neighbor?' Jesus replied with a story: 'A Jewish man was traveling from Jerusalem down to Jericho, and he was attacked by bandits. They stripped him of his clothes, beat him up, and left him half dead beside the road. By chance a priest came along. But when he saw the man lying there, he crossed to the other side of the road and passed him by. A Temple assistant walked over and looked at him lying there, but he also passed by on the other side. Then a despised Samaritan came along, and when he saw the man, he felt compassion for him. Going over to him, the Samaritan soothed his wounds with olive oil and wine and bandaged them. Then he put the man on his own donkey and took him to an inn, where he took care of him. The next day he handed the innkeeper two silver coins, telling him, 'Take care of this man. If his bill runs higher than this, I'll pay you the next time I'm here.' Now which of these three would you say was a neighbor to the man who was attacked by bandits?' Jesus asked. The man replied, 'The one who showed him mercy.' Then Jesus said, 'Yes, now go and do the same.'"
(Luke 10:25-37 NLT)

Lead By Example

Lead by example. Following others, while sometimes beneficial if they possess more wisdom than you in a certain circumstance, more often will put you into a place you don't need to be. I would go as far as to say that it can put you into a place that you shouldn't be.

Lead by example. If you want peace, foster it. If you want justice, encourage it. If you want love, give it. If you want equality, treat all others (even those you don't like) equally. If you want honesty and integrity, exhibit those. The list goes on and on. You will see in others the things you set before them - even those things that are undesirable such as violence, undermining, hatred, deception, and unkindness. Stick with the positive and beneficial traits.

Lead by example. Never tell half-truths. While the truth may sting at times, half of the truth is harmful to you and those listening. A half-truth will render any chance at growth stagnant. A half-truth could risk or ruin a life. Half-truths are the same as lies. They benefit nothing.

Lead by example. Do not pepper your speech with expletives to get the point across or to demean others. Keep your words forthright, kind, and clean. You will find that others are more willing to listen when you are respectful.

Lead by example. Give grace when it is needed. We all need grace and forgiveness at any given point in our days. Think of the ultimate grace you have been given and extend it to others. On the other side of that coin, always be ready to ask for grace and forgiveness when you have misspoken or done wrong. It's not a weakness; it's strength of character.

Lead by example. Listen first. Listen intently. Listen with purpose. Be willing to learn before speaking your mind and heart. By listening well, you will find that you are listened to well.

Lead by example. Leading does not mean standing above, walking ahead, or prodding from behind. Leading is not boasting that you are leading. Leading means standing shoulder to shoulder, eye to eye, and heart to heart. Leading is quietly setting a good example without unneeded explanation. Leading is simply walking with others in love, lighting the way when you are able, standing aside when someone else has light to shine, and showing compassion and kindness.

Lead by example. Leading means following Him who possesses all wisdom and has the best interests of the entire human race at heart. Ask Him and He will show you the way you should go.

Lead by example. As far as it concerns you, live in peace with everyone. Show the graciousness of patience. Speak only words of encouragement. Be kind. Be understanding. Love others. Think of others as more important than yourself.

Lead by example.

"The Pharisees and the scribes occupy the seat of Moses. So you should do the things they tell you to do—but don't do the things they do. They heap heavy

burdens upon their neighbors' backs, and they prove unwilling to do anything to help shoulder the load. They are interested, above all, in presentation: they wrap their heads and arms in the accoutrements of prayer, they cloak themselves with flowing tasseled prayer garments, they covet the seats of honor at fine banquets and in the synagogue, and they love it when people recognize them in the marketplace, call them 'Teacher,' and beam at them. But you: do not let anyone call you 'Rabbi,' that is, 'Teacher.' For you are all brothers, and you have only one teacher, the Anointed One. Indeed, do not call anyone on earth 'Father,' for you have only one father, and He is in heaven. Neither let anyone call you 'leader,' for you have one leader— the Anointed One. If you are recognized at all, let it be for your service. Delight in the one who calls you servant. For whoever exalts himself will be humbled, and whoever humbles himself will be exalted."
(Matthew 23:2-12 The Voice)

The Foundation of Praise

Why is it we seem to concentrate on the oddities of life (usually the negative ones) instead of the beauty of everyday occurrences? We focus on the one thing we didn't accomplish, the one moment we felt insulted or offended, and that one event of disappointment we endured instead of the joy that accompanies our days.

God's blessings abound in everyday life if only we take the time to dwell on them! Yet we concentrate on those annoyances that pop up from time to time and miss out on what we need - the joy of everyday circumstance, the moments of kindness, contentment in a job well done, and the love brought by those around us. We take those things for granted and virtually ignore them because we are "used to them."

The simplicity of watching a sunrise or sunset, the undemanding walking in step with our own beat, the effortless moments spent with friends and family, the uncomplicated truth of knowing we are loved - these are the things on which we should concentrate to recognize the blessing and beauty in our lives. These will bring the confidence and joy for which we long. We need only recognize them and focus on them. Thanksgiving needs to be the foundation on which we build our lives, along with the solid rock that is Jesus..

"With praise and thanksgiving they sang to the LORD: 'He is good; his love toward Israel endures forever.' And all the people gave a great shout of praise to the LORD, because the foundation of the house of the LORD was laid."
(Ezra 3:11 NIV)

Everyday Blessings

It seems we all wish for the big or extreme blessings in life. We long for that winning lottery ticket that will pay off our mortgage or buy a new car. We long for the chance to go on a lengthy cruise to anywhere, just to get away and relax. I don't know anyone who doesn't wish for a cure for cancer and so many other debilitating or terminal diseases. If only we received this, if only we solved that - if only.

While all of these are not out of the question because nothing is impossible with God, they are improbable. Yet we ruminate on them and complain (dare I say, "whine") when they don't come to pass. In doing so, we miss out on so many of the everyday things that have the wondrous capability to bring us joy.

I have been absent from the keyboard for a bit simply because of these everyday blessings. While focusing on the larger things I desired since I last wrote - an end to the incessant rain, the demise of the nasty lantern flies that have invaded our state, and a complete lack of time to sit down and get words onto paper or screen - I was also reminded of the blessings some of those things have caused.

We'll start with the rain. Yes, it has been terrible with all the flooding in our region. Roads become impassable, basements fill with water, and in some cases back yards and stone driveways are completely washed away. It's devastating in some ways yet a blessing in others. I grieve the loss of many of my perennials that couldn't take all that water. While some crops are severely stunted by the deluge, others are producing at a tremendous rate. Just look at your local farm stand (or perhaps my modest backyard garden). I've noticed that watermelons and cantaloupes are in great supply. My eggplants are coming in by the half-dozen at a time, but the cucumber vines were rotted and had to be pulled from the ground. And tomatoes! I have a modest six plants, yet there have been tomato sandwiches for lunch and fresh garden salads at dinner for weeks now, as well as quarts and quarts of sauce and pints and pints of salsa. The funny thing about those plants is that the vines are dying from the ground up (probably because of root rot), but the tomatoes are still ripening at a steady rate. There will be more canning to come shortly.

Another of the larger desires we've experienced was the wish for packing and moving my dad's belongings quickly and easily. That didn't quite happen. It took much longer than we thought and was fraught with annoying little problems along the way. Since my mom's passing in January, he decided to sell his home and move into an apartment. He was placed on a waiting list for the apartment back in April, but his house sold more quickly than anyone thought, and his apartment isn't available yet. So, his things are now in storage. The blessing is that my dad now resides with us. Yes, it was an adjustment for us to add another person to the household just as it was an adjustment for him to be with two other people and two dogs. However, the blessing of having him with us is wonderful. Hopefully, it is for him as well.

I have even found a blessing in the lantern fly infestation. Yes, I still want them gone in the worst way, but their existence has made me aware of and thankful for so many of the other insects that are beneficial to our trees and gardens and to the birds that I love to watch each morning.

Lastly, you all know how I love to sit and write. However, taking the time to can and freeze the bounty of the garden for the winter months and being able to spend more time with my dad definitely brings much more blessing to the table!

We all want the big things, but it's just as important (if not more so) to not miss the little things. The lottery ticket might not show up, but the provision is there to pay the mortgage or the car loan. You might not get to go on that cruise, but there is relaxation and peace to be found in your backyard and in the company of loved ones. The cure for cancer or other diseases may be far off in the distance, but there is much to be learned about the love, determination, courage, and faith of those who live with those illnesses and of those who are caregivers to them every day.

As for my previously mentioned absence, I have a feeling it will be happening again very soon. There are more tomatoes to put up for the winter, and the apples (hopefully not too damaged by the weather or the pests) to do soon, too.

Just remember this: there's a harvest of blessing out there waiting for you. Don't miss out by overlooking it!

"The Lord is my shepherd; I have all that I need. He lets me rest in green meadows; he leads me besides peaceful streams. He renews my strength. He guides me along right path, bringing honor to his name. Even when I walk through the darkest valley, I will not be afraid, for you are close beside me. Your rod and your staff protect and comfort me. You prepare a feast for me in the presence of my enemies. You honor me by anointing my head with oil. My cup overflows with blessings. Surely your goodness and unfailing love will pursue me all the days of my life, and I will live in the house of the Lord forever."
(Psalm 23 NLT)

The Necessity of Accountability

Being accountable in all areas of life is important. Yet in today's world of technology with its online capabilities, many don't feel the need to keep proper accounts.

I spoke recently with someone who no longer feels the need to reconcile their bank statement to their checkbook. The logic they gave me went something like this: "When I pay a bill online or use my debit card, I just check the balance using the automated system if I need to do so. They tell me how much money I have." Granted, this person was of a younger generation than myself and much more trustful when it comes to technology. However, my OCD still stood there (mentally) with eyes bulging and mouth gaping. How can you not understand that just because the bank's system tells you that you have X-amount of dollars, it may not be accurate to what you really have? There are, perhaps, payments or direct deposits (since no one gets a paper paycheck for the most part anymore) that haven't cleared your account. There could be fees of which you're unaware. There could be errors in the bank's system. Yes, banks do make mistakes. Automated equipment reads numbers wrong from time to time – maybe not as often as a human being might, but it still happens. And on occasion, creditors' systems enter double payments in error, causing amounts to be doubly deducted. I've seen it on my own bank statements and those at work. Any of these could lead to overdrafts and unnecessary fees, wasting your hard-earned money.

All of this may sound ridiculous to those who no longer feel the need to keep a bank register of any sort. I am here to tell you it is a necessity (whether in a paper check register or on your laptop or desktop in an Excel document). In the end, you are responsible for keeping track of your money, no one else - only you. To not do so is irresponsible.

Not keeping proper accounts is like stumbling blindly down a darkened alleyway holding your wallet loosely in one hand as a thief approaches you. The wallet and your money will be gone in an instant, perhaps your physical well-being also. Much better to be in a well-lit area while your wallet is safely tucked into your pant pocket or your purse. You are - and must be - responsible to keep your financial accounts in a fastidious manner just as you are responsible for keeping proper accounts in your life.

Life has its own set of accounts. There are relationships - family, friend, and work relationships, new and old relationships. There are standards, whether we choose to live to them or not. There are behaviors that are appropriate and those that are not. There are checks and balances, debits and credits, wrongs and rights. No one else can keep an accounting of such things in your life; only you can do that. Only you are responsible to do that.

There are mental columns, which we all should keep current - words spoken, deeds done, and thoughts thought as well as words, deeds, and thoughts stopped dead in their tracks. There is good and bad in each one of these. The key in accounting for our life is to be sure that the good is what comes forth into the columns and the bad presents itself rarely, if at all.

Yes, there are times when the bad will surface despite our best efforts or due to the lack of our best efforts. We are, after all, only human. It is then that accountability is crucial. Corrective entries must be made to keep our rights in higher balance than our wrongs. Sincere apologies, reversing of costly actions whenever possible, and keeping closer track of our thought processes leading us to act or react - in other words, living with purpose and integrity - can up the end total in those good columns.

Thinking of others before ourselves, choosing our words to encourage and not harm, and kindness in action and deed should be the accounts we want to have grow and thrive. The "fees" of life - those things that are the consequences of unkind words, deeds, and thoughts - are the accounts we want to avoid just as we want to avoid overdraft charges from the bank. Both are costly, one to the wallet and one to the heart.

Everyone can be a good accountant. It takes persistence, understanding, and integrity. It means taking the moment to make a choice between stumbling as easy prey down that darkened alley into the hands of the waiting thief and keeping that which is valuable close to us and in hand by shining an honest light on ourselves and the path before us.

We are meant to live richly - not so much in the monetary sense but more in the character and joy sense. Opening our eyes to accountability and shining the light on our path will help bring the abundance of life we are meant to have.

"The eye is the lamp of the body. So, if your eye is healthy, your whole body will be full of light, but if your eye is unhealthy, your whole body will be full of darkness. If then the light in you is darkness, how great is the darkness!"
(Matthew 6:22-23 NRSV)

Here's To the Overcomers

Life is not always a bowl of cherries; neither is it spent perpetually in the pits. Instead, it is the perfect balance of the two meant to create character, endurance, and all of the qualities needed to be a shining example to others as well as to mold us into a wondrous and closer-to-perfection specimen driven to purpose.

Memories of times past might bring a smile. They might bring tears and fears as well. Yet if you map your life in reverse, you will find all of them served to bring you to where you are and make you the person you are - just as future memories will bring you further and mold you more.

The past few days have been some of those moments for me. I have this blessed (or cursed) ability to remember dates and times very easily. That means I can remember exact moments, from the smallest and most insignificant happenings to the biggest and most significant ones. Michael says it's weird to be able to do that. Sometimes I wish I couldn't. Sometimes he wishes I couldn't. However, that is not the point here.

The things we wish we didn't remember are often the very things we need to remember - not because we should relive how terrible they may have been, but because we should look on them with gratitude for the changes they made in our lives. At the risk of repeating myself, which I do quite often when I'm writing, they have brought us to where we are, and the outcome is not always a bad thing even if the event itself was.

None of these events seem easy or desired when we are experiencing them. As a matter of fact, some of them are blatantly catastrophic. However, there is always a way through to the other side. How long it takes to get there is our choice. We can wallow in the pain or trudge through the muck to solid ground - easier said than done to be sure but well worth the effort it takes.

So, here's to the ones who went through what seemed like the fires of hell to emerge stronger. Here's to those who have learned and grown from the catastrophes they've endured. Here's to all who walked with them, extended a hand to help them up and steady their steps, and those who remember the pain and difficulty of watching someone they love struggle every day.

Here's to the overcomers. Thank you for making your way through and showing others how to do the same. You know who you are, and you know (hopefully) how much you are loved.

"You know that in a race all the runners run, but only one gets the prize. So run to win! All those who compete in the games use self-control so they can win a crown. That crown is an earthly thing that lasts only a short time, but our crown will never be destroyed."
(1 Corinthians 9:24-25 NCV)

The Uncomfortable but Indisputable Truth

This truth is going to be uncomfortable: God sees all sin in the same way. He cannot look at it. He does not see one act of sin as greater or lesser than another. *All* of it grieves Him.

Our human perspective is quite different. I am not sure if it is because of our flawed vision or our flawed sense of right and wrong. We put murder further up the ladder than thievery because murder is taking a life, whereas thievery is stealing things. We put hatred higher than gossip because hatred is forbidden by the commandment that tells us to love one another, whereas gossip isn't directly mentioned in a commandment. However, bearing false witness is. The two could be fraternal twins. Besides, gossip doesn't hurt anyone, right? The Apostle Paul, however, denounces it in his letters and says to rid ourselves of anger, rage, malice, slander, and filthy language. Prioritizing sins for punishment and/or human forgiveness is truly misguided. Prioritizing is an act of human nature not God's nature. Sin, my friends, is sin.

Trying to explain this concept is difficult. We are better off simply accepting the word of God in this area without question. Our righteousness is all filthy rags. All sin is black as blackest night. All sin needs redemption. All sin needs to be washed white. If not, God could not look upon any of us - ever.

Here is my take on trying to explain it from a human viewpoint.

Yes, killing someone takes a life. We cannot imagine how someone could do such a thing. Stealing things doesn't seem nearly as bad to us, but let's look at it from a different perspective. What if the thing the thief steals is a necessity for the life of the victim? What if the loss of that thing causes the loss of the victim's life? To me, that seems to put it on a more even playing field.

Hatred takes on many meanings. Hatred can be a feeling, words, or actions. Biblically, the word hatred is defined as intense hostility or sustained ill will, sometimes accompanied by malice. Hatred often harbors the desire to cause harm to someone. Now, in bringing harm to someone, we're heading back up the ladder towards murder on the human scale of thinking. The playing field is leveling with this one, too.

Gossip couldn't possibly reach any of those heights of sin, could it? We often think of gossip as a fun past time that is harmless. In reality, such a thing can be devastating to a life. Reputations can be ruined. Character can be questioned. The fun past time of a friendly chat about others can, if taken to others and expanded as it goes, take away someone's standing in their community, their employment, their family relationships, or friendships. It has the capability to garner irreparable damage. Whether we want to acknowledge it or not, gossip is malicious and hateful, stealing valuable things from the life of another. In the most extreme cases, it can cause such despair in the object of the gossip that the person will attempt to take their own life.

And now, we're back to the top of the ladder again. There is a reason our Father looks at all sin from an even perspective. It is all detrimental to His creation - those He created in His image and loves more than we could ever fathom.

Let's come down from our pedestals and stop thinking of ourselves as better than others based on our human scale of measurement. We have placed ourselves on them for far too long. Sin is sin. It all looks the same in the eyes of our Father. God tells us that the wages of sin is death. There is only one way around that. That way is to place ourselves on the level ground at the foot of the cross and let Jesus take over. That is where our forgiveness is found and where our life is guaranteed.

Matthew 5:21-24
(Same scripture, two versions today)
*"You have heard that our ancestors were told, 'You must not murder. If you commit murder, you are subject to judgment.' But I say, if you are even angry with someone, you are subject to judgment! If you call someone an idiot, you are in danger of being brought before the court. And if you curse someone, you are in danger of the fires of hell. So if you are presenting a sacrifice at the altar in the Temple and you suddenly remember that someone has something against you, leave your sacrifice there at the altar. Go and be reconciled to that person. Then come and offer your sacrifice to God." **(NLT)***

"You're familiar with the command to the ancients, 'Do not murder.' I'm telling you that anyone who is so much as angry with a brother or sister is guilty of murder. Carelessly call a brother 'idiot!' and you just might find yourself hauled into court. Thoughtlessly yell 'stupid!' at a sister and you are on the brink of hellfire. The simple moral fact is that words kill. This is how I want you to conduct yourself in these matters. If you enter your place of worship and, about to make an offering, you suddenly remember a grudge a friend has against you, abandon your offering, leave immediately, go to this friend and make things right. Then and only then, come back and work things out with God."
(The Message)

Sift Through the Chaos to Pursue Peace

As I sit here on this humid and cloudy Saturday morning, the dogs are at my feet... and barking loudly. It is what should be the last day there are craftsmen in our home doing work on the kitchen. The noise in this room is deafening - Sally's spinal cord rending, high-pitched bark and Angel's bass-toned boom. Ah, the love of pups!

And yet, the young man grouting our backsplash that he so beautifully tiled yesterday continues his work unperturbed. It's like he has found some secret to peace amid the cacophony of barking. As for me, I keep trying to shush my two beautiful girls (Daddy is still sleeping...maybe), which only seems to force them to make themselves known more loudly.

"When peace like a river..."* Keep moving, folks - no peace here, only the whitecaps of rapids.

Still, the longer I sit and listen to the words flooding my mind and heart in their insistence to be put on this page, peace indeed does begin to insert itself into my being.

The noise of the world is quite chaotic. Peace is, at best, elusive. There seems no way to find it, let alone get our hands on it and take it for ourselves.

Did you ever think there's a reason for all of that noise? Agreed, some of it is quite unnecessary and brought on by our own tendency to allow it. Then there is the rest of the noise. It's there for a purpose. It's there because we need to listen. It's there because that's where the peace is found.

106

The incessant barking of my dogs, which has now subsided, has a purpose. "Mommy, there's a stranger in the house!" That's something I would need to know had I not been expecting Ben's arrival early this morning. The equally incessant noise of many of the voices in the world has just as much purpose.

The cries of help, need, and sometimes warning consistently seem to go by unnoticed other than the irritation of their clamor for attention. The sound of God's voice in our hearts and minds, sadly, goes unnoticed as well. The two are intertwined, and peace resides in the center. If you notice the cries and pay close attention, the still, small voice of the Father comes through loudly and clearly and reveals their purpose. Paying attention to that will bring you straight into the presence of peace.

And so, my advice is don't block out the noise. Don't ignore it. Sift through it, separate the necessary from the contrived, and find the purpose; then act. Whether the action is the actual helping of another lost and needy soul or sitting at the feet of the One who loves us most and has something to tell us, we will find the peace we crave.

"When peace like a river..."* Stop and let it attend your soul.

"Thou wilt keep him in perfect peace, whose mind is stayed on thee: because he trusteth in thee. Trust ye in the LORD for ever: for in the LORD JEHOVAH is everlasting strength."
(Isaiah 26:3-4 KJV)

*It Is Well With My Soul, written by Horatio Spafford and set to music by Philip Bliss, first published in "Gospel Songs No. 2" by Ira Sankey and Philip Bliss, 1876.

Thoughtful, Loving, Kind

Social media is a tricky beast. So much can be misconstrued through these letters typed on a screen. Relationships are strained, friendships are stressed, and the rules are muddled at best.

I found recently that I had been unfriended by someone. Were we close? At one time, perhaps. However, having not seen each other in several years, the closeness had dissipated, and simple acquaintanceship was what remained at face value. For me, the caring and loving friendship was still very real.

We still spoke amiably and shared things via Facebook. I considered that we still had an open and honest friendship. When she posted and asked for an opinion on things, my input was not quite what she thought it should be. That is where the problem began. It continued when I was truthful after she asked for clarification. Somehow, truth is not always desired by most, even when sprinkled with grace and forgiveness. And so, my friends list is minus one.

At first, I was hurt by the gesture. Then I realized that all we can do in this life is love our friends, do what we can to maintain the relationship despite time and distance, and maintain the integrity of an honest, loving, and caring relationship.

While we must carefully consider our words, we must also remain true to a character of integrity. Our words must always be salted with the generosity of kindness, graciousness, and (when required) forgiveness. Truth is more easily relayed and (for the most part) more readily accepted when our words are simple, straightforward, and not confrontational or insulting.

The bottom line is that our words, whether spoken or on paper/screen, must be thoughtful and never impulsive. In being sure of this, we can remember that though we may have been "unfriended," we did what we could to maintain the love and care needed to continue an encouraging and fruitful relationship and to let the other person know that they are loved - even if we disagree.

"Be wise in the way you act toward outsiders; make the most of every opportunity. Let your conversation be always full of grace, seasoned with salt, so that you may know how to answer everyone." **(Colossians 4:5-6 NIV)**

Yes, I'm Crazy

Many people think I'm crazy, including my husband at times. I've ceased trying to deny it. Here is the reasoning.

I don't find relaxation in the normal outlets. Yes, I like leisurely soaks in a hot bath on occasion, long drives in the country, and reading a good book. Naps may be a necessity at times, but they are not my preference. I find no relaxation in "shopping therapy;" as a matter of fact, shopping makes me tense. Just give me a list of what I need, and I'm in and out of any store in a flash. Dining out is nice, but not if the restaurant is overly crowded and there is an extensive wait time for a table. Honestly, I can make a homecooked meal that will rival any restaurant - if not in presentation, definitely in taste and cost - and I don't mind the cleanup afterwards.

Instead, I find my relaxation in what others would call "work." Before you get the wrong impression, I don't find it in the day-to-day work at the office. I find it in getting my hands into the dirt, fighting Mother Nature for the harvest, and preparing what I've reaped for consuming over the cold winter months. I find it in cooking and baking and passing on the fruits of my labor to others.

There's something about the feel of the soil on my hands, rinsing and drying veggies and fruits to a polished shine, and chopping, dicing, and mincing that calms me. Give me some cucumbers, peppers, and onions that need to be cut into tiny pieces for a relish, and I'm a happy girl. Put me in my kitchen, and I never want to leave. This morning is the perfect example.

Yesterday was filled with errands of a practical nature to be accomplished before heading to the office for work. Things that should have taken minutes took much longer. First, there was the pharmacy where I needed to pick up medication for one of my pups. The line was five people deep in front of me. They were all picking up, too. My first thought was that this shouldn't take long; get your meds, pay the clerk, and be on your way - ten minutes tops until I would be at the counter. To my dismay, each person in line felt the need to have a personal conversation with the clerk. Ten minutes turned into twenty, and twenty turned into twenty-five. Finally, I was on my way. I imagine the clerk wondered why I was so quick about my business instead of staying to chat. The answer? There were three more people behind me and there was no need to hold them up, too.

Next came the drive to my dad's to make a few phone calls for him to take care of some business with utility companies. On the way, a gentleman chose to run a stop sign in front of me. I felt the panic rise in my throat as I slammed the brake pedal to the floor. Thankfully, the accident was avoided. I was more than relieved. He, on the other hand, felt the need to tell me I was "number one" even though I had the right of way and he had run the stop sign. Shaking my head, I continued on (when I really wanted to follow him into a nearby parking lot and let him have it) and arrived at dad's safely. Surprisingly, and contrary to my experience when I have to do it at work, this errand was finished within fifteen minutes - not fifteen minutes each but

112

fifteen minutes total for three utility companies. Hallelujah! It seemed things were turning around and going my way.

The final stop before work was the bank. This was a simple matter of changing some information, no more than a five-minute chore as I had all the required paperwork with me. The young man behind the counter was pleasant but had no sense of urgency (in any definition of the word) to accomplish the task. His trip to the copier, which was eight feet away at most, to make copies of the required documents I brought with me seemed an eternity. He then returned to stare at his computer screen for several minutes before asking me another question or two only to stare at his screen once again for several more minutes. Was he binge-watching Netflix? I was finally able to leave the bank and start the trip to work some twenty minutes later - all for a small task that took as much typing on the keyboard as I am able to do in two minutes along with making a few copies that should have taken another two minutes.

It's the little things in life that drag us down and try to hold us there. While it did drag me down slightly, I refuse to let it keep me there. Today is a new day. This morning there are no outside errands to run. The morning started at 5:00 with me in my kitchen, a cup of tea on the counter, and several veggies to chop. It is heavenly. The relish is now soaking in salt water, the brine of vinegar, sugar, and spices is simmering, and all is right with my world. When the time comes to leave for work, I will be as relaxed as one of my pups when they are receiving their much-loved belly rubs. I will also be relaxed enough to see others in need of some joy and good news so that I can pursue my first passion - helping others.

Crazy? Maybe, but it's a good kind of crazy. Paul mentions the concept of crazy in his second letter to the church in Corinth. His passion is for spreading the good news of the love and redemption of Christ. Find what you love and what takes all the tension from your mind, heart, spirit, and body. Do it whenever you feel the urge and need. The little errands will wait. Feel your spirit lift and your mind clear. Allow the healing to reach your heart and body. You're no good to anyone if you're tense, frustrated, and snappish. Only when your heart, mind, spirit, and body are calmed and healthy can you uplift others and impact them in a loving, nurturing way.

And when people call you crazy for playing in the dirt, chopping to your heart's content, or whatever it is you do, just smile and say, "Yes, I am. But it's a great kind of crazy to be."

"If it seems we are crazy, it is to bring glory to God. And if we are in our right minds, it is for your benefit. Either way, Christ's love controls us. Since we believe that Christ died for all, we also believe that we have all died to our old life. He died for everyone so that those who receive his new life will no longer live for themselves. Instead, they will live for Christ, who died and was raised for them."
(2 Corinthians 5:13-15 NLT)

Darkness to Light

Life will give us just as many dark or cloudy times as it will give us times full of light and bright sunshine. While it may not seem so in the moment, there is beauty to be found and growth to be attained in the dark. This is not to say we should seek the darkness, only that when it comes upon us there is much thanks to be given in its midst.

God created both the darkness and the light. Darkness brings the coolness of night and the time for rest. It is a time of rejuvenation from the tasks of the day. Light brings the opportunity for accomplishment, both in work and in play. Both darkness and light bring fortuitous moments (whether we see it at the time or not) for the pursuit of the One who loves us so much - a pursuit that helps us to thrive. No matter in which we find ourselves, we are surrounded by possibilities to blossom.

The moon flower opens its blooms to the encroaching darkness each night. The reason for this is that they are pollinated by nighttime insects. Their large and glorious white blossoms fill the air with sweet fragrance as their beauty glows without the sun to light them from above. This is the lesson they give.

We can find sustenance in the darkness as well as the light. We don't need to have sunshine in our lives for our spirits to shine. We don't need perceived perfection to surround us to bring sweetness to the lives of others. We simply need the faith to know, much as the moon flower opens knowing the pollinators will come as night falls, that our Nurturer is there through all things, planting seeds of growth and purpose in our hearts.

So, do not fret when the darkness begins to fall into your life. First of all, there is always another sunrise just on the other side of it, whether that sunrise be here on earth or in Heaven in God's presence. Next, remember that there is rest, provision, beauty, and purpose in this dark time, and give thanks for them. Embrace those things knowing you are growing, being strengthened, and enabled to shine for and bring joy to all you meet. You are being turned into a beautiful and fragrant blossom for the glory of God.

"I am ADONAI—there is no other. Besides Me there is no God. I will strengthen you, though you have not known Me, so they may know, from the rising to the setting of the sun, that there is no one besides Me. I am ADONAI—there is no other. I form light and create darkness. I make shalom and create calamity. I, ADONAI, do all these things."

(Isaiah 45:5-7 Tree of Life Version)

Don't Turn Back

Bridges can be a good thing in life. They cross deep waters, lead us safely to where we need to go, and provide clearer vision and new insights from their heights.

They can also be detrimental to life. There are old bridges that should never be recrossed. Once passed over, they should be left where they are as nothing more than a reminder of how far we have come and the lessons we have learned. While burning them is not always necessary, leaving their entrances to become overgrown and impassable is.

If we are to live to our full purpose, we must not attempt to clear the way to return to them. We must not yearn for what came before them but only for the land into which they have brought us. One step up and two steps back is never an option.

We all have those bridges in our lives. Current or future circumstances may make it appear as though the land before those bridges was easier and better. This is nothing but a lie! It only seems easier because it is a land known to our spirits as opposed to the unknown land ahead of us. It only seems better because the trials and pitfalls of that land have faded from memory.

While the truth of our lives may seem fearfully difficult to handle, it is the only way to fully live. The lie of the easy and better past must be put in its place. The only way to do this is to fully take responsibility for all of our bridges, good and bad, and to learn the lessons, take that wisdom and experience, and move forward into the open space of the unknown with confidence that we have come through and need never return to that place.

When you happen upon that bridge already crossed today, look at it and smile. No, the place you are in now might not be ideal by any definition. However, the place from which you have come will only take you back through the thorns and briers you fought so desperately to escape. That is why you must smile; the knowledge of the past holds no power over you. Instead, you own the power through taking the responsibility for it. Once you take that responsibility, you will move forward with sure steps, and the land behind the bridge you have crossed will flee from you.

"That night all the members of the community raised their voices and wept aloud. All the Israelites grumbled against Moses and Aaron, and the whole assembly said to them, 'If only we had died in Egypt! Or in this wilderness! Why is the Lord bringing us to this land only to let us fall by the sword? Our wives and children will be taken as plunder. Wouldn't it be better for us to go back to Egypt?'"
(Numbers 14:1-3 NIV)

Let's Get Uncomfortable

Love is seldom comfortable. It encompasses a multitude of things. Love is obedience. Love is responsibility. Love is caring. Love is giving. Love is compassion. Love is kindness. Love is enduring difficulty. Love is standing in the face of hatred and still loving. Love is doing what you don't want to do. Love is all of these and more, but it is seldom comfortable.

Love covers all things God desires us – and commands us - to do. "Jesus replied: 'Love the Lord your God with all your heart and with all your soul and with all your mind.' This is the first and greatest commandment. And the second is like it: 'Love your neighbor as yourself.' All the Law and the Prophets hang on these two commandments." (Matthew 22:37-40)

There was certainly no comfort (an understatement if there ever was one) in the love Jesus poured out upon us. It caused great injury and suffering for Him to love us. Then why is it that we complain about doing even the simplest of things to show love?

We have grown way too secure in our comfort. We have grown way too adjusted to walking our own path and picking and choosing when, where, how, and why we will show love. I don't think any of us can deny those facts.

It's time to be uncomfortable. It's time to love in the context of true love. It is how we are loved by the Father and our Lord. It is time to love in spite of any and all circumstances and to do all the things love does - care, give, have compassion, be kind, endure difficulties, love in the face of hatred, and yes, be obedient and responsible. The truth of the matter is this: "For this is the message you heard from the beginning: We should love one another." (1 John 3:11)

Let's love fully with an open and whole heart. Let's hold nothing back. Let's do all the little things as well as the big things that show love. It is nothing less than we've received and nothing less than we've been commanded.

"You have heard that it was said, 'Eye for eye, and tooth for tooth.' But I tell you, do not resist an evil person. If anyone slaps you on the right cheek, turn to them the other cheek also. And if anyone wants to sue you and take your shirt, hand over your coat as well. If anyone forces you to go one mile, go with them two miles. Give to the one who asks you, and do not turn away from the one who wants to borrow from you. You have heard that it was said, 'Love your neighbor and hate your enemy.' But I tell you, love your enemies and pray for those who persecute you, that you may be children of your Father in heaven. He causes his sun to rise on the evil and the good, and sends rain on the righteous and the unrighteous. If you love those who love you, what reward will you get? Are not even the tax collectors doing that? And if you greet only your own people, what are you doing more than others? Do not even pagans do that? Be perfect, therefore, as your heavenly Father is perfect."
(Matthew 5:38-48 NIV)

Freedom for All

"We hold these truths to be self-evident, that all men are created equal, that they are endowed, by their Creator, with certain unalienable Rights, that among these are Life, Liberty, and the pursuit of Happiness." (The Declaration of Independence)

It's Independence Day. The above words birthed a country and an ideal - *our* country and *our* ideal.

Notice that the words are not placed in a doubtful way as if to say, "Perhaps they are endowed..." or "They might be endowed..." They do not state that, "All men may be created equal." They are straightforward and blunt - all men *are* created equal; they *are* endowed, by their Creator...

The meaning of these unequivocal words escapes us at times (at best) and on a consistent basis (at worst). The context of these words and the birth of this nation were fought for with blood, sweat, and tears. They were attained with passionate intent and without thought of self. Has it remained that way? Do we have passionate and selfless intent?

These words do not place conditions of color, creed, origin, financial or social status, gender, or gender preference. They are, simply, unconditional ideals that all people deserve the same treatment and the same unalienable rights. For those who profess faith in a loving God or anyone who professes humanism, these are words by which we should live. Living otherwise is hypocritical and self-righteous, and much as we hate to admit it, we can all be just that.

Today, take a moment to consider the weight of these words. It was a weight our founders embraced and carried willingly and boldly. In order for freedom to continue and this nation to thrive, it is a weight we must embrace and carry in the same way. The war for freedom was fought on this ground and won. The peace of equality and unalienable rights followed. It is up to us to continue that peace as well as fight, if necessary, to ensure that freedom is for all people and not just those who feel they are entitled to it because they think they are better than others. The biggest enemy of the freedom we inherited and enjoy is not someone with whom we don't agree or someone who looks or lives differently from us or whose life originated elsewhere. It is not with someone whose faith differs from ours. The biggest enemy to freedom we face comes from within ourselves.

"For you have been called to live in freedom, my brothers and sisters. But don't use your freedom to satisfy your sinful nature. Instead, use your freedom to serve one another in love. For the whole law can be summed up in this one command: 'Love your neighbor as yourself.' But if you are always biting and devouring one another, watch out! Beware of destroying one another."
(Galatians 5:13-15 NLT)

"Finally, brothers and sisters, rejoice! Strive for full restoration, encourage one another, be of one mind, live in peace. And the God of love and peace will be with you."
(2 Corinthians 13:11 NIV)

Stop the Thief

Imagine nature devoid of color - nothing in existence but shades of grey. It would be easy to miss the important things, simple to walk a path without noticing even the most effortless form of beauty. Now imagine life without experiences, whatever they might be. It would be just as easy to live every day without noticing each necessary miracle of breath, each growing moment, or each second of nourishment gained by the spirit through experience. Sure, there would be no trial or frustration; just as surely, there would be no joy or peace. There would be no up, down, right, or left. There would be only level, straight-forward steps to more level, straight-forward steps. There would simply be existence and boredom - lots of boredom.

Choose life over existence. Choose experience over aimless meandering. Don't miss the moments of beauty, growth, joy, and peace because you are fearful of the trial, sadness, and chaos. Don't miss the miracle of breathing and knowing you are actually living. A bee floats from flower to flower unafraid of obstacles in its path. It seeks out the beauty, nourishment, and pure joy of the nectar. Cast out the fear and allow yourself to be held in perfect love, even carried through to the other side where joy and peace abound. Be nourished by each step and amazed by each moment. Fear is simply a thief. Stop it in its tracks and cast it aside.

Scripture tells us multiple times that we should not be afraid. The reason not to fear is quite simple. God is always with us. We never walk alone, whether through easy days or difficult ones. Our paths, when we are on the right one, will not be broad or smooth. They may be fraught with holes, rocks, and flooded areas. Yet we must keep going. We must see the beauty in each step and the color in each moment, and reach out for the hand that steadies, strengthens, and guides us. Just like the bee in search of its much-needed, lifegiving nectar, we must travel unafraid through our days. Our travels also take us to that which gives life - abundant, joyous, miraculous life.

"Therefore Jesus said again, 'Very truly I tell you, I am the gate for the sheep. All who have come before me are thieves and robbers, but the sheep have not listened to them. I am the gate; whoever enters through me will be saved. They will come in and go out, and find pasture. The thief comes only to steal and kill and destroy; I have come that they may have life, and have it to the full.'"
(John 10:7-10 NIV)

The Perfection Trap

Perfectionism - it's a curse. That fact is something I've only relatively recently come to realize. I had always looked at it as a blessing. Things were done properly. The house was always clean and completely organized. Meals were prepared and on the table on time. Dishes were done right after dinner and put away before bedtime. The bed was made every morning - even if I was running late - because I couldn't stand the idea of coming home to something undone. Laundry was done when it needed to be and folded and put away immediately after coming out of the dryer.

At work, my desk was always neat. I knew where everything was and what needed to be done with each task by where it was placed in my space. I could always tell when someone else had used my desk while I was away from it. Depending on who that someone was, it would drive me crazy because there was absolutely no attempt to put things back where they belonged.

When it came to schedules, my "skills" really shone. I knew how much time something should take and how to arrange things for maximum time efficiency. The only problem was that operative word: should. Should did not mean would. Should is not an exact science. Should leaves room for the unexpected, and that, my friends, is the bane in a perfectionist's existence.

The fact is that I fancied myself a perfectionist. It was a goal to be attained. It was the ability to execute

126

and accomplish. It was a learned and practiced skill. It was…oh, who am I kidding? It was none of those things. It was a misguided attempt - a downright sinful attempt to control my world and my life.

Hi, I'm Carol, and I'm a recovering perfectionist. Here the operative word is: recovering. I slip back into the perfectionism habit very easily. I have to stop myself from doing so several times a day, sometimes by completely removing myself from the room in which my task resides or from the house completely for a period of time until the urge passes. It's an ongoing battle that I am not equipped to win on my own. Yet it's a battle I must win.

There are just certain things that should not be taken into our own hands. We are not meant to be in control. We do not possess the wisdom, power, strength, foresight, or forethought to be in control. We simply cannot see the entire picture with our finite vision.

There is something to be said for doing things right. However, there is a big difference between perfectionism and right. We are not able to be perfect. We are not even able to be good. Our human nature precludes both of those. What we are able to be is covered in the grace and mercy of our Father, who *is* perfect and good.

Trying to control things so that they are perfect is nothing more than telling God that this is what we want, this is how it's going to be, and we will not settle for less. The sad part is that, in most cases, we are striving for that perfectionism because we want to be noticed, loved, accepted, and acclaimed by others.

We're looking in the wrong direction! We already have those things from the most important One of all! We've been noticed as we struggled, loved beyond measure, accepted in spite of our flaws, and will be acclaimed by our Father for our obedience and the good we have done for Him on the day we enter Heaven to live in His presence for eternity. If we already have all of that, what are we striving for?

Here's the thing: perfection does not reside within the human realm. There will always be a flaw to be found, an error to be corrected, and a do-over to be done. Stop fighting for that which is not possible. Instead, give thanks for the ability you *do* possess: the grace to try again, and the love and acceptance you are given freely. To do less than this is opening up the door to grieving Father God and a lifetime of heartache.

No one cares if there are dishes in the drainer to be put away or dog hair on the rug. No one notices if you wear the same jeans two days in a row because you didn't get to the laundry yesterday. Your company, if they truly love and appreciate you, doesn't come to see your rugs or your clothing. They come to spend time with you. And if the bed isn't made, you're going to sleep in it again tonight anyway.

What God does notice is a heart that stays on Him, that pours forth thanksgiving and praise, and that gives Him all the glory instead of trying to gain glory for itself. That heart is what makes Him smile. That heart is what makes Him say, "Have you noticed my servant...?" or "Well done, child."

"And you were dead in the trespasses and sins in which you once walked, following the course of this world, following the prince of the power of the air, the spirit that is now at work in the sons of disobedience— among whom we all once lived in the passions of our flesh, carrying out the desires of the body and the mind, and were by nature children of wrath, like the rest of mankind. But God, being rich in mercy, because of the great love with which he loved us, even when we were dead in our trespasses, made us alive together with Christ—by grace you have been saved— and raised us up with him and seated us with him in the heavenly places in Christ Jesus, so that in the coming ages he might show the immeasurable riches of his grace in kindness toward us in Christ Jesus. For by grace you have been saved through faith. And this is not your own doing; it is the gift of God, not a result of works, so that no one may boast. For we are his workmanship, created in Christ Jesus for good works, which God prepared beforehand, that we should walk in them."
(Ephesians 2:1-9 ESV)

Finding and Embracing Humility

While reading several social media posts and scrolling by several memes, the word humility kept rolling around my mind. Why? Because what I was seeing was promoting exactly the opposite of that word. The dictionary's definition of humility is as follows: "a modest or low view of one's own importance; humbleness." However, biblical humility is that and much more. In one article I read it stated that "Biblical humility is grounded in the nature of God" (Christianity.com, Brannon Deibert). Now we're getting somewhere!

It is beyond the ability of our human nature to exhibit humility. First, we think we know it all. Secondly, we think we are good. The world tells us we are, so it must be true. Neither of those things exhibits the quality of humility, and lest we think we have this particular trait down pat, remember that as soon as you think that, you are no longer humble. Do not pass Go; do not collect $200.00.

Let's start with the first problem. We simply do not know it all. Our wisdom is finite, and what wisdom we do have is less than someone's wisdom who has had more life experience and more of a desire to listen to the wisdom of others. It's certainly much, much less than God's wisdom. As a matter of fact, let's multiply that word much by 1,000,000.

The second problem is that while we think we are good, we are not. We may do good things for others from time to time. We may strive for goodness in our behavior and thoughts. However, the good in us will not be perfected and reach fruition for quite some time.

This brings me back to the social media posts I've been seeing. They indicate that we should only be around those who love us, respect us, and appreciate us or that we should only give to those who show gratitude and will give back when we need it. Some say that we should stop giving so much of ourselves to others before we lose ourselves. These are not the definition of humility. They are the definition of self-interest.

Humility will put others before itself. Humility will bear burdens even though it has burdens of its own. Humility will give beyond what seems practical or logical to extend help to someone else. And - here's the important part - humility will expect nothing in return for any of it.

The humility modeled by Jesus is our example. He gave up unimaginable riches to come into this impoverished world. He poured out his strength to heal and help others. He gave all that He had to show the Father's love to the world, and then He gave some more. He was homeless and possessed nothing on this earth in spite of His heavenly riches, but that didn't stop Him from giving. At any time He could have returned to the heavens from which He came, but He stayed. He left His Kingship to be a servant to mankind, and He saw it through to its conclusion.

When the strength left Him from performing so many healings and casting out so many demons, He didn't give up and leave. He paused to regenerate and be refilled. When gratitude wasn't forthcoming, He

131

didn't rescind the gift. He moved on and gave to the next person. When He was not respected, He didn't stop working. He went to the next town and started again. He never rolled into Himself and said, "No more." And if we think we have ungrateful, grabbing people in our lives, just think about those in His!

His humility was truly grounded in the nature of God. He gave it all, refilled, and gave it all again. He kept nothing for Himself. He knew there was more whenever He needed it because God would provide. And in the end, He gave life and blood for everyone - those who knew Him and those who didn't, those who loved Him and those who hated Him, those who respected Him and those who mocked Him, those who gave their hearts in return and those who just took what they needed and walked away. Humility is Christlike and selfless.

We are not humble. We are like the little girl who plays at being mommy with her dolls or the little boy who plays at being an Army general. They have a lot to grow into before those goals are reached. So it is with us. We have much to grow into and much to learn.

We must start by thinking of others – all others – as better than ourselves. And when we think we've got that part down, start over again and go even further. Humility is a constant renewing of our hearts and minds. Humility is a constant pouring out of everything we have regardless of response. There can be no worry that we will ever exhaust ourselves or run out of something to pour into others - as long as we are humble enough to realize that we must allow ourselves to be refilled by our Father and to pour out again, we will never run dry.

"Don't be selfish; don't try to impress others. Be humble, thinking of others as better than yourselves. Don't look out only for your own interests, but take an interest in others, too. You must have the same attitude that Christ Jesus had. Though he was God, he did not think of equality with God as something to cling to. Instead, he gave up his divine privileges; he took the humble position of a slave and was born as a human being. When he appeared in human form, he humbled himself in obedience to God and died a criminal's death on a cross."
(Philippians 2:3-8 NLT)

(**Please take note:** I am not suggesting that anyone endure abuse of a physical or emotional nature. Abuse is never acceptable and should never be condoned. That is not what humility is about.)

Self- or People-Serving

We've all been told at some point in our lives, "You don't have to do that!" Our typical answer is, "I know I don't have to do it; I want to do it!" It's very easy to carry that attitude when whatever the act might be is simple, gratifying, and/or brings us recognition (in other words, self-serving). It's easy to do when we "have time." However, bearing that attitude on a daily basis through the twists and turns of life is a completely different matter.

We seem to find our days filled with rules and regulations on many levels. There is the normal level of legality, which we all must deal with unless we want our names in the police log of the local news or citations issued should we choose to ignore the statutes. Then there is the level of regulation put upon us by our employment or by our social circle. Since, for the most part, we all need our jobs and would like to keep them, following the rules of our employers is as important as following the laws imposed by government.

The rules of our social circles are, more often than not, self-imposed out of a desire to keep our friends and avoid conflict. Please keep in mind that I am not referring to our manners - manners are a must (in my mind) in all situations. I am referring more to the need we all seem to have to (whether lightly or emphatically) force our views, opinions, and such on those with whom we have contact on a frequent basis. If someone we associate with doesn't agree (i.e. doesn't obey the "rules"), we tend to cast them to the side and move on, particularly in the current world of social media. This does not constitute friendship. What it does constitute is a need to be validated or an attitude of narrow mindedness, which isn't what friendship (or any relationship) is all about.

There are the rules and regulations of religion. I take particular issue with these. Following a strict set of rules to be accepted by God is not why Jesus sacrificed everything. We would never be able to follow all of God's laws in our own strength without backsliding anyway. We are human; we're going to mess things up at some point and probably on many points. Relationship with God is not based on rules. It's based on the relationship between a Father and child, the unconditional love we are given, and the grace and mercy we are extended through Christ so that we are able to say, "I was wrong, please help me and forgive me," knowing that we will receive what we need to move forward - including consequence.

Lastly, the rules of family are quite simple. Family is family. There will always be disappointments, disagreements, and the like. There will be times of distance, whether that distance is purposeful or not. There will be moments when we are hurt and sometimes disgusted. However, as I said, family is family. The one rule of family is that of love. Come to think of it, that is the rule that applies to all of life. Love first, last, and always.

Now that we've gotten the rules out of the way, we need to look at ourselves. We all do things for a reason. The question is this: what is the reason? Motive in action is very important. We cannot claim to be loving and compassionate if the desire in our hearts is to be recognized and rewarded for our actions - like receiving a paycheck from our employer. We cannot claim to be good when, in the darkest recesses of our hearts and mind, our actions are decided by what is good for us before what is good for others. (The truth is that none of us are good anyway.) It all comes down to a willingness to sacrifice for the betterment of the lives of others (both those known to us and those who are not) as opposed to the pseudo sacrifice that benefits our own circumstance first and foremost.

Old Testament sacrifices were the law. Yet not a single one of those sacrifices had the effect of releasing sinners from their sin. In truth, all God really wanted was their heart - not the physical heart, but the heart and soul that has the capability of love, compassion, kindness, and grace because it was created in His image. He didn't want the Israelites to do something out of fear or selfishness or out of a need for validation and recognition. He wanted them to do something strictly out of the loving and compassionate response of their hearts. It's what He wants of us too.

Here's a simple and true story from a dear friend and pastor: while vacationing, the family stopped at an eatery for lunch. On the way in, they held the door for an elderly gentleman who was entering at the same time. After finishing their meal, they walked past the older man on their way out. He stopped them and asked for help. He had not been able to open the packet to put the sauce on his sandwich. My friend and his son immediately opened the packet for the man, who was extremely grateful because he had been trying for quite some time to accomplish the task. This took all of about fifteen seconds. The little boy thought it was pretty cool to help the man.

I'm betting that the older gentleman thought it was even more cool that someone didn't pass him by but stopped to help. How many others walked by while he sat there trying desperately to open a sauce packet? Granted, he had probably not asked as he did with my friend. However, that is not the point. The point is that we are most often so wrapped up in ourselves that we don't see the need right in front of us. Fifteen seconds is a small sacrifice to show love to a stranger, as well as to show a little boy what it means to be compassionate. That fifteen seconds will remain with both of them for a lifetime.

The sacrifices of love and kindness can be fifteen seconds or fifteen days. They may take even longer. It doesn't matter. What matters is that they *are*.

And the only rule that truly matters is the rule of love - first, last, and always.

"The kind of fasting I want is this: Remove the chains of oppression and the yoke of injustice, and let the oppressed go free. Share your food with the hungry and open your homes to the homeless poor. Give clothes to those who have nothing to wear, and do not refuse to help your own relatives."
(Isaiah 58:6-7 Good News Translation)

Instruction For Life

In my daily reading lately, there seems to be a common theme. Of course, this is the time of year when the holidays are fast approaching. Thanksgiving is later this year than most - November 29th. Quick to follow will be Christmas and then New Year's Eve and Day when a sense of renewal settles into our hearts and minds. Resolutions and promises will be made - and broken.

The book of Galatians is full of encouragement and instruction as to exactly how we are to live. It starts simply enough with the statement that there is no other Gospel than that of Jesus. I say "simply" because we all know what that Gospel is. We've all read why Jesus came to this world and how and why he left it. We know the gift he came to give and how to receive it. Simple, right? Yet, as Paul warns, so many take that Gospel and twist it into their own interpretation for their own means, even within the church.

Paul goes on to tell the story of his opposition of Peter due to hypocrisy. Peter was acting in such a way that he did one thing with one group of people, but as soon as others came onto the scene he acted differently and separated himself from the first group. We cannot pretend to be one way and then claim to be another. We cannot live in grace yet force others to live by the law. We must live by the faith we've been given and the Gospel we've been taught. Truly, all ground is level at the foot of the Cross. All living in repentance and faith are welcome on that ground, as are those just coming to repentance and faith and those seeking

138

answers yet still living in their sin. God certainly doesn't play favorites, and just because we have received the gift of Jesus Christ and the salvation He offers doesn't mean we are above those who sin or above sinning ourselves. We cannot "set aside the grace of God" for the gaining of righteousness through the law - for ourselves or anyone else. This denies the Gospel of Jesus. This denies the very faith we say we have. It negates the freedom Jesus died to give us.

What freedom were we given? Freedom to live without fear of condemnation, freedom to speak with the Father directly, and freedom to love others, give to others, and have great compassion for others. Along with this wondrous freedom, we were also given the gift of the ability to leave our selfish, jealous, and self-isolated selves behind and replace those things with "love, joy, peace, patience, kindness, goodness, faithfulness, gentleness, and self-control." All these things live in us thanks to the Spirit. All these things are ours to grasp and pass on to a hurting world.

For me, the verses in chapter 6 are a wakeup call. We live in a busy world with busy lives. We can always come up with an excuse not to do something, but how often do we come up with an excuse TO do something?

Verses 2 and 3 read, "Share each other's burdens, and in this way obey the law of Christ. If you think you are too important to help someone, you are only fooling yourself. You are not that important." (NLT)

And before anyone jumps on this, let me state the faith-based obvious: we are *all* important in Christ. I think what this refers to is the fact that we are all *equally* important. We cannot consider ourselves more important than the next because it's simply not the truth. Again, this ground is level.

In my opinion, it is so vital to remember that everyone is important, that we need to share burdens, and we need to live humbly enough to put ourselves aside for the bettering of the lives of others. And we don't just need to do this during the upcoming holiday season and for certain people, but during all seasons and for all people. Humility is a tough pill to swallow but a necessary one if we're going to live out our faith, please our Father, and show others just how much love we have been given and have to give. The holiday season starts with Thanksgiving. Personally, I don't look at that as just being thankful. I also look at it as giving - no matter how busy we think we are.

The bottom line is really quite simple: be real and not contrived. Be free to be fruitful and not imprisoned in isolation and self-centeredness. Be humble and giving and not self-important and selfish. Live each day passing on what you've been given so that others in a world of hurt can gain the freedom and gifts you so easily take for granted at times. Hold onto the Gospel of Jesus and let go at the same time.

"But as for you, continue in what you have learned and have become convinced of, because you know those from whom you learned it, and how from infancy you have known the Holy Scriptures, which are able to make you wise for salvation through faith in Christ Jesus. All Scripture is God-breathed and is useful for teaching, rebuking, correcting and training in

righteousness, so that the servant of God may be thoroughly equipped for every good work."
(2 Timothy 3:14-17 NIV)

Simple Living Brings Abundance

The trappings of life - we all get caught up in them. The word itself brings to mind (at least for me) its very root: trap. The things that matter in life are so simple - family, friendship, faith, love, kindness, and compassion. Why do we make them so complicated? Why do we make the trappings as important or more important than the things that truly matter?

There are basic things we need to live. We need breath, sustenance, and shelter. Yet we take those things for granted and add to the list. We need the 3-bedroom, 2-bath house that comes with a large mortgage when a 2-bedroom, 1-bath house would suffice. We need the latest iPhone or Samsung Galaxy and the ultimate TV provider with 1,000 channels at astronomical prices. The simple truth is that a basic cell phone that provides talk, text, and minimal internet data would do the job, and basic cable would provide enough viewing pleasure. Who watches 1,000 channels? We need that big SUV when a simple sedan without the price tag would meet our travel needs. We need 500 or 1,000+ "friends" on Facebook when our handful of true friends are waiting for us to nourish that relationship and our family is waiting for us to look up from social media and just be present. We need...

Then there is the matter of our faith. There are no requirements for a huge, fancy building with stages, lighting, instruments, video screens, and all that goes with them. Don't get me wrong, I love an upbeat worship service where I can close my eyes, raise my hands, and be lifted into the presence of the God I trust and love with all my heart, but all of those trappings don't really matter. If I were to be completely honest, some of the most meaningful moments I've been in His presence were in the darkness of the wee hours, walking the streets, and tossing papers on my route with the only instrument being my voice and the only stage being the only one that matters - God's stage. Those are the only things required - my voice, His voice, and His stage. His lighting as the dawn approaches is sheer perfection. The message His voice purveys is something that moves the depths of the spirit if surroundings and the heart are quiet enough to hear it, and it's done without a sound system.

Life, family, friendship, faith, love, kindness, and compassion are not a show. We don't need the trappings; they do, indeed, only trap us. They take away what is important and leave a pseudo meaningful life behind. They take reality and replace it with impossible standards that can never fulfill us, even if we can attain them.

In the words of one of my favorite Christian singer/songwriters, Ross King, "Clear the stage" - in life, family, friendship, and faith. Find what's important and hold onto it, then share it with all you meet. Things become crystalline and life is easier and more fulfilling when the trappings are reduced or even discarded altogether.

"But the Lord answered her, 'Martha, Martha, you are anxious and troubled about many things, but one thing is necessary. Mary has chosen the good portion, which will not be taken away from her.'"
(Luke 10:41-42 ESV)

1,440 Minutes

I was reminded a couple of days ago of the impact we all have on others. It doesn't matter if we know each other well or not at all. It doesn't matter if we see each other daily or if it's been years since we've been physically present in the same space. The simple fact is everything we do and say has an impact one way or another. It is up to us to determine what the outcome of our words and actions will be. We can employ careful thought to make sure our impact is beneficial and encouraging, leaving others feeling loved. On the other hand, we can forego that and leave others with the feeling of having barely escaped with their hearts intact due to our thoughtlessness.

The truth is that long after we have left this earth, our words and actions will still be impacting the lives of those we leave behind. The reminder came to me after messaging with the daughter of a very dear friend who left us way too soon. Adam's loss was tragic for so many, but it was his appointed time to travel to Heaven. However, he did not leave us without pieces of himself instilled in our hearts and day-to-day lives. The imprint he had on each of our lives remains and is shared between us as easily as we breathe and many times without knowing we are sharing it. He left us with his love and his selfless way of caring for and bringing joy to the lives of others. There is nothing he would not have done for his family or his friends, nothing he would not have given up for their happiness and well-being.

We will all face the day of our leaving. The question is what imprints will we leave behind us? What words and deeds will be embossed on the hearts of others? Whether we realize it or not, the answers to those questions are our decisions to make. We have a choice as to whether the memories and legacies we leave will be those that bring smiles and tears of love and joy or those that bring feelings of emptiness and pain.

I am not saying we must be perfect in our lives. We all have moments when the wrong words escape our lips or the selfishness that is inherent in human nature rears its ugly head. We also have the moments right after those things happen to begin to cover our missteps with love in the hopes of making reparation for damage done. The key is in examining our actions, words, and motives and correcting them, turning them into loving moments as immediately as possible.

We have so many opportunities to spread joy through our love and the love of Christ to so many - just as many opportunities as we have to be short, callous, and mean-spirited. There are 1,440 minutes in every day. The choice is ours. The remembrance others who cross our paths will have of those minutes is in our hands. It could be the person in the car next to you on the highway, the one ahead of or behind you at the store, the client at work that tries your patience, the friend you haven't seen in years or the one you see regularly, or the family members who depend on your love and support. They all take up those minutes. How will they remember their 1,440 at the end of the day?

How will they remember them when it is our time to leave?

I want those in my path to remember each 1,440-minute day with smiles and tears of thankfulness and joy. I'm far from perfect, but I pray that I can be loving and selfless in my giving - and honest about the times that I'm not those things. I want to leave the imprint on the hearts of others that my dear friend left on mine and on the hearts of those who loved him most.

"Love must be sincere. Hate what is evil; cling to what is good. Be devoted to one another in love. Honor one another above yourselves. Never be lacking in zeal, but keep your spiritual fervor, serving the Lord. Be joyful in hope, patient in affliction, faithful in prayer. Share with the Lord's people who are in need. Practice hospitality. Bless those who persecute you; bless and do not curse. Rejoice with those who rejoice; mourn with those who mourn. Live in harmony with one another. Do not be proud, but be willing to associate with people of low position. Do not be conceited. Do not repay anyone evil for evil. Be careful to do what is right in the eyes of everyone. If it is possible, as far as it depends on you, live at peace with everyone."
(Romans 12:9-18 NIV)

The Impression We Leave

The examples we set for the onlookers in our lives leave the deepest of impressions. Whether we are a leader, follower, or sitting on the sidelines in a quandary of which choice to decide upon, we are making an impression on someone.

We often look at our leaders and place blame for what happens in the world based on their words and actions or lack thereof. Yes, it is true that they are more exposed to the general public and therefore seem to garner greater exposure for their words and behavior. However, it is we, in our everyday lives, that need be concerned as to the impressions we are leaving on those who cross our paths.

We cannot change how others behave in any given moment. We can, however, be an influence as to how they will behave going forward. The world, as they say, is watching. What behavior will we emulate as they wait to see what will come to pass? What behavior will we emulate as we watch the happenings all around us?

We simply cannot and will not survive in a climate of hatred. We cannot expect to perpetuate the bullying and degradation of others and still hope and pray things get better. Words and actions have implications and consequences. No, we might not see them directly as the word or action escapes our person, but they will come.

Those "sitting on the fence" are waiting to see in which direction we will turn. Will we backtrack, leaving a wake of potential destruction in our path? Will we stand still and be silent as the emotional and cultural

148

climates worsen and crumble around us? *Or will we take steps forward, showing those who watch that we do care, we do love, we do have compassion, and we do accept that not everyone is just like us?*

Will we leave a legacy of harmony and peace to the generations that are now growing and learning from our example, or will we encourage them, also by our example, to shun and detest that which is different from them - that they may see as the enemy?

The choice seems simple to me. The world and its people cannot and will not survive in a climate of hatred. We scream for someone to do something about global warming because the earth is changing and probably will become inhabitable and incapable of sustaining human life in the future. Yet we allow and perpetuate the current climate of "not my brothers' keeper" and "my way or the highway" that will most certainly destroy the earth and our fellow humankind long before global warming has the chance.

Christian, Judaic, Muslim, Atheist, or non-committal; black, white, Hispanic or Asian; straight, homosexual, or transgender; we are truly all the same. We are all redeemed by the blood of Jesus. Judgment is not ours to render and stones are not ours to throw. We inhabit this planet *together*. We care for each other and this planet or destroy each other and this planet *together*. The choice is ours. Our children and children's children are watching. The world is watching and deciding which way they will choose based on the example set by all of us, individually and collectively. I choose love.

"Let no debt remain outstanding, except the continuing debt to love one another, for whoever loves others has fulfilled the law. The commandments, 'You shall not commit adultery,' 'You shall not murder,' 'You shall not steal,' 'You shall not covet,' and whatever other command there may be, are summed up in this one command: 'Love your neighbor as yourself.' Love does no harm to a neighbor. Therefore love is the fulfillment of the law."

(Romans 13:8-10 NIV)

The Season of Grace

Without Grace

What would life be like without grace? I really don't want to know the answer to that question. The only thing that comes to mind is that without grace, we would not have life. Grace is at the root of everything - at least as much as I can tell when I sit to think about it. It is only by the grace of God that we have breath in our lungs, light and warmth, darkness and cool, nourishment for our bodies, and love for our hearts.

Everything we have, we have because of grace. That alone should be enough to make us want to extend grace to others as it is extended to us. It's the only fair exchange, right? Of course! Then why is it so hard to do? It takes practice. It takes recognizing even the smallest bit of grace being poured into our lives and realizing we would not be here without it. It takes shoving our flawed human nature into the background in the power of Christ and bringing the love of Jesus to the forefront.

Father God pours His grace over us every day. We have opportunities to extend that grace to others every day. Every season is a Season of Grace, from Him to us and from us to others.

"For while we were still helpless, at the right time Christ died for the ungodly. For one will hardly die for a righteous person; though perhaps for the good person someone would even dare to die. But God demonstrates His own love toward us, in that while we were still sinners, Christ died for us."
(Romans 5:6-8 NASB)

The Journey Home - January 3, 2018

All of my writing is personal in the sense that it comes from my heart and experiences. Today, it is even more personal because it comes from the experience of my family. Many of you who are on my personal Facebook page will already know its content, but for those of you who aren't, I ask your indulgence in these moments.

I am convinced that we were born with two eyes for a reason. The capability for sight is the obvious reason, both forward sight and peripheral sight. Our eyes also cry. Tears fall in many forms - as joy, as sadness, as frustration... Until yesterday, I never realized (at least I don't think I did) that it is quite possible to cry more than one kind of tears at a time. Hence the theory of other reasons for having two eyes.

Our family suffered a loss yesterday, and while our tears are those of grief and sadness, they are also tears of joy. My mom is now an angel in heaven, much as she was on this earth. Her struggles and pain no longer contain her just as they never defined her. She is free. She now resides in true grace; the grace Father God poured into her life on earth has been realized in its purest form in heaven.

My mom was, in my opinion at least, the greatest woman whoever walked this earth. Her standing was not one of social, political, financial, or celebrity stature, but a stature of deep and constantly abiding faith. She faced life head on, whatever each day would hold, with a quiet yet formidable strength of spirit grounded in her Lord knowing that He indeed knew what that day held and how she would walk through it in His power while holding His hand.

Her first thought in any situation was of Him. Her second thought, close on the first's heels, was of those she loved without limit and held closely in her heart. She had the heart of a servant, the soul of a worshiper, and the spirit of a prayer warrior. My brother John and I talked yesterday about her constant prayer for us, as well as all those she knew and some that she didn't know. We both agreed that we didn't know where we would be now had she not had that spirit of unceasing prayer.

This perfection of character, or as close to perfection as any of us walking this earth would ever come, was never more evident than in her last hours with us. True to her earthly life, she thought of Jesus first and His waiting for her with open arms just across the bridge in eternity. She knew without a single doubt that His hand was reaching for hers. She held no fear but instead held encouragement for the rest of us. Some of the last thoughts she shared with us were those of love, joy, and reconciliation.

She told us how much she loved each of us and her grandchildren. She named each one and mentioned how proud she was of each one. No one was left out. Not any single one was more important than the next because she loved all of us without boundary. She encouraged us to reach for her hand and to understand that she wasn't fearful, and we shouldn't be either. And it was her wish that hearts and lives that had become pulled apart for some reason would be reconciled.

156

Most of all, there was that incredible love. It filled the room like a bright ray of sunshine and enveloped all of us in its warmth. She was, in those last hours, totally at peace. She was about to experience the ultimate joy, the culmination of her deep faith - to be in the presence of Christ.

As I write this, I find it hard to fathom that there could be a joy any greater than having had her in our lives, except for the joy of knowing her faith has brought her home, healthy and whole. And, of course, that my faith and the faith of all of us will bring us home to meet her again.

"Behold, the tabernacle of God is with men, and He will dwell with them, and they shall be His people. God Himself will be with them and be their God. And God will wipe away every tear from their eyes; there shall be no more death, nor sorrow, nor crying. There shall be no more pain, for the former things have passed away."
(Revelation 21:3-4 NKJV)

Strength to Rely On

We all go through tough times in our lives. Some aren't as tough as others, but some are downright unbearable. It's like a rite of passage. The storm clouds gather, the deluge begins, and all of it seems to last forever. Yet we always come out into the brilliant, sparkling rays of sunlight on the other side.

Regardless of the saying we've all heard - God doesn't give you any more than you can handle - we all learn the lack of truth in those words at some point. The real truth is that God does allow us to go through more than we can handle. This isn't because He doesn't love us but because He does. He wants us to realize we need to rely on His strength and not just our own. And He will walk beside us the entire journey and send others to fall in step.

I can think of two examples of someone experiencing more than they can handle. The first is a dear friend whose husband fell and suffered a brain injury. He did survive and even regained some abilities but needed care for the rest of his earthly life. She, like most of us, is a doer. If it needs to be done she will accomplish the task. However, this was a monumental task, the likes of which she had never experienced. She was not equipped physically, emotionally, or educationally to do it. Yet do it she did - for over 17 years.

The second example is Michael and me. Over a period of five years, we dealt with critical illness in three of our four parents. We cared for them daily, saw them through treatments and surgeries, and made sure they could spend their last days at home in the midst of those they loved. Added to that was our son's catastrophic accident and the following health issues. It was an extremely rough five years. Our weakness was evident. Our ineptitude was evident. Our devastation was evident. Yet we did it and came out on the other side. The reason we were able to survive all of it was because God was loving us, leading us, and carrying us every step of the way. Without Him we would have faltered and ended up face down in the mire of tragedy.

Were we to wander around in our own strength, conquering demons of all kinds and winning at everything, we would never grow. If we could do it alone, why would we need God?

In His grace, He allows certain circumstances to present themselves so that we can realize our weakness and our need. Those are the moments where we feel we cannot take one more step, take care of one more person, or get out of bed to face one more day. In those moments, we cannot bring ourselves to see the shimmers of light beginning to break the storm clouds. We lose hope. We lose perspective. We lose function.

The fact is that these moments are when God's gracious strength pours into us. He sends His angels to minister to us - sometimes in unseen form and sometimes in the form of beloved family members and friends. Neither my friend nor Michael and I accomplished what needed to be done alone. We didn't have the strength or capability. However, both of those things flowed in and through us in a supernatural way. At least it did once we admitted to ourselves and everyone else, including God, that we couldn't do this alone.

Once that admission became reality, we felt renewed inside. We also felt renewed outside. Friends and family showed up to shovel pavements and driveways during snowstorms. Others dropped by with meals for our parents and us. Still others cleaned houses and visited with our parents. And even more than that prayed, sent cards, called, and provided what we sometimes needed most - a nonjudgmental listening ear, a prayer partner, a moment of laughter, and love. All of these people helped lead us through the clouds into the sunlight.

Weakness and admitting the weakness aren't bad things. It allows God to send His strength through angels, unseen and seen. It allows others to do what they were meant to do in assistance. It allows us to be led through the storm and into the sunshine. It lets God be God and replace our weakness and other lacking areas with His pure grace to see us through. Admitting our weakness makes us strong.

We can't do it alone. We can try, but much more will be accomplished successfully with our Partner and Friend.

"Each time he said, 'My grace is all you need. My power works best in weakness.' So now I am glad to boast about my weaknesses, so that the power of Christ can work through me. That's why I take pleasure in my weaknesses, and in the insults, hardships, persecutions, and troubles that I suffer for Christ. For when I am weak, then I am strong."
(2 Corinthians 12:9-10 NLT)

Small Town Tranquility

I love the feeling of living in a small town (population 5,059 as I write this). The reality that, when we cross the town boundary, we are surrounded by the calm and quiet acreage of farmland consisting of farmers' fields, dairy cows, and horses is a daily blessing. The tranquility is almost tangible. Even after a long day at work and sometimes a trying drive home, I can feel the tension melt away as I turn off of the main roadway and onto the winding thoroughfares that meander between corn and soybean fields and country lanes.

I love the fact that we can walk to almost anything we need from our home. Our favorite restaurants, the grocery store, the hardware and drug stores, and small shops are all within a 10-to-15-minute stroll from the front door. Professional services are also within walking distance - dentist, optometrist, attorney, and others. And of course, there is my personal favorite: the bookstore.

There is something warm about a small town. Life's pace is a bit slower, the sights are more easily accessible, and the sunsets and nature's other occurrences seem deeper in color and intensity. In the quiet of small-town living, you can actually hear snowflakes as they land on the ground.

Each day at noon, the church bells ring out in an old hymn. Today's selection was "The Church's One Foundation." The sound was especially beautiful ringing out into air whose other sounds were muted by the

162

snowfall. Listening closely, I could actually hear my mom and grandmom singing as I had heard them so often while growing up.

After spending most of my years living in the city or just outside in the suburbs, small town living is quite a treat for me. I never realized how many things I'd missed. Walking to beloved eateries or shops was not the norm because most everything required transportation. There were no calming scenes of cows lounging in the field or horses feeding on the grasses. Sunrises and sunsets were, for the most part, viewed between houses. Did church bells ring out at noon? I'm not sure, but if they did, they were unheard amid the sounds of traffic and people hurrying from one place to another.

It occurs to me that this small-town feel is something I want to hoard and never release. Everything I need is here. Then it occurs to me that everything I need was always here, no matter where "here" was.

We have the ability to bring that tranquility to our lives every day. We have the wherewithal to gaze upon beauty and let it calm our spirits. We have nourishment for our souls within walking distance, just as those favorite restaurants and grocery stores are from my home - and not just within walking distance but within simple steps.

The truth is that all we need is within us thanks to the blessed gift of God. By His grace alone the Spirit within us can exhibit calm, beauty, peace, and nourishment at any given moment if we only stop to listen and look with the ears and eyes of our hearts.

Tranquility can overtake us, and tension can be released exactly where we are now - no commute required.

Take a deep breath and close your eyes. Do you hear the snowflakes landing after their floating journey downward from the heavens? Are the church bells ringing out in a favorite tune? Now open your eyes and take another deep breath, looking to the skies. Are the hues of the Master's palette showing themselves in a colorful display that soothes your soul?

All we need is within us because it was purposefully placed there. Thanksgiving will open the floodgates of grace to recognize it. I'm so thankful I live in a small town. I'm even more thankful I can access whatever I need through the Spirit that God has gifted within me.

"He causes the springs to gush into the valleys; they flow between the mountains. They supply water for every wild beast; the wild donkeys quench their thirst. The birds of the sky live beside the springs; they make their voices heard among the foliage. He waters the mountains from his palace; the earth is satisfied by the fruit of your labor. He causes grass to grow for the livestock and provides crops for man to cultivate, producing food from the earth, wine that makes human hearts glad—making his face shine with oil—and bread that sustains human hearts."
(Psalm 104:10-15 Christian Standard Bible)

Redemptive Beauty

The sunrise was gorgeous on Wednesday morning from the balcony of our vacation spot, and I know that subsequent sunrises (once the cloud cover leaves us) will be just as beautiful - different but beautiful.

Each sunrise and sunset are unique. All are perfect in their own right. Variations in tint, color saturation, brightness, and any cloud cover that catches the hues will present themselves, but no sunrise or sunset is in any way diminished when placed beside another. And amazingly, we never (at least not that I've ever heard) judge one against the other or claim that one isn't good enough at all. Instead, we always find at least one quality in the variations we like or love. There is always something redemptive in a sunrise or sunset. Either there is the start of another day and the chance to start anew, or the end of an old one and the chance to look forward to starting anew after a good night's rest.

Why is it we don't look at our fellow travelers in life the same way? Like the sunrise and sunset, there is a uniqueness and beauty to be found in each one. There is something to be realized, pondered, and then tucked away for later reflection. Variations in brightness and hue emanate from each spirit - all with a gift to give and a lesson to teach. Yet we seldom look beneath the surface to the spirit inside.

"He doesn't have my level of education. She doesn't dress in appropriate style. They don't agree with my thought processes or beliefs."

"His tattoos offend me. Her piercings are off-putting. They don't come from the right neighborhood."

Oh, what we miss when we refuse to delve beneath the uniqueness of personality and background! Oh, what treasures of spirit connection we forfeit! And sadly, our lack of taking the time or using wisdom to realize we are not really so different and there is beauty in the differences we do have opens us up to the same hurtful judgment with which we judge. Would we turn our backs on a beautiful sunrise just because there wasn't enough pink in the clouds for our liking or a sunset because the purples and blues didn't meet our standards of grandeur?

Education, clothing, agreement, and presence or lack of tattoos, piercings, or money to live in "acceptable" neighborhoods are only as important as the amount of nourishment they bring to the spirit within. I am fairly confident in saying the spirit doesn't grow or thrive on any of these things.

The spirit thrives on the beauty of relationship, not on the temporal things of worldly covering. It finds its nourishment in things like love, kindness, faithfulness, grace, mercy, and compassion. It lives not in neighborhoods but in the constant search of and transition to places of focus on wisdom, beauty, truth, and the wonder found not in the likeness but the uniqueness of other spirits. It is ever growing, ever changing for the better, and ever mindful that perfection manifests in different hues, contrasts, and the redemptive qualities of everyday people - both known and unknown. Like the sunrise or sunset, each encounter is a new chance to start fresh, strengthen the beauty that has come before it, and build the anticipation for what comes after it.

The choice is ours to strengthen, remain stagnant, or weaken. It is our decision to thrive or flounder. These are the things that happen through snap judgment. We can only gain what we set out to achieve - not in terms of the world's eyes but in terms of what will grow our spirit to its fullest and most perfect potential - when we choose rightly. The choice is ours as to whether to enrich our hues and contrasts with the interaction of others or to go it alone, never growing and never changing.

I believe the better choice is strength, growth, and change - focusing on those things that are true, noble, right, pure, and lovely. In this choice, our spirits will soar. The redemptive beauty of the grace of God will be realized for us and for others.

"And now, dear brothers and sisters, one final thing. Fix your thoughts on what is true, and honorable, and right, and pure, and lovely, and admirable. Think about things that are excellent and worthy of praise. Keep putting into practice all you learned and received from me—everything you heard from me and saw me doing. Then the God of peace will be with you." **(Philippians 4:8-9 NLT)**

Loving the Storm

I love thunderstorms. I love watching the power of the heavens, listening to the booming voice of thunder, and seeing the brightness of lightning strikes as they stretch toward the earth. I love the sound of the rain as it pounds on the roof. I love the way the winds turn the air cooler and bend the tree branches. I will watch the skies as the storms approach, thrilled at the show I know is about to start.

The key is that I love all of this as long as I can watch from the safety of my deck or through a window inside my home. I admit, however, that if I am out in the midst of the storms, I can become quite terrified. I don't think anyone wants to be in the midst of the storm or the potential danger it contains.

I write this because of a simple Facebook status I posted. It read, "The garden needs attention, but there's no point in doing it until today's storms come through. My morning just doesn't seem complete without time in the dirt." I was told by a dear friend and pastor that I should "...go get dirty...don't wait for tomorrow's storms, do it today...there's a sermon in there somewhere I'm pretty sure." I answered that perhaps he and I should collaborate. Well, Pastor Brett, here is my part of the collaboration.

Weather is changeable, as is life. There are days that will be spent bathed in sunshine without a care in the world. You will be able to dance among the flowers, enjoying every second with a joy you wish would last into eternity. However, flowers don't thrive

168

without rain, too. Were there to be sunshine at all times they would wilt, turn brown, and die from the lack of moisture. And so, the rains will come, sometimes with thunder, lightning, and wind so that the flowers can grow into their full, beautiful potential. And here's the thing: they're okay with that! They raise their heads to the sky, almost as if inviting the storm. They're flexible by nature and bend with the winds. They soak up every last drop of rain, as if knowing it is for their good. They are oblivious to the possible danger at hand and instead revel in the elements coming from the heavens.

As our human nature dictates, we are not so flexible or fearless. Yet our faith dictates that we should be. Storms are just that - storms. They come and they pass. The key is to dance with joy through the storms, just as we do through the sunshine. Even more, the key is in knowing that even the storms are part of God's grace. Both things, I know, are easier said than done.

I think we should let the storms come; we should invite them. Let the mountains be moved and the earth shaken because my faith promises that though that may happen, our Father's love will never be removed from us. The waters will not overtake us. Instead, they will cultivate the gardens of our lives, and we will grow. We will thrive. On the other side of the storm, the skies will brighten with promise, and our promised hope and future await us.

We can dance in the sunshine, and we can dance in the storms. Why? Because we *know* that which we are promised. Be flexible. Be fearless. Raise your gaze to take in whatever may come your way, confident that it will grow your spirit. Take joy in each day, whether it is sunny or stormy. Take heart in the truth and goodness of God's planning.

I think the true joy of the storm is that you can see God's light in the thunderbolts. You can hear His voice in the loud claps as air masses collide. You can feel His cleansing in each drop of rain that falls. You can revel in His presence in the wind as it passes.

Do you know what I love most about thunderstorms? It is the rainbow of promise that the skies will clear once again, that the storm will not destroy me nor will it destroy the gifts of hope, faith, and joy I have been given.

So, my friends, watch in anticipation. Listen. Revel. Dance. It is *all* for our good. He promises.

"While they were sailing, Jesus fell asleep. A very strong wind blew up on the lake, causing the boat to fill with water, and they were in danger. The followers went to Jesus and woke him, saying, 'Master! Master! We will drown!' Jesus got up and gave a command to the wind and the waves. They stopped, and it became calm. Jesus said to his followers, 'Where is your faith?'"
(Luke 8:23-25 NCV)

Unburdened

Yesterday was Ash Wednesday. Our church service last evening was not truly a service but instead a time of personal reflection and communion. You came in the door between the appointed hours as you were able, sat in the pew, and had a quiet time of introspection, confession, and cleansing before walking to the altar rail, kneeling, and receiving communion and if you chose, the ashes marking the cross on your forehead.

It's amazing to me the burdens we willingly carry with us over a period of time. They go seemingly unnoticed in our hearts and minds as we plod through our days while bending under the sheer weight of them. To others we look completely normal (whatever normal is). We convince ourselves that carrying this weight is just a part of life, that we are not really bending under it but strengthening. We feel that our mistakes, our wrongdoings, our past and present actions are something we must hold like a banner of some sort so that we don't repeat them. What we are truly doing is crushing the budding spirit within us that would allow us to step forward onto new paths and better days filled with true purpose.

I can say this because I know it to be true in my life. I am also quite certain that I am not alone.

As I settled into a seat and read the inspiring words on the paper that was given to me, I felt the weight of my personal burden. I won't bore you with the list (it would take hours or days for me to write and you to read), but I will tell you that I was inspired and compelled by the crushing of my spirit to let it lift. After reading, I stood and turned toward the pew and knelt with my head in my hands to pray.

As tears began to fall, I immediately felt, ounce by ounce, my burden lifting. Why did I wait so long to give this over into God's hands? Why did I ever think I needed to carry it with me every second of every hour of every day? The thing is, He already knew what I was carrying. And according to the faith I hold dear in my heart, He had already forgiven my mistakes and blatant wrongs. I didn't need to carry them any longer, but I insisted on it anyway. I hadn't forgiven myself.

Leaving the sanctuary and walking out into the sunlight, I felt increasingly lighter with each step. The drive home was easy in spite of the traffic. The little things just don't bother you as much when you're not carrying extra, unneeded burdens.

As I drove along the back roads closer to home, the sunset was in full color. I had to stop and take a picture because the beauty was so overwhelming. It was almost as if someone was whispering in my ear, "You can see so much more when you're not bending under unbearable weight."

Shed the weight, my friends. Don't carry what you are not meant to carry. You cannot walk purposefully through the next days of your life when you are bent under the past. Forgive others; forgive yourself. Let the burden lift. Accept the grace of God, and then give it as God gives it to you every day.

Last evening, I took the ashes upon my forehead. As I gazed upon this magnificent sunset, they were traded.

172

Ashes for beauty, mourning for gladness, and sorrow for joy. Amen.

"'They will come and shout for joy on the heights of Zion; they will rejoice in the bounty of the LORD—the grain, the new wine and the olive oil, the young of the flocks and herds. They will be like a well-watered garden, and they will sorrow no more. Then young women will dance and be glad, young men and old as well. I will turn their mourning into gladness; I will give them comfort and joy instead of sorrow. I will satisfy the priests with abundance, and my people will be filled with my bounty,' declares the LORD."
(Jeremiah 31:12-14 NIV)

Take the Less Traveled Path

Are you keeping yourself from being the person you were created to be? Do you feel, whether justifiably or not, that you have been wronged by someone? Are you harboring bitterness and anger that block the road to your best, abundant life? These are the hard questions we must ask every day if we are to grow and fulfill our purpose.

We have all been wronged just as we have all wronged someone else. The key is in not letting the wrongs define us or our actions. Bitterness and anger set deep roots in the soul and spirit. They are like the vines of poison ivy that thrive in damp, darkened spaces and wrap themselves around trees, eventually draining the life from them as they take on a life of their own - a life much bigger and stronger than should ever be.

We all feel the hurt of being abused, ridiculed, or simply lied about by others. If we are to be completely honest, we have done the same. That honesty is hard to come by since we are human, and human nature is to be blind to the true flaws of oneself. It takes that same honesty to realize when we have gone beyond the moment of hurt and rage that is normal and have allowed the poison to take root in the darkness of self-pity. It is not wrong to feel hurt or angry. It is, however, wrong to let those things grow and overtake the person you are, turning you into something that is unrecognizable and stagnant.

As much as we may hate the words "forgiveness" and "grace" in these situations, they are

174

words we need, both for those we feel have wronged us and for ourselves. We need to let grace flow over and through us to ease the pain and bitterness, allowing us to forgive others. Forgiving the one who hurt us in no way means that we condone their behavior. It simply means we have come to a place where our desire to grow and move forward on the path set before us has blessedly overcome our need to publicly present our pain and self-pity constantly in the desperate hope of bringing others to our side. We then need to forgive ourselves for letting our emotions control our destiny instead of us controlling our emotions. It is at that precise moment our desire to grow will be realized, and we can take the first step towards a full, unfettered life.

I suppose the question truly is this: what do we want for our lives? Do we want the feel-good moment of others rushing to our sides to give comfort and support to our bitterness, or do we want the life for which we have been created, which is ultimately more satisfying and joyful? It is not a simple choice in our human imperfection. Yet the difficult road is, in reality, the one we need to take. Anyone can be bitter, angry, and hurt. Particularly in today's society, it seems only a few have the courage to take that first step out of the box in which they have placed themselves into the sunshine of new life where grace and forgiveness flow and joy awaits on the horizon.

Perhaps today is the day to make a concerted effort to forgive yourself and then forgive others - to extend grace and concentrate on what is ahead rather than what has been. Maybe, just maybe, it is time to sprout new growth and reach for the sun. As you open the eyes of your heart, you just might find that the light of joy on the horizon beats the darkness of twining vines with deep roots. Of course, the best reason for making the effort is because we have all been extended grace and forgiveness by our heavenly Father, and we are instructed to be "perfect as He is perfect."

Live the best, abundant, purposeful life that awaits. It will be well worth the difficult choice to take the less traveled path and move forward in the grace of Jesus.

"He does not punish us for all our sins; he does not deal harshly with us, as we deserve. For his unfailing love toward those who fear him is as great as the height of the heavens above the earth. He has removed our sins as far from us as the east is from the west." **(Psalm 103:10-12 NLT)**

Grace in Friendship

There is not much that measures up to the sweetness of true friendship. Being able to share your innermost feelings, talk through the most difficult of days, rejoice in each other's blessings, offer an embrace of comfort, or just sit in contented silence are all gifts that nourish our spirits.

Friendship is one of God's greatest blessings that is poured over us with His grace. In turn, it shows us that we must extend that same grace to our friends - in their presence or away from it, in good times and not-so-good times, and whether the relationship is just beginning, has existed for some time, or has ended. Yes, friendship is still friendship no matter what its current state might be. God in His loving grace has provided it, nurtured it, and sometimes will take it away.

You might be wondering, "Just how is taking away something so sweet also showing His grace?" I'm glad you asked.

I met this particular friend when I was in the 7th grade. My parents had moved from one district to another, and I started at a new school about halfway through the year. I was nervous. I expected teasing, and I received it. I felt like there wasn't a friend I would be able to count on during those first days.

When we first met, friendship seemed almost instantaneous. We made each other laugh. We liked a lot of the same things. Of course, that's not saying much for two twelve-year-old girls, but it was all a starting point. We went through the rest of our school years together and were inseparable for the most part.

We were married just seven months apart. She had her first daughter and I had my son within eight months of each other. Our husbands got along very well. We spent time together as friends and time together as couples. We called each other with our good news, bad news, and frustrations. Our bond simply grew stronger with the passing of the years. I viewed her, our individual relationship, and our relationship as couples as incredible gifts.

What I forgot along the way was the Giver. I forgot that it was by God's grace alone that I had this wonderful woman in my life. I also forgot that He was an even better best friend than she was. Those things led me to two huge mistakes: I began to take the Giver and the gift for granted.

Don't get me wrong. This was not something intentionally done. Deep in my heart I was and am grateful for this incredible friendship and for the friendship with my Lord. The problem is that the world worms its way into your vision, and your remembrance and sight aren't what they should be. It happens to all of us. The good news is this: in God's redemptive grace and mercy, He will fix the problem. The not-so-good news is it might hurt a bit at first.

Some 36 years into our friendship, the fabric of our relationship was torn. It was not beyond repair, mind you; it just seemed that way. I was devastated. I can see now that God was just rearranging things according to His plan. He was cementing our relationship in His perfect timing, but even more, He was cementing my relationship with Him. What I saw as the pain of losing a beloved friend was really the emptying of buckets and buckets of grace into my life and probably hers as well.

He wanted me to go back to the beginning when I realized that I needed Him more than anything. *He wanted me to remember that I still need him more than anything.* He wanted me to look at that scared, nervous twelve-year-old girl who had prayed for just one friend at her new school. He wanted me to see that as my dearest friend, He gave me the wonderful gift of friendship here on earth as well. *He not only wanted me to love the gift, He wanted me to renew my love and recognize my need for the Giver.*

Twelve years passed before He had finished pouring those particular buckets of grace into my life. While being soaked in His grace, I realized the love He has for me, the relationship He wants with me, and the friend He is to me. During those years I also realized the love I continued to have for the friendship that was in the past and the fact that I not only took God the Giver for granted but the friendship, too. I was and am deeply sorry for both of those things.

Once the realizations came over me and I expressed my deep sorrow to the Father for my mistakes, the buckets of grace began to pour over my life again. It started out as a drizzle and ended in a deluge. I cried out in thanksgiving and danced in the downpour. The Giver gave me a precious gift for the second time as the friendship was restored. He then reminded me that the gift of His friendship had never waned and never will.

Grace doesn't always present itself as we think it should. Sometimes grace means taking something away to remold it, refine it, and polish it to a restored shine. Sometimes grace means reminding us of just who it is we need, who we should treasure and not take for granted, and who we should thank - both on earth and in heaven. One thing is certain: there is always grace and thanksgiving in friendship, and that's as it should be.

"Sweet friendships refresh the soul and awaken our hearts with joy, for good friends are like the anointing oil that yields the fragrant incense of God's presence."
(Proverbs 27:9 The Passion Translation)

There Is Light Even If You Don't See It

(In honor of the birth of Clayton Michael, 4-1-2020.
We're so glad you're here!)

I had a bad day yesterday. I knew it almost from
the moment I woke. It's not surprising. I am quite sure
all of us are having those days lately. There's so much
darkness that is pervasive in our lives. It doesn't matter
that it's all pretty much beyond our control; the fact
that we can't control it just adds to the gloom. We are
human beings that, for the most part, are determined
to control our surroundings. When we can't do that,
even a small sliver of the brightest light doesn't seem to
break through into our field of vision.

I got out of bed with big plans. I've been doing
my much beloved chore of spring housecleaning. That's
right, I said "beloved." I look forward to it every year.
With non-essential businesses closed (no work for me)
and stay-at-home orders in place, I started early this
spring. Monday began with the living room and
yesterday was the dining room.

My routine began when Michael left for work.
For those who don't know, his job as a produce
manager is essential. No sooner was he out the door
than the dark clouds gathered in my mind. I worry
about him going to work these days; his contact with
the general public concerns me, and that's putting it
mildly.

I tried to push the clouds away. I really did. They
weren't moving any faster than the ones in the sky

outdoors and blocked out just as much light. I started the morning task of going through the house and disinfecting surfaces that are touched constantly - countertops, doorknobs, light switches, remote controls, bathroom surfaces. Somewhere in the middle of that, I began to break down. I didn't completely realize it until I felt the tears on my cheeks. I continued with my rags and disinfectants until I was finished. I then pushed the clouds back once more and started the dining room.

The day ended up being dark all around. No matter what I tried - prayer, praise music, counting the many blessings I have, scrubbing harder, and being sure to get all the nooks and crannies - the darkness just seemed all that much darker. I finished the last of the dining room with a sigh just in time to start dinner as Michael came back through the door, said hello to me, and headed directly for the shower.

Bedtime came early last night. I was suffering from the sheer exhaustion of my worry and my fervent but inept attempts to glimpse the light through the clouds. I told myself, "Tomorrow is another day," as I prayed for some semblance of peace to permeate my soul. A message notification came across my phone just before I fell asleep. It was Erin, my son's other half. She was letting me know that her son's girlfriend had gone into labor. The sliver of light that simple statement gave me was breathtaking! My Heavenly Father was pouring grace over us in this difficult time!

The peace finally came, and with it, sleep. This morning I woke to find another text message on my phone from Erin. The time of the message was

5:32 a.m. It read, "Clayton Michael has arrived!!!!! Everyone is doing fine!!" Next to her words were emojis - baby footprints and a blue heart. My heart soared at the news. Rich and Colleen had a baby boy!

The sliver of light that had dawned just before I closed my eyes last night became a full-blown, brighter than bright, larger than life sun this morning. A new life! A sweet baby boy that came into this world weighing 7 pounds, 15.6 ounces and measuring 21 inches long was chasing away the darkness for his parents, grandparents, great-grandparents, and great-great Pop Pop. Such a big responsibility for a tiny boy, but he handled it with the determination and stamina of his Irish heritage. I am convinced that young Clay is headed for great things. I'm still coming to grips with the fact that this, in essence, makes me a great-grandmother, but I'm doing that with a huge smile on my face.

The point of all this is that there is always light behind the darkness. Sometimes we just need to step back from ourselves and our human nature to see it. Sometimes we have to allow someone else to show it to us. And sometimes it's as simple as opening our eyes. Open your eyes to find the light in the midst of this gloom. When you do and if you still can't see it, push down the worry inside you until it shines through. And if that doesn't work, lean on a trusted and beloved friend. The light is there; I promise it is. God created light and what He creates will stand.

"Then God said, 'Let there be light.' And light appeared."
(Genesis 1:3 The Living Bible)

Today Is the Day the Earth Was Shaken

He had walked among them for three years. He took them from their mundane lives and gave them everything they needed to live abundantly according to heaven's standards if not the world's. They wanted for nothing. Yet one betrayed Him, one denied Him, and they all scattered. The betrayer, in doing so, lost the very earthly life and its riches he so dearly treasured, and he lost it horribly. The denier panicked and uttered the words Jesus had prophesied, sobbing in remorse the moment the words left his tongue. He would wander in the deepest of sorrow until the day Jesus stood before him once again.

It was all preordained. The plan was set in place long before the births of any who witnessed the horror and glory of the cross. The birth, ministry, and death of Jesus had been purposed, and nothing could change it. All of the apostles and followers thought they had lost. Evil clapped its hands in glee thinking it had won. None of them could have been more wrong.

He was arrested, accused, and spat upon. He was ridiculed, bullied, and beaten beyond all human recognition. He was stripped, crowned King of the Jews with thorns and heckling, and forced to carry His manner of death on his shoulders as onlookers - both those who loved Him and those who hated Him - shouted from the sides of the road. His only relief, if you could call it that, was when Simon from Cyrene was forced to carry the cross for Him because His broken

184

body could no longer shoulder the burden in a timely enough manner to satisfy his torturers.

They pushed Him to the top of the hill, laid the cross on the ground, and excruciatingly hammered the spikes through His flesh to attach Him to it before placing it upright in the ground. None of us can imagine the pain He endured. None of us can conceptualize the darkest of black moments when God turned His face away as this humble servant took on the sin of the world that had been before Him, was now, and would be after this treacherous act took place. None of us can fathom the final humiliation of having His killers cast lots for His clothing or thrust the sword through His side in one final act of degradation.

As He uttered the final words, "It is finished," some cried, some laughed, and the Jewish leaders heaved a sigh of relief. They took Him at His word as they understood it. It was over. His family and friends would mourn Him. The soldiers who had been charged with the task would head home from a tough day's work. The Pharisees could go back to wielding the power they so loved over the people.

Once again, evil clapped its hands in glee. Jesus had lost. None of them could have been more wrong. The veil had been torn and nothing would ever be the same.

Sunday is coming!

"Surely He has borne our griefs And carried our sorrows; yet we esteemed Him stricken, smitten by God, and afflicted. But He was wounded for our transgressions, He was bruised for our iniquities; the

chastisement for our peace was upon Him, and by
His stripes we are healed. All we like sheep have gone
astray; we have turned, every one, to his own way; and
the LORD *has laid on Him the iniquity of us all."*
(Isaiah 53:4-6 NKJV)

Sunday Has Come!

Early this morning, the earth quaked with such force that the very foundations of hell crumbled. It still exists, but it cannot and will not stand because it is built on a base of nothing more than sinking sand.

With strength only God can muster, the angel rolled the stone away and took his seat upon it. The grave clothes laid in a heap inside the tomb, and the head cloth sat neatly folded where once a body had lain. As the women came with their spices to anoint the body of Jesus, these simple words opened their hearts and eyes: "Why do you look for the living among the dead? He is not here. He is risen!"

They were so sure they would find Him as they had left Him - cold and still, His life's blood absent from His body. They had seen Him die. The had spent their tears in horror and grief and then cried even more. They came to honor Him and they expected... well, they certainly hadn't expected this, even though they had been told. All they found in the tomb was emptiness. And that emptiness filled their hearts and lives to overflowing.

At the same time the realization hit them, the brilliant light of dawn came over the earth. The darkness of Friday and the sorrow of Saturday were banished in its rays. The confusion of being certain they had known the Messiah yet seeing Him suffer and die like any other human being was lost in the knowledge that what He had promised had happened. The result was pure joy.

He had done what He had said. He gave His life so they could keep theirs and we could keep ours. God's grace flowed with His blood so that none of us can ever be separated from the love of God through Jesus Christ. Our path is clear; our destiny is certain just as theirs was.

The distant yet distinct sound of evil groaning in painful defeat is still heard every Resurrection Sunday, even as the kingdom it has built sinks deeper into the sands of oblivion. Even in times of perceived darkness, the light of the Son prevails. God's Kingdom has come. The grave has no victory. Death has lost its sting.

Jesus Christ is risen. He is risen indeed!

"The one who loves us gives us an overwhelming victory in all these difficulties. I am convinced that nothing can ever separate us from God's love which Christ Yeshua our Lord shows us. We can't be separated by death or life, by angels or rulers, by anything in the present or anything in the future, by forces or powers in the world above or in the world below, or by anything else in creation."
(Romans 8:37-39 Names of God Bible)

Her First Love - Living in Christ's Grace

On May 10, 2018, Daddy and I spent an afternoon together for the purpose of going through Momma's closets and dressers. To say it was emotional doesn't even begin to cover the myriad of feelings that floated in and through both of our hearts and minds, leaving their trail of smiles and tears behind.

There were outfits that were her go-to items - comfy sweatpants and sweatshirts for the colder months, and light and airy shirts and capris for the warmer ones. So many of those shirts spoke to things she loved. Many were adorned with birds, butterflies, or flowers - and of course, there were lighthouses. Oh, how she loved her lighthouses!

Others held images of flags, stars, and fireworks. Momma was very patriotic. I don't remember a single national holiday passing without several small flags adorning the outside of their home or her not sporting a red, white, and blue shirt of some kind. As a matter of fact, most of her clothes were the shades of red, white, and blue contained in the American flag. She loved her flag and its colors as much as she loved her birds, butterflies, and flowers.

For most of the items I folded and put into boxes for donation, memories would flood my mind as to when they had been bought and for what occasion. Some were gifts I had purchased for birthdays, Christmases, and Mother's Days. And then there were those outfits that had a very special meaning.

In the spring of 2006, after claiming victory over her months-long battle with breast cancer and all of its complications throughout 2005, she and I went on a shopping spree of sorts. First, we went to lunch. Then we spent the entire afternoon between two stores, acting much like schoolgirls shopping for a school dance or vacationers shopping for that once-in-a-lifetime trip. I remember her smiling and talking with me as she tried on outfit after outfit before choosing a handful to take home. The joy came not so much from the new clothes themselves but almost completely from the realization that she had graciously been given a new start. Thanks to the healing mercies of her heavenly Father, she was healthy, happy, and embarking on her future: a future that was filled with the promise that cancer tried and failed to take from her.

There were also other items - purses, newspaper clippings, special keepsakes from here and there - and there was her wallet. I opened it to be sure there were no identification cards, medical cards, or money left inside. While I didn't find any of those things, I found something of much greater value to my mom.

As with many wallets, the first thing you see when you open it is the section containing pictures. There was a picture of her and my dad, one of her and me that we had taken for Daddy one Christmas, one of my brother and me, as well as several each of Jason, Bryan, Sabrina, John Jr., Jacob, and Thayer. However, it was the first picture that grabbed my attention and brought even more memories to mind. The first picture you saw when opening the wallet was a picture of

Jesus. On the back of the picture were the following words: "Only one life, 'Twill soon be past; Only what's done for Christ will last." Beneath those words were the words of Philippians 1:21: "For to me to live is Christ."

My heart and soul filled to overflowing as I gazed upon this picture. Tears filled my eyes at the realization that this told the entire story of exactly who Momma was and how she lived her life. This is the One she loved and relied upon most. While Daddy was the love of her earthly life and she loved all of us with an overflowing heart, she loved Jesus with everything she was and was to become thanks to His sacrifice. She knew that her life and strength came from Him. She knew that He would carry her through anything that this world threw her way. She knew He had gone to prepare a place for her. And she carried His picture in her wallet as the image of the One she loved and trusted beyond any earthly person or power. Oh, to attain her level of faith!

Behind the pictures was the section for credit cards. Instead of credit cards, this section held business cards of a sort. They were the business cards of Father God. They contained beloved verses that she carried with her for whenever a need would arise, or simply to gaze upon and be reminded that she was loved beyond human reason.

The first card held this verse from Isaiah 40:31: "But they that wait upon the Lord shall renew their strength; they shall mount up with wings as eagles; they shall run, and not be weary; and they shall walk, and not faint."

I cannot imagine how many times Momma opened her wallet and looked at that card, even though I know she knew that verse backward and forward without having to read it. What I can imagine is her taking out that card and holding it in her hands during the most difficult moments of her life simply because of the promise it held. It was the promise contained in the first picture along with those cards in her wallet that defined her life with us. They were the gifts she gave to each of us each day she lived on this earth - the gifts of grace, faith, and immeasurable love, just as Christ had given those gifts to her.

The picture of Jesus she carried now sits here on my desk. I look at it every day and remember the gift of life He has given me along with the gift of Momma. I read the writing on the back of the picture frequently. I remember that His strength is flowing through me, His love surrounds me, and for me to live is Christ. At least I pray that is what I show to the world just as Momma did.

Each Mother's Day, I will miss her more than words can express. My tears fall and are innumerable. Yet I remember the gifts she gave to all of us, gifts she continues to give even today, and smile. And I will whisper a prayer of joy and thanksgiving even through my tears of grief for the incredible gift that is Momma, for all she taught each one of us along the path of her life, and for the grace that covers all of us.

"But let your adorning be the hidden person of the heart with the imperishable beauty of a gentle and quiet spirit, which in God's sight is very precious."
(1 Peter 3:4 ESV)

Be Light

There is a quiet beauty present, even on the mornings where clouds prevail. It lies in the muted tones of the birdsong, the soft feel of the gentle mist that falls, and the sweet sway of the trees in the cool breeze. The sun always shines, even though it might be obscured to our vision. So should that light shine in your soul, permeating any dark place. Let it fill you, warm you, and spread outward. It is not meant to be hidden but to be released to a waiting world! Grace abounds to you; let grace also abound to all you meet. The beauty of this grey, misty morning greets you with promise and joy. Embrace it and realize the promise.

"No one lights a lamp and then puts it under a basket. Instead, a lamp is placed on a stand, where it gives light to everyone in the house."
(Matthew 5:15 NLT)

Days We Can't Forget

We all have those dates that stay in our minds forever. Today, May 15th, is one of those for me.

Today in 1977, at the age of just one day shy of eleven months, we rushed our son to the hospital in the middle of the night. He awoke and let out a scream and then was silent. We jumped from our sleep to his crib, where we found him laboring to barely breathe as his lips began turning blue. His skin was very hot to our touch. We grabbed him, wrapped him in a blanket, and ran half a block down Buttonwood Street to the hospital emergency room. It would have taken longer to get to the car, get him safely in, and drive there.

As we checked him in with the receptionist and began to answer questions, I wanted to scream. He was having so much trouble breathing! After a period of time - too long in my opinion - he was seen by a doctor. The doctor diagnosed him with croup, and he was placed in an oxygen mist tent. We were told that croup wasn't too serious of a condition and he would be fine.

Fast forward a few hours later and he was getting worse. The doctors on duty didn't understand it. They ran blood tests and did chest x-rays. The results all came back good. Scratching their heads as I was panicking and crying, they called in two more doctors. One was an ENT and the other was a young pediatrician.

After examination by these two new doctors, Jason was swept out of my arms and off to the operating room. They told me they had to do a tracheotomy to enable him to breathe. My heart, which was already in my throat, felt like it was about to come out of my mouth. By this time, Michael's parents had arrived to sit with us. My parents were on the other side of the state visiting relatives. We were placed in a small employee locker room across from the ICU to wait...and wait...and wait.

I was inconsolable. We all were. For me, a young mother of not quite 19, my emotions were all over the place. I wanted so desperately to be calm so I could understand whatever they might tell me when they returned. I wanted, even more than that, to hold my son and take him home. And yet even more, I wanted to be at home with none of this having happened.

The doctors returned after quite some time. The ENT explained that Jason had a viral infection that had caused a swelling that was cutting off his windpipe. They had managed to put a thin tube through his nose and bypass the swelling in his throat to allow him to breathe. The tracheotomy, thankfully, would not needed as long as this continued to work for him. I listened quietly. The last sentence I heard was the one that made my body quake inside and out, and still does somewhat to this day: "There is a 75% chance he will not survive the next 48 hours."

I spent the next 48 hours at the hospital. I waited in the ICU waiting room until the prescribed time that I could visit with Jason - ten minutes of time with him and then one hour and fifty minutes waiting for the next time. It was excruciating, and even that word doesn't describe it accurately.

He was in an oxygen tent with all kinds of tubes and wires attached to him. His arms and legs were restrained so he couldn't pull any of those things off of his body. I couldn't hold him, couldn't touch him, and wasn't even sure he could hear my voice because he was so heavily sedated. I talked to him, sang to him, and prayed with him regardless.

When I wasn't with him, I was yelling at God. *Why did this happen? Please don't take him from me! Please heal him! I want my baby home! I'll do anything!*

The truth is there was nothing I could do. I had to trust. I had to believe the doctors knew what to do and that the medications would work. It was difficult at best and impossible at worst. And yet, what choice did I have?

The first 48 hours passed, and Jason began to improve. A feeding tube was placed in the other nostril so he could gain more substantial nourishment than the IV provided. He managed to get his arms out of the restraints at least once a day after that and pull the wires from his chest, giving the nurses a scare every time. I stopped listening to the visitation rules and flat out refused to leave his side. I watched God heal my son one minuscule step at a time. It was nothing short of amazing, but it was a long recovery.

He was in the hospital for a total of two weeks, and ten days of that were spent in the ICU. There was a second surgical procedure halfway through his stay. He was left thin and weakened. It was probably a full month before his strength returned completely and longer until he regained the weight he had lost. But he survived and he thrived.

I learned at that young age that God is gracious and faithful. I learned that it's okay to be scared, but it's also okay to trust at the same time. I learned that God sends exactly the right people at exactly the right time, and I learned to trust that timing and be thankful. I am beyond thankful for Dr. John and Dr. Mark, the ENT and pediatrician that were sent that day. I am more than grateful that God knew who and what Jason needed and provided it, thereby showing His wisdom and glory.

Each year on this day, I say a silent prayer of thanks... for the gift that is Jason, for those who took care of him and saved him, and for God the Father's wondrous grace, mercy, and provision.

Cry out, learn to trust, and be thankful, for God is faithful in all things. Dates are to be remembered for a reason. In my experience, they are the times God showed up in a huge way and gave us a glimpse of His glory. Even in the midst of our pain, we experienced His grace.

"Lord, you are my God; I will exalt you and praise your name, for in perfect faithfulness you have done wonderful things, things planned long ago."
(Isaiah 25:1 NIV)

Uniquely the Same

The beauty of flowers comes in their uniqueness. Each bloom differs in shade, tone, highlight, size, and number of petals. It is the same with people. Just as with flowers, it is our uniqueness that separates us just as it is our likeness that binds us.

Ultimately, flowers and people all need the same things to thrive, regardless of unique traits. Without rain in their seasons, neither would grow. Without sunshine in their days, neither would bear the buds of new bloom. Without the coolness of nights, neither would be restored to face the heat of the day to come. And without loving care, both will die. The likenesses far outweigh the differences when it comes to living. The differences are nothing more than our perception.

Look with new eyes. Remember these simple facts as you walk through your days. Without the storms, there will be no growth in faith. Without the calm, there will be no rest to face the next storm. Without all of the circumstances of life, we will remain stagnant, never reaching our full potential. Without our differences, the picture of God's creation would not be complete in its beauty. And without love, care, and kindness, we cannot survive, but with those things we can rise up into the abundance for which we were created.

"For just as the body is one and has many members, and all the members of the body, though many, are one body, so it is with Christ. For in the one Spirit we were all baptized into one body—Jews or Greeks, slaves or free—and we were all made to drink of one Spirit. Indeed, the body does not consist of one member but of many. If the foot would say, 'Because I am not a hand, I do not belong to the body,' that would not make it any less a part of the body. And if the ear would say, 'Because I am not an eye, I do not belong to the body,' that would not make it any less a part of the body. If the whole body were an eye, where would the hearing be? If the whole body were hearing, where would the sense of smell be? But as it is, God arranged the members in the body, each one of them, as he chose. If all were a single member, where would the body be? As it is, there are many members, yet one body. The eye cannot say to the hand, 'I have no need of you,' nor again the head to the feet, 'I have no need of you.' On the contrary, the members of the body that seem to be weaker are indispensable, and those members of the body that we think less honorable we clothe with greater honor, and our less respectable members are treated with greater respect; whereas our more respectable members do not need this. But God has so arranged the body, giving the greater honor to the inferior member, that there may be no dissension within the body, but the members may have the same care for one another. If one member suffers, all suffer together with it; if one member is honored, all rejoice together with it."

(1 Corinthians 12:12-26 NRSV)

200

Rain Makes You Beautiful

The skies began to darken dramatically, and the rain fell as I made my way home from work last evening. I felt the inner cringe my thoughts give each time I see even a single drop lately, as we've had more than our share of rain in the last month. Yet even as that feeling made itself known, the words Momma used to say spoke rather loudly in my mind and heart. "Rain makes you beautiful," I heard her say. I had just enough time to begin to ponder the truth of those words through the rest of my drive.

The benefits of a soaking rain are quite obvious, particularly in the spring and hot summer months. During early spring, the rains wake up the landscape from winter's browns and greys to the vibrant greens of new growth. They nourish newly planted flowers and vegetables and wash away the stagnant air of the cold months. As Momma's words said, those rains bring beauty. They bring growth.

During the heat of summer, the rains fall more furiously as storms move through. They give much-needed quenching to parched ground. The rains revive the greenery and help it to produce fruit as they recede, and the sun's rays once again warm the earth.

The rains of nature and of life are much the same. We experience cold and grey periods where we are stagnant. We reach for the sun to grow but can't seem to find the strength. We go through dry spells where our spirits are parched and thirsting for relief. We wilt under the heat of everyday life. Circumstance seems to scorch us, and we cannot push forth the fruit in our lives that we feel budding within us.

We need rain. We need to soak in the nourishment that will bring the vibrancy and growth to help us withstand the dry periods and the cold seasons. When those times arrive in their cycles, we need the rain again and again to bring life to our spirits that seem brittle and broken. We need it to pour over and into us and to soak it in so that the budding flowers of fruitfulness don't wither and die, never accomplishing their purpose.

We need, as my mom would say, to let the rain make us beautiful.

When Heaven's rains come, act as you did as a child. Run into the deluge. Splash in the downpour. Dance in the puddles. Lift your face to the sky and laugh as you soak in its benefits. Cast the encumbrance of properly-acting adulthood aside for as much time as it takes to renew and revitalize. Let your childlike faith take over and your inhibitions flee in the moment. Be filled, be nourished, and be satisfied as only Heaven's rains can satisfy. And then be thankful.

Let the rains from the Father above make you beautiful.

"The LORD says, 'People of Jacob, you are my servants. Listen to me! People of Israel, I chose you.' This is what the LORD says, who made you, who formed you in your mother's body, who will help you: 'People of Jacob, my servants, don't be afraid. Israel, I chose you. I will pour out water for the thirsty land and make streams flow on dry land. I will pour out my Spirit into

your children and my blessing on your descendants. Your children will grow like a tree in the grass, like poplar trees growing beside streams of water.'"

(Isaiah 44:1-4 NCV)

Let Yourself Be Comforted

Somehow, over the years, I've learned (or perhaps needed) to keep my emotions in check. It's not that I don't feel them; it's simply a matter of not making them a priority. Whether it's because of the need to appear strong for someone else, a need to concentrate on any particular matter at hand, or (banish the thought!) fear of letting things out because I may not be able to stop or someone may see and think it weakness, I keep my emotions under wraps. The only time I allow them to take over is when I'm alone or with someone I deeply trust, usually Michael.

I can't remember when this talent or skill (if you want to call it that) made itself known. I only know it's there. The first time I actually remember making a concerted effort to portray calm and concentration was when Jason was eleven months old. He was admitted to the hospital, unable to breathe. As they looked for a reason, they rushed him into the operating room to perform a tracheotomy. In the end, the procedure wasn't needed, and they were able to thread a small tube through his nose and bypass a swelling in his throat. He was diagnosed with epiglottitis, a potentially life-threatening condition where the epiglottis swells and keeps air from entering the lungs. I was a panicked young mom waiting in a very small, private room with my husband and in-laws (my parents were away visiting relatives) when the doctors walked in and pronounced that his chances of survival were 25% over the next 48 hours. Everyone shattered into pieces, including me. Yet something rose up inside of me and pushed those pieces to the side so I could understand what the doctors were telling me about what needed to happen next. I continued to be (apparently) calm as I looked at his small body inside an oxygen tent, unclothed except for a diaper and the myriad of leads and wires that were attached to him. It was only when I left the hospital for a very short period of time after being there for 24 hours that I fell apart. The scream that had been bottled up inside me came out forcefully, driving me to my knees and into the waiting arms of my husband.

This behavior became a habit for me. Through 13 more hospitalizations for various reasons during the first four years of Jason's life, through my dad having and surviving surgery for an abdominal aortic aneurysm, through my mom's battle with breast cancer, to Jason again going through major medical problems and a catastrophic accident in his adult years, and losses of my mom and beloved family members and friends, I "keep it together" in the public eye.

For those who enact this same charade frequently, I know you understand. For those who don't, please know it is not that I am hard-hearted or cold. I just function on a somewhat different plane for the purpose of simply that word - function. I feel just as deeply. I sympathize. I empathize. Inside, I am torn to shreds and soaked with tears, even if I am smiling on the outside.

This may not seem like much of a problem, other than the perception it creates in onlookers. However, it is always a problem eventually.

You see, emotions have a way of sneaking up on you when you least expect them, especially if you tend to hold them in. You can be walking through your day, going about your own business, and thinking everything is fine when bam! You become similar to a wet dishrag unable to hold shape or substance. The tears break out. The memories flood. The feelings run rampant through your well-intentioned and organized heart and mind. Everything brings a reminder of the reason for the emotions and makes them more intense, causing the barely healed, shredded parts of your heart to open afresh. For me, this process can last moments or days. It's frustrating. And it's scary.

I am particularly prone to the surprise attack of my emotions at this time of year. From the autumn through the holidays, my senses overwhelm me as the memories grow sharper while forcing their way into the forefront of my days. It creates chaos where none need be created.

There's a solution to all of this: feel the feelings. Let them wash over you and through you. Share them with someone you know cares about you. Get over the fear of being judged or of appearing weak, and open up to let them out into the air - perhaps easier said than done but necessary.

Emotions are not a bad thing. They are quite beautiful even if it may not seem so at the time. We were created to feel them and share them. So, let yourself feel. Mourn loss, cry out in sadness, and feel the pain of not being able to fix something. Let others help you through the moments. Let God help you. Let yourself be comforted in the way God intends.

On the other side, there is purpose. Once you have allowed them to come to the surface, comfort and

206

hope will envelope you. More importantly, you will be able to use all of it to comfort others when they need it most because you've been there, and it is at that moment they will find hope. It's a gift meant to be received and then given away.

"Blessed are those who mourn, for they will be comforted."
(Matthew 5:4 NIV)

Grace In Every Moment

Let's talk about grace - the grace we are given every moment of each day and the grace we (should) give every moment of each day.

None of us would be breathing without the grace that pours over us throughout our lives. Grace surrounds us and permeates each second. We've all heard the saying, "May lightning strike me if..." That's where grace comes into play. We all have those moments where that lightning should strike, the moments where we should no longer be walking this earth. Yet here we are.

While on vacation with my husband a few weeks ago, we walked the quiet main street of Chincoteague to have dinner at a beautiful bayside restaurant. Sitting at an outdoor table, the view was nothing less than breathtaking as the sun set over the water. Our meals were delicious, the tones of an acoustic guitar and vocals filled the air creating the perfect setting, and gratitude settled in as we enjoyed the evening, lingering long after our meals were finished.

At a nearby table, another couple was having dinner. Sadly, it became apparent they were not enjoying their time as much as we were. The gentleman called the server over to the table and began complaining about the entrée he had been served. The complaint would have been remedied easily enough, as it seemed a matter of personal preference and not the dish itself. However, he had already eaten his food. As he voiced his displeasure, the server offered to have the manager come to speak with him. His displeasure grew along with the heightening volume of his voice. He indicated that he didn't want the manager, he just wanted his check. The server left the table a bit red-faced with embarrassment. Truth be told, there was no reason for her to be embarrassed. She had done everything she could to avoid the raising of his voice and to make things right. She returned with the check and asked again if he would like to speak with the manager, only to be met with the same reply. "No." The server returned a few minutes later and accepted the payment from the gentleman and returned his change. She thanked him and his wife for coming and wished them a good night. This was greeted with silence as far as we could tell.

The couple soon left the table and headed for the parking lot. A minute or two later, I went to use the restroom and passed by the table. They had left just a few dollars in tip money for the young woman. My heart broke for that poor girl. The fault was not hers, yet she took the brunt of the displeasure, tried to fix what was wrong, and then shouldered more displeasure. There was no gratitude for her attempts, no "You do the same" for her good night wishes. The tip was less than ten percent of what the meal would have been.

Part of me wanted to try to find this couple in the parking lot and let them have a piece of my mind. Part of me wanted to find this young woman and comfort her to let her know she'd done all she could. Mostly, I was appalled at the lack of grace allowed to someone who was just trying to do their job and doing it well from all indications.

Yes, I understand that the server was the person with whom the couple had contact. I have been in that position much of my professional life. However, there is much truth to the phrase, "Don't shoot the messenger." There is also much truth to the phrase, "You deserve a break today," as the old commercial sings. Everyone deserves that break. Everyone deserves a little grace poured upon them by those whose paths they cross. Even that gentleman deserved a little grace, which is why (for the most part) I didn't hunt him down in the parking lot.

Grace could have come in the form of a simple statement: that they knew it wasn't her fault but wanted her to know there was something with which they were not quite happy. Grace could have come in the form of not raising his voice but agreeing to let a manager speak with him. It could have come in the form of wishing her a good night as well. And it could have come in the form of the standard tip of 15% to 20% for her efforts in actually serving the two of them (we noticed she was a very attentive server as we sat there observing) as well as trying to validate their wishes to be heard so that whatever had been wrong might be made right in some way, even though the food had already been eaten.

So much time and so many ways to give grace, and yet so little is given by those of us inhabiting this world.

Where would we be without grace? We would be living in self-centered misery while everyone around us was living in their own self-centered lives. There would be no one to help and encourage us and no one to care. Looking at our past would be excruciating. Living our present would be agonizingly lonely and sparse. There would be no future beyond our numbered earthly days - at least not one that is in any remote way one in which we'd want to live.

Jesus poured out His life so that we might obtain grace. He hung on that cross so that our pasts are simply that - our pasts, forgiven and forgotten. He gave it all so that we could live abundantly now and in the future. He did it so that we would see that we should do for others just as He did and does for us.

Do we deserve it? No. Do those with whom we come in contact deserve it from us? Yes. It is not meant for us alone. It is meant for everyone.

Let the grace you are given every day have an effect on you. Give a little grace. Sprinkle it like seasoning on everyone you meet in your daily life - even those who aggravate you. Let me rephrase that - especially those who aggravate you. It is certain that you don't see perfection when you look in the mirror. Neither does anyone else. Yet Jesus sees you and everyone else as perfect through His 20/20 vision of grace and love.

"But because God was so gracious, so very generous, here I am. And I'm not about to let his grace go to waste. Haven't I worked hard trying to do more than any of the others? Even then, my work didn't amount to all that much. It was God giving me the work to do, God giving me the energy to do it."
(1 Corinthians 15:10 The Message)

Beautifully Broken

Brokenness is not weakness. Even the cup whose handle is broken is still more than capable of serving its given purpose - to hold the drink that satisfies your thirst.

The way I look at it, brokenness is strength. It is quite able to reinforce the determination to move forward toward the goal, even if - for a time - moving forward means crawling up onto the shoulders of someone stronger. True strength comes in knowing you are broken and admitting your need for that time when others must carry you until you can walk on your own.

Brokenness in body or in spirit is not a bad thing. It is simply one step along a path designed to build upon that which resides within you. You might lose sight for a moment. You might take some time to wallow in self-pity. We all do that. The key is in always taking the second moment to look upward and see the light shining with the intent to soak up your darkness.

Brokenness allows for more room to grow. It allows for the things not needed to leave you and the needed things to take up residence. Once the needed things gather, the cracks and fissures begin to close - yes, leaving scars, but in closing becoming stronger than they were. This is healing. This is the grace of Jesus.

Never be afraid of being broken. Instead, be aware of the healing that immediately starts upon breaking. Watch as others rush to aid in that healing; let them aid in the healing. Their encouragement and help to you might just be a healing process in their own brokenness.

Brokenness is beautiful. It is a humble beginning from which great things happen. It is the first step toward the goal and your purpose. It is strength and beauty disguised as darkness and despair. Even the caterpillar spends time in the darkness of the cocoon before it is broken and the glorious butterfly emerges.

The bottom line is this: Be humble. Be beautiful. Be strong. But first, be broken. Being broken releases the beautiful fragrance that is you to the world.

"And when Jesus was in Bethany at the house of Simon the leper, a woman came to him having an alabaster flask of very costly fragrant oil, and she poured in on his head as he sat at the table."
(Matthew 26:6-7 NKJV)

214

A Time to Rest

Speaking as someone who almost never took the time to rest - I didn't feel like I needed it - recovery from this Covid-19 virus is quite frustrating. I am the kind of person who keeps going until a task is complete. Not only do I keep going, but I also multitask. It seems I don't have that capability right now either.

My body is tired. We are trying to regain strength each day by walking. Prior to becoming sick, we would walk anywhere between three and five miles a day at a very fast clip, usually completing five miles in sixty minutes, perhaps a little more than that. Our latest venture outdoors amounted to two miles, and that took us a full forty-five minutes. We needed water and a nap upon returning home.

My brain is tired. My mind doesn't want to focus completely. I find myself needing lists where I didn't need them before. I must force my mind to concentrate fully on only one thing at a time in order to do things the way I want them done. This is something completely new and different for me. This is something I want to go away - now! I am praying this is not a lasting effect of this illness.

On the other hand, Michael's mind is working nonstop. He has trouble shutting it down at night when it's time for bed. This leaves him awake several times a night and more tired during the day. This is the opposite of his usual behavior. He is an asleep-before-his-head-hits-the-pillow kind of guy. It seems we have traded places. It is equally as frustrating for him as it is for me.

Rest. It's the prescription to remedy all kinds of ailments whether they be physical, mental/emotional, or spiritual. Yet as human beings with a self-sufficient nature, we all fight taking the prescription.

It's highly probable that the tendency comes from the society in which we live. The world has become a constant flurry of activity. Everything takes place seven days a week, twenty-four hours a day. Companies exhaust their efforts for maximum production. Workers exhaust themselves for that overtime pay. Customers exhaust themselves (and their credit cards) placing their orders at all hours. Entertainment can be found around the clock, and there is always an audience available and exhausting themselves to take advantage of it. Social media runs 24/7, leaving no relief from the exhaustion of dissension, discord, and fractured relationships.

Rest. We need it. We crave it, admittedly or not. If we don't get what we need we are, very simply, doomed. We may think we're above needing it. We may think we're quite capable of completing our tasks, crossing off our lists, fulfilling our obligations to work, family, and friends, and able to get our fill of enjoyment without giving in to the urge for even five minutes of downtime - not just body downtime but mind and heart downtime as well. Newsflash: we're not! We may complete all of those things, but we won't complete them properly or well.

So please take a moment or moments to close your eyes and focus your heart, mind, soul, and spirit on the One who gives you rest. Stay in His presence for as long as you need and as long as He asks. Let His grace flow over you. He will heal you in whatever ways healing is needed. He will restore your strength, your focus, your capabilities, and your complete health. He will make sure that what needs to be done is done and the remainder will wait. I, for one, am counting on that.

"Do you not know? Have you not heard? The Lord is the everlasting God, the Creator of the ends of the earth. He will not grow tired or weary, and his understanding no one can fathom. He gives strength to the weary and increases the power of the weak. Even youths grow tired and weary, and young men stumble and fall; but those who hope in the Lord will renew their strength. They will soar on wings like eagles; they will run and not grow weary, they will walk and not be faint."
(Isaiah 40:28-31 NIV)

"Yes, my soul, find rest in God; my hope comes from him. Truly he is my rock and my salvation; he is my fortress, I will not be shaken. My salvation and my honor depend on God; he is my mighty rock, my refuge. Trust in him at all times, you people; pour out your hearts to him, for God is our refuge."
(Psalm 62:5-8 NIV)

The Season of
Thanksgiving

Always Thankful

As 2020's days became short, I think we have all been thankful to have simply survived. As I am trying to put together this draft to send to Stef for editing, I am reminded that there is always something to lift to God in thanksgiving.

I think the key to a constant attitude of thanksgiving is to never take anything for granted. Everything in life, small and large, is orchestrated just for you. This in and of itself is miraculous. It starts with the gift of mercy at Christmas, when Father God saw our desperate need for His compassion. It continues with the gift of ultimate grace at Easter as He fills our need for forgiveness, not only for past sin, but for present and future as well. We anticipate, celebrate, and give thanks for these special days as they draw closer.

The calendar year continues to move from spring into summer, and we often sink into those lazy and warm days without a thought to the bounty from above we experience every day. The fact is that every day is Christmas, and every day is Easter. The gifts of mercy and grace are poured over us *every day*.

The truth is that Thanksgiving is and should be every day, too. Just waking up to a new day each morning is something to celebrate - a time to sing praises to our Father. No matter your circumstances, try to remember to give thanks. Your troubles actually will seem smaller when you thank God for them because it will remind you that God is in control and has it wrangled and put in its place. It will also remind you of the Season of Lessons because you're growing, as well as the Season of Grace because you couldn't do this on your own.

The Season of Thanksgiving is a year-round perfect mix of blessings and blessings in disguise. Each one brings us one step closer to perfection in Jesus. I am thankful for all of it.

I chose the month of November to indicate daily thankfulness because there are many dates in that month that represent the people I love who inspire me. With each of those people also comes the reminder of biblical gifts and promises. As I reflected on my gratitude, I discovered that every day contains something or someone placed in my path that correlates with scripture. That realization brought – you guessed it – more thanksgiving.

I challenge you to find gratitude in each day. As you go through this section, you will notice blank space on the pages. Use that space as an opportunity to spur your own gratitude, no matter what month you're in. Think of what you're most thankful for and write it down. It will start a daily habit that will become a constant Season of Thanksgiving – even on the days it seems there's nothing extraordinary happening, even on the days that are fraught with trials.

Being thankful is a lesson in grace learned as we anticipate what lies ahead in our journey. That anticipation will always bring joy, no matter the circumstance, as we travel the path our faith sets before us.

"Be anxious for nothing, but in everything by prayer and supplication, with thanksgiving, let your requests be made known to God; and the peace of God, which surpasses all understanding, will guard your hearts and minds through Christ Jesus."
(Philippians 4:6-7 Jubilee Bible 2000)

Rushing Headlong Into Thanksgiving
Thankful, Day 1

Last night we said goodbye to October. Today we're transitioning into the month of November and all it has to offer. We leave behind the ghosts, goblins, and jack-o-lanterns to embrace pumpkin pies, turkeys, and cornucopias. We're running headlong into a month of gratitude - at least we should be. Truth be told, we should be running headlong into gratitude each morning upon waking to a new day, no matter the time of year.

Why is it we spend way too much time questioning our situations, whining about our conditions, and crying for something better? Everything we need to have joy in our lives is right in front of us every day. Why don't we see it? The truth is our blindness is self-inflicted. We allow the world and circumstances to darken our vision. We can't see the joy that's right where we are because we won't take our eyes off of the perceived problems we have. We're choosing despair, choosing disappointment, and choosing misery because we won't be grateful for all that comes into our lives. That's right - all of it.

There is joy in all things if we only express our gratitude for all things. Think about it in broader terms than just what you allow yourself to see. Gain a different perspective from the tunnel vision you force upon yourself, because here's the thing: problems bring solutions, trials bring endurance, tears bring cleansing, emptiness brings fullness, and gratitude changes perspective and brings joy.

I am not minimizing the circumstances we all go through at any given time. Things like illness, pain, loss, and disappointment are serious issues for us whenever we experience them. However, we must allow ourselves to be picked up out of them rather than wallow in them. God does not allow these things into our lives to crush us. He allows them to mature and refine us. He allows them to fulfill His purpose, whether the purpose fulfilled is for us in our struggle or for someone else who enters to stand in the struggle with us. He is making us a light for others who are shrouded in darkness, and He is making us joy for someone stuck in despair - perhaps not in this instant but in moments to come. *He is bringing us through so that we have the experience to help bring someone else through.*

And so, let's look at this month as a transition into gratitude. Go into each new day with the attitude that there is something for which to be thankful, and then thank God for it. If it seems difficult to do that, pray for the ability to see what should make you grateful in any situation. Watch how that gratitude will shape your days while turning despair into joy and darkness into light. See how just one moment of thankfulness will bring many moments of peace that is unsurpassed.

I wish you all a month full and a life full of gratitude. I plan on finding something for which I am thankful each day. I write the first thirty days here to give God glory. Feel free to join me. Let's let the light of joy and gratitude shine for others to see.

Today I am grateful for the recent ability to touch the heart of an old friend who has been absent from my life. I don't know where it goes from here, but I know I always am thankful for her regardless.

"Praise be to the God and Father of our Lord Jesus Christ, the Father of compassion and the God of all comfort, who comforts us in all our troubles, so that we can comfort those in any trouble with the comfort we ourselves receive from God. For just as we share abundantly in the sufferings of Christ, so also our comfort abounds through Christ."
(2 Corinthians 1:3-5 NIV)

Thankful, Day 2

Today I am thankful for the grace to begin each day with a clean slate...a new chance to do what I should, to touch the lives of others in a positive way, and to give to others the grace I've been given. I am deep down in my soul, jump for joy, shout from the mountaintops thankful for the grace that is Jesus Christ in my life. Without Him, each day would be a blank page that would remain blank, for without Him, what story could my life possibly write for others?

"And God is able to make all grace abound to you, so that having all sufficiency in all things at all times, you may abound in every good work."
(2 Corinthians 9:8 ESV)

Thankful, Day 3

This morning I am thankful for true freedom - not the freedom of the world but the freedom to be who I am in Jesus because of His gift. Earthly freedoms are fragile and can be broken, stolen, or revoked. The treasure that is real freedom can never be taken away from us once we have claimed Jesus as our Lord. The prophet Isaiah wrote, "And the government shall be upon His shoulder" (Isaiah 9:6). While earthly governments last but the blink of an eye, His Kingdom and the freedom He brings are eternal.

"Do not let sin control the way you live; do not give in to sinful desires. Do not let any part of your body become an instrument of evil to serve sin. Instead, give yourselves completely to God, for you were dead, but now you have new life. So use your whole body as an instrument to do what is right for the glory of God. Sin is no longer your master, for you no longer live under the requirements of the law. Instead, you live under the freedom of God's grace."
(Romans 6:12-14 NLT)

Thankful, Day 4

I am thankful for the ultimate love. Knowing I am loved and accepted in all my flawed humanity by the One who created me fills my heart with gratitude and joy. When I feel rejected or frowned upon by others, He is always there to hold me, place me on higher ground, and remind me of who I am. I am a beloved child of God and joint heir with Jesus. Thank You for Your love!

"How precious also are Your thoughts to me, O God! How great is the sum of them! If I should count them, they are more in number than the sand; when I awake, I am still with You."
(Psalm 139:17-18 Modern English Version)

Thankful, Day 5

Today - *every* day - I am thankful for the man God richly blessed me with as a dad. He, along with my mom, taught me what love is, how to live with integrity, how important it is to give kindness and have compassion for others, and that forgiveness is something that must be given as well as received. He has been my biggest supporter, cheering me on throughout my life, helping me up when I fall, and has shown me that there are no failures but only mistakes from which to learn valuable lessons. He has been an example of faith in action. He is one of the greatest gifts given to me by God, the Father. Today, on your birthday and every day, I am thankful for you, Daddy! I love you and pray I am as much a blessing to you as you have been to me.

"Children, obey your parents in the Lord, for this is right. 'Honor your father and mother'—which is the first commandment with a promise— 'so that it may go well with you and that you may enjoy long life on the earth.'"
(Ephesians 6:1-3 NIV)

Thankful, Day 6

This morning my heart overflows with gratitude for friendship. Whether it be friendships that have waned due to time and distance, friendships where distance separates but keeping in touch regularly is the norm, or friendships that are close in every way, you have all had a profound impact on my life that I deeply treasure. I think of you all with love every day. Most of all, the friendship that is found in Jesus brings words of thanksgiving to my heart and lips - what a friend we have in Him. He is always here, available to listen, gives the best advice, and will never leave our side. Thank You for Your friendship and the earthly friendships You bring into our lives!

"I no longer call you slaves, because a master doesn't confide in his slaves. Now you are my friends, since I have told you everything the Father told me. You didn't choose me. I chose you. I appointed you to go and produce lasting fruit, so that the Father will give you whatever you ask for, using my name."
(John 15:15-16 NLT)

Thankful, Day 7

    I am so thankful I don't have to worry over all the details of my life. (That doesn't mean I don't worry at times; it just means I'm thankful I don't have to!) I am thankful for the joy of knowing that God is in control of every detail, large and small, that goes into my life. Nothing happens that He doesn't allow, has not predestined according to His perfect will, and does not intend for my growth and good.

    My joy is found in His perfect vision and planning - it's found in Him!

"You made my whole being; you formed me in my mother's body. I praise you because you made me in an amazing and wonderful way. What you have done is wonderful. I know this very well. You saw my bones being formed as I took shape in my mother's body. When I was put together there, you saw my body as it was formed. All the days planned for me were written in your book before I was one day old."
(Psalm 139:13-16 NCV)

Thankful, Day 8

Today I am grateful for people; not just those people who harbor beliefs and opinions like mine but also people who completely differ from me. There is much to be learned from those who are different. There is much to be gleaned from the knowledge and wisdom (yes, they are two different things!) we each have.

The key is in not holding the unfounded belief that any one of us is always right or has all the answers (we are not, and we seldom do) along with having the openness and respect to listen to and hear each other without the goal of proving one another wrong or berating one another for our differences. The key is in seeking common ground, understanding, mutual compassion, and ultimately, peace. Thank You, Lord, for people - all people!

"Listen before you speak, for to speak before you've heard the facts will bring humiliation."
(Proverbs 18:13 The Passion Translation)

"Blessed are the peacemakers, for they will be called children of God."
(Matthew 5:9 NIV)

Thankful, Day 9

This morning I am thankful for gardens, both the ones I love to spend time in during the spring, summer, and fall, and the ones we cultivate in our hearts and relationships. There is something so calming and encouraging about tending our gardens - sowing quality seeds and waiting for them to sprout, nurturing their growth, seeing their blossoming promise, and harvesting the good things they produce at just the right moment. Today, remember to tend your garden with gratitude, patience, and great care. Doing so will produce sweet fruit that will last and bring a smile to your heavenly Father's face.

"Sow for yourselves righteousness. Reap in accord with covenant love. Break up your unplowed ground. For it is time to seek ADONAI, until He comes and showers righteousness on you."
(Hosea 10:12 Tree of Life Version)

Thankful, Day 10

I am so thankful for children. You cannot witness the actions and antics of a child without smiling, no matter your mood. You cannot dispute their honesty in emotion or their zeal for life. You certainly cannot dispute their faith. Since their world has not yet been jaded by experience or the opinions of others, we can learn much from their unbiased approach to living each day to its fullest. Their joy is boundless. They present the simplest of solutions when they encounter a problem. Their love is uncomplicated. Children, whether our own or someone else's, are one of life's greatest gifts if we only take the time to look beyond their wrapping to see the beauty inside!

"Some people brought their little children for Jesus to bless. But when his disciples saw them doing this, they told the people to stop bothering him. So Jesus called the children over to him and said, 'Let the children come to me! Don't try to stop them. People who are like these children belong to God's kingdom. You will never get into God's kingdom unless you enter it like a child!'" **(Luke 18:15-17 CEV)**

Thankful, Day 11

Today I am thankful for selflessness. I have witnessed selfless acts in all kinds of people. I have met those who put their lives on the line for this country and its citizens. I have seen those who have nothing refuse a gift of compassion because "someone else needs it more." I have met people who selflessly give of their time and treasure so that the lives of those less fortunate are enriched. I have seen those who drop everything to rush to the side of a friend in need. And in this year, I have seen many who put their health and safety aside to see that others have medical care, food on their tables, and comfort in their times of loss. Thank you, veterans, for your selfless service. Thank you to everyone who gives to someone else without thought of personal need or comfort. Most of all, thank You, Jesus, for the ultimate selfless act that has given us life now and in eternity.

"Greater love hath no man than this, that a man lay down his life for his friends."
(John 15:13 KJV)

Thankful, Day 12

  Today's grateful post is going to be a bit long as well as tough to write. I am having one of those "off" days. I know, after a tearful morning, that it's because the holidays are upon us. It's also because Momma's birthday is Saturday; this will be the third one she's celebrating in heaven. It may take longer to write this than to actually come up with the words simply because the screen will blur before me.

  Michael and I were discussing a couple of weeks ago how the holidays just aren't the holidays anymore. I suppose it gets that way when those you love have ended their earthly journey, especially when your family was close-knit and holidays were times of celebration together. So it's no surprise that I feel this way right now. This grey weather isn't helping either. I'm longing to get out and walk, but it's too wet yet. Hopefully that will change this afternoon. Back to the matter at hand...

  Today I am thankful for grief. Yes, grief. I'm not sure who originally said the words, but I've read them many times: "You grieve because you loved." The truth of these words struck me this morning as tears streamed down my face. I loved Momma deeply and still do. The grief isn't always so much at the forefront; it comes in waves. When it does, there's not much I can do but give in and ride the wave to the shore of loving remembrance.

  The remembrances today were of little things - little things that brought big smiles. The first was that Momma was always singing, or so it seemed to me. I can hear her voice singing hymns along with the radio as she worked in the kitchen, sharing a duet with Nat King Cole, Perry Como, or Andy Williams on the stereo as she cleaned in the living room, and singing to some of my friends when they would call on the phone. I'm talking about a time when I was a teen and the telephone hung on the kitchen wall of our home. You answered it, asked who was on the other end of the line, and then called for the person they wanted to come to the phone.

If you had a name that resonated with a song she knew, you could be sure she would sing it to you before handing the phone over to me. Two in particular stick out in my mind. The first was "Oh, Johnny" by the Andrews Sisters. There was a boy who lived a few blocks away that would call from time to time. His name was John. He wasn't really a boyfriend, although I suppose I had a crush on him. I knew when he was on the other end of the phone because she would start singing, "Oh, Johnny! Oh, Johnny!" much to my dismay. Teenage girls are so easily rattled! The second was the loving teasing of my childhood best friend, Robin. Everyone called her "Bird." Whenever Robin called, whether I answered or Momma did, she would immediately break into song: "She's only a bird in a gilded cage, a beautiful sight to see!"

Another thing about Momma was that she always had room for someone extra at the table. I can remember countless times that she welcomed my friends for lunch or supper, even though she wasn't expecting an extra guest. I can remember the first time Michael came for supper when we began dating. I asked her at the last minute - actually, he was already on his way. She looked at me and said, "But we're only having French toast!" It wasn't that there wasn't room for him; it was that she would have made something better had she known he was coming. Truth be told, breakfast meals were and are his favorite type of meals, so he was thrilled. The simple fact was that the table was never too small to add one more seat. It was the same with her heart. It's no wonder my friends called her "Mom."

The final memory that came to me was the way the dogs made her smile. Sally and Angel basked in the sunshine of that smile so often. When we lived across the street from each other, Momma would carefully walk across with her walker to visit with them as they laid on the deck. And when she wasn't feeling strong enough to walk across the street, she would open her sliding glass door and take one step out onto her deck. "Hi Angel! Hi Sally!" she would call, smiling broadly as they would jump up on the chairs so they could see her and bark a greeting back to her.

A smile began to creep onto my face and into my heart amid the tears as these things came to my mind and heart. The tears of grief mingled with tears of joy. The fact is, while I think of her every day, these little things and the joy they brought might not have come to mind without that wave of grief today. I have been truly comforted in riding the wave to the shore.

And so, today, I am grateful for grief.

"The Spirit of the Sovereign Lord is on me, because the Lord has anointed me to proclaim good news to the poor. He has sent me to bind up the brokenhearted, to proclaim freedom for the captives and release from darkness for the prisoners, to proclaim the year of the Lord's favor and the day of vengeance of our God, to comfort all who mourn, and provide for those who grieve in Zion—to bestow on them a crown of beauty instead of ashes, the oil of joy instead of mourning, and a garment of praise instead of a spirit of despair."
(Isaiah 61:1-3 NIV)

Thankful, Day 13

I am so grateful for sunshine! After the damp and gloom of the last few days, the brilliant light of the sun is warm and welcoming this afternoon. It brings to mind and heart the truth that even in our darkest moments or days, there is a light that shines and warms our surroundings. And so, I am extremely grateful for *Son*shine every day!

"In the beginning the Word already existed. The Word was with God, and the Word was God. He existed in the beginning with God. God created everything through him, and nothing was created except through him. The Word gave life to everything that was created, and his life brought light to everyone. The light shines in the darkness, and the darkness can never extinguish it." **(John 1:1-5 NLT)**

Thankful, Day 14

This morning I am thankful for inspiration. Inspiration comes in many forms, but one of the most important ones for me is the woman God gave to me as a mom. She has inspired me for as long as I can remember and continues to do so from heaven. She inspires me to wait in quiet patience, to hope, and to love beyond measure. She inspires me to never quit but to keep climbing. She inspires me to reach for the deep faith she always modeled. Happy 90th Birthday in Heaven, Momma! I thank God for giving me the inspiration that is you!

This is her favorite passage of scripture, which inspired her favorite hymn, both of which are favorites of mine and inspire me just as she does.

"It is of the Lord's mercies that we are not consumed, because his compassions fail not. They are new every morning: great is thy faithfulness. The Lord is my portion, saith my soul; therefore will I hope in him. The Lord is good unto them that wait for him, to the soul that seeketh him. It is good that a man should both hope and quietly wait for the salvation of the Lord." **(Lamentations 3:22-26 KJV)**

Thankful, Day 15

I love and am very thankful for laughter. Laughter has the ability to heal, transport, and transform any given moment. I believe relationships that contain an abundance of laughter also contain an abundance of love, and they thrive in spite of any circumstances the world can throw at them. If we can laugh at ourselves and with others, we can climb any mountain that rises before us. Michael and I both know that our marriage is built on a firm foundation with God as our center. We also know that the beams of every wall and ceiling of our marriage home are strengthened even more by laughter. It might seem to some that we are just silly and to others that we're being irreverent in some way, but laughter has seen us through almost 45 years of every kind of circumstance. We laugh with each other almost every day, knowing it is one of the glues that holds us together. Laughter is truly a gift from the Father, who had the foresight to know there would be "days like this" and wanted us to have the perfect tool to turn those days into blessings for others as well as ourselves. Pass on the gifts of laughter and love in all circumstances!

"God will let you laugh again; you'll raise the roof with shouts of joy."
(Job 8:21 The Message)

Thankful, Day 16

Today I am grateful for music. It doesn't matter if it is the music of nature through the sounds of raindrops or birdsong, the music of instruments, the music of voices raised in song, or the music of children laughing. Music is a gift from above with the power to bring forth emotions, heal hearts, and send up praise. Psalm 8:2 (The Passion Translation) tells us that when the music of praise is lifted the evil one is silenced - "You have built a stronghold by the songs of babies. Strength rises up with the chorus of singing children. This kind of praise has the power to shut Satan's mouth. Childlike worship will silence the madness of those who oppose you." Fill your life with healing, restorative music and songs of praise!

"Praise the Lord. Sing to the Lord a new song, his praise in the assembly of his faithful people. Let Israel rejoice in their Maker; let the people of Zion be glad in their King. Let them praise his name with dancing and make music to him with timbrel and harp." **(Psalm 149:1-3 NIV)**

Thankful, Day 17

I am thankful for correction. I was raised by parents who lovingly corrected me when it was needed and a heavenly Father who does the same. It's not always easy, but there are just times when it is needed. Being of open mind and open heart to accept discipline and correction that will spark growth in character and faith is so important in life. To understand how important it is, we sometimes must sit down and plot the course life might have taken without accepting wise and loving input from others. The choice is ours - the miry pit or solid ground. Correction will place us on the solid ground of wisdom and steady our feet for the next step.

"My child, guard the commands of your father and do not forsake the instruction of your mother. Bind them on your heart continually; fasten them around your neck. When you walk about, they will guide you; when you lie down, they will watch over you; when you wake up, they will talk to you. For the commandments are like a lamp, instruction is like a light, and rebukes of discipline are like the road leading to life."
(Proverbs 6:20-23 New English Translation)

Thankful, Day 18

I am beyond thankful for answers to prayer. Whether the answer is yes, wait (it's not time yet), or no (it's not good for you or I have something exceedingly better for you), I know that prayers are always answered. We may not see it at the time, but as we look back on our lives, the answers and the hand of God working are quite evident. Because of the sacrifice of Jesus, we can approach Father God with our concerns, requests, confessions, praises, just to chat, or simply to sit in silence with confidence. Look back at your life and be amazed at the answers and wonders you missed simply because you weren't expecting the answers you received. I promise it will be breathtaking to realize the healing that's taken place, the protection that's been given, and the gifts that went way beyond your expectations.

"So then, since we have a great High Priest who has entered heaven, Jesus the Son of God, let us hold firmly to what we believe. This High Priest of ours understands our weaknesses, for he faced all of the same testings we do, yet he did not sin. So let us come boldly to the throne of our gracious God. There we will receive his mercy, and we will find grace to help us when we need it most."
(Hebrews 4:14-16 NLT)

Thankful, Day 19

I am grateful for rest. I saw a meme the other day that said, "Next week has been exhausting." While we could all probably have a good laugh at that, the truth of it is tragic on some levels. Life doesn't have to be exhausting. We tend to make it that way simply because we refuse to take the time and invitation to rest. We are not Energizer™ bunnies. We are not meant to keep going at all times. We are built for rest as well as activity. We are not meant for exhaustion on a daily basis; our bodies won't tolerate that for very long. We must choose to rest. We must make a conscious decision to quiet our hearts and minds, seek a peaceful place, and rest in the arms of the One who created us and knows exactly what we need. Even He rested after His labors. Thank God that a peaceful place of rest and restoration is only a heartbeat away!

"Thus the heavens and the earth were completed in all their vast array. By the seventh day God had finished the work he had been doing; so on the seventh day he rested from all his work. Then God blessed the seventh day and made it holy, because on it he rested from all the work of creating that he had done."
(Genesis 2:1-3 NIV)

"Come to Me, all of you who work and have heavy loads. I will give you rest. Follow My teachings and learn from Me. I am gentle and do not have pride. You will have rest for your souls. For My way of carrying a load is easy and My load is not heavy."
(Matthew 11:28-30 New Life Version)

Thankful, Day 20

Thank you for the journey. Destinations are nice, but there is so much to be appreciated on the path - life lessons, helping hands just when you need them, the accomplishments of boulders surmounted, rivers crossed, or chasms spanned, the warmth of sunshine and cool of shadow, and the beauty observed along the way. Oh, if we would only embrace the journey instead of taking shortcuts to quicken our arrival! We wouldn't miss out on so many wonderful and important things. The journey is a gift, and the hand of God is in its every step. This truth is certain: we never take any journey alone.

"Then the cloud covered the Tabernacle, and the glory of the Lord filled the Tabernacle. Moses could no longer enter the Tabernacle because the cloud had settled down over it, and the glory of the Lord filled the Tabernacle. Now whenever the cloud lifted from the Tabernacle, the people of Israel would set out on their journey, following it. But if the cloud did not rise, they remained where they were until it lifted. The cloud of the Lord hovered over the Tabernacle during the day, and at night fire glowed inside the cloud so the whole family of Israel could see it. This continued throughout all their journeys."
(Exodus 40:34-38 NLT)

Thankful, Day 21

This morning I am thankful for long walks in the countryside. There's something about them that instill a quietness of heart and mind, allowing me to focus on what's truly important. Whether walking in silence or with worship music playing from my phone in my back pocket, I experience a closeness to the Lord that melts the world away for a time and makes the rest of the day flow more easily when I return home. I know that's because when my heart and mind are focused on Him, I walk more closely within His footsteps.

"LORD God of Israel, there is no God in heaven above or on earth below like You, who keep Your covenant and mercy with your servants who walk before You with all their hearts."
(1 Kings 8:23 NKJV)

"He lifted me out of the pit of despair, out from the bog and the mire, and set my feet on a hard, firm path, and steadied me as I walked along. He has given me a new song to sing, of praises to our God. Now many will hear of the glorious things he did for me, and stand in awe before the Lord, and put their trust in him."
(Psalm 40:2-3 The Living Bible)

Thankful, Day 22

I am thankful for opportunities to serve. Whether it be family, friends, neighbors, an individual I don't know, or the homeless/impoverished community, there is so much joy in serving others. Even more than the joy is the knowledge that it's not that God can't do it on His own (He can) or that He needs my help (He doesn't), but that He lets me see where He is working and invites me to join in that work. It's amazing to know that He cares about my growth and my joy so much that He would risk me making a mess of things in order to allow me to give joy to others and experience joy in my giving. Oh, how humbling and joyous to be a child of the Father!

"Therefore Jesus answered and was saying to them, 'Truly, truly, I say to you, the Son can do nothing of Himself, unless it is something He sees the Father doing; for whatever the Father does, these things the Son also does in the same way. For the Father loves the Son and shows Him all things that He Himself is doing; and the Father will show Him greater works than these, so that you will be amazed.'"
(John 5:19-20 NASB)

Thankful, Day 23

Today I am thankful for being "old fashioned." I write first with pen and paper before typing any text into Word or converting to PDF format to publish. All of my books were written in plain spiral notebooks before hitting the keyboard. I can't see the emotion of my words on the screen, but I can see it in the little glitches, zigs, and zags in my handwriting. In the kitchen, I make things the way my mom and grandmother did - no bread machine, the dough gets kneaded by hand; no fancy food mill for my applesauce, I use Momma's applesauce strainer every time. At Christmas, I still sit down to send out physical cards in the mail. There's something about that personal touch that email and social media just don't have - at least for me. Perhaps it's because I remember watching my mom sit at the kitchen table to write a card to beloved friends and family each year. Traditions and practices handed down and honored touch the heart deeply. Each one of the things I am old fashioned about spurs a treasured memory or emotion in me. Technology is okay; it certainly helps with many things, but how many memories or emotions can actually be connected to a laptop or smart phone? I am truly grateful to be old fashioned. It keeps me connected in heart and spirit to those I love who came before me as well as to those that are still here. It keeps me grounded in my life and in my faith.

"I will teach you hidden lessons from our past—stories we have heard and known, stories our ancestors handed down to us. We will not hide these truths from our children; we will tell the next generation about the glorious deeds of the Lord, about his power and his mighty wonders. For he issued his laws to Jacob; he gave his instructions to Israel. He commanded our ancestors to teach them to their children, so the next generation might know them— even the children not yet born—and they in turn will teach their own children. So each generation should set its hope anew on God, not forgetting his glorious miracles and obeying his commands."
(Psalm 78:3-7 NLT)

Thankful, Day 24

Today I am thankful for trials and difficulties. No, they are not fun. No, I don't wish them on myself or anyone else. However, there are benefits to having them enter our lives. The first is the realization that we can't do this on our own. We need help. We need God. We need family. We need friends. We need our village - because sometimes it takes a village.

The second is the way in which all of those people rally around us in prayer, providing for our needs during tough times, and giving us gifts of encouragement and hope. Lastly, there is the building of character that always happens in the midst of troubled days. I don't like trials and difficulties, but I am thankful for what they bring to life.

"Therefore, since we have been justified through faith, we have peace with God through our Lord Jesus Christ, through whom we have gained access by faith into this grace in which we now stand. And we boast in the hope of the glory of God. Not only so, but we also glory in our sufferings, because we know that suffering produces perseverance; perseverance, character; and character, hope. And hope does not put us to shame, because God's love has been poured out into our hearts through the Holy Spirit, who has been given to us." **(Romans 5:1-5 NIV)**

Thankful, Day 25

This morning I am very thankful that God's got this. Our daughter-in-law was diagnosed with the virus via test results on Monday. She began with symptoms last Thursday. At this time, she is home but struggling. Her asthma does not help the situation. Our worry skyrocketed upon hearing the news. First, of course, for her health and well-being. Quickly on the heels of that worry came the concern that our son could become ill as well. He, too, has some underlying conditions that would not help him battle this illness and could complicate it. I immediately rallied my closest prayer warriors to join me in the task of praying for healing for Erin and protection for Jason and for Tom (Erin's son, our grandson). Regardless, I didn't sleep the first night after the diagnosis came. The what-ifs kept running through my mind. We all know what that feels like, and we all know it's never a good feeling.

The next morning, I was reminded during my quiet time that God's got this. Not only does He have this, He's through the middle of it and out on the other side. He's already on to solving whatever the next bump in the road of our lives might be. It's been handled. It's been solved. The healing has begun and will be completed. Perhaps not in the immediate timing we would all like, but completed according to His timing, and we all know His timing is perfect and in our best interests.

I will say it again, for myself, for Jason and Erin, and for whoever else is out there that is going through a time of struggle: God's got this. He's got it for Erin, for Jason, for Tom, and for those of us who love them and are so concerned for them. And dear readers, He's got it for you. All of you are loved beyond limit by a God who has planned every day of your life and watches over you, never sleeping.

" I will lift up mine eyes unto the hills, from whence cometh my help. My help cometh from the LORD, which made heaven and earth. He will not suffer thy foot to be moved: he that keepeth thee will not slumber. Behold, he that keepeth Israel shall neither slumber nor sleep. The LORD is thy keeper: the LORD is thy shade upon thy right hand. The sun shall not smite thee by day, nor the moon by night. The LORD shall preserve thee from all evil: he shall preserve thy soul. The LORD shall preserve thy going out and thy coming in from this time forth, and even for evermore."
(Psalm 121 KJV)

Thankful, Day 26

Today I am just thankful. That's very general, I know. I've been thinking of Thanksgivings past this morning, and it just brings a smile to my face. I remember Thanksgiving Eves at worship services with my mom and dad when I was growing up. I remember tons of Thanksgiving dinners both as a child and as an adult. I remember my favorite meal as a child - fried oysters! Yum! That's still a favorite, although I don't prepare it for holiday meals. I remember the first Thanksgiving meal I cooked as a new bride. I remember helping Momma cook meals for this day throughout my childhood and adult years while the Hallelujah Chorus filled the air with the first sounds of the Christmas season. It was her first step in welcoming Baby Jesus once more into our home for His birthday. And at this moment, I remember the first Thanksgiving meals that both Jason and Thayer helped me prepare. Both were so eager at a young age to get into the kitchen and get their hands into the assembling and cooking of special dishes. That eagerness and passion for bringing joy to others through food has stayed with them. Today, they are preparing their own meals and will be celebrating separate from us due to this awkward season in time. I will miss them. I pray their day will be blessed beyond measure even though there will be the challenges of illness in Jason's household, and the anxiety of wanting his first holiday meal to be perfect for Thayer. No worries, Thayer. You are the product of wonderful grandmothers and great-grandmothers who have passed down their passion and talent in the kitchen to you. Three of them are watching over you with proud smiles on their faces from heaven today. And if there's a glitch, that's what this is all about - not perfection, just family, love, and gratitude no matter what life throws at us. You'll do a fantastic job!

So, dear readers, this morning I am just thankful - for everything. It is my prayer that you would find a quiet moment or moments today amid the preparation and chaos to be thankful as well. May your day be filled with an awareness of the love and grace that surrounds you both from heaven above and from all of your friends and family here on earth. Happy Thanksgiving!

"So be very careful how you live. Do not live like those who are not wise, but live wisely. Use every chance you have for doing good, because these are evil times. So do not be foolish but learn what the Lord wants you to do. Do not be drunk with wine, which will ruin you, but be filled with the Spirit. Speak to each other with psalms, hymns, and spiritual songs, singing and making music in your hearts to the Lord. Always give thanks to God the Father for everything, in the name of our Lord Jesus Christ."
(Ephesians 5:15-20 NCV)

Thankful, Day 27

   Today's gratitude post is long and has been difficult in arriving. While I know there's always much to be grateful for, the events of the last 24 hours have been taxing at best and monumentally frustrating, worrying, and sleep-depriving at worst. I had no clue what to write or where my gratitude was. I knew it was somewhere, but where and how would I find it? Then I had a talk with a wonderful friend.

   So, today I am so thankful for Lisa. We grew up together in the Baptist church. Over the years, distance often has separated us, but the heartfelt bond we share never wavered, even though sometimes years went by without any real contact.

   She was checking in with me this morning to see how Erin was doing since being taken to the hospital last night. For that matter, she's been checking in with me every day since we found out that Erin was battling Covid. This morning I filled her in on the latest, which is another item of gratitude, and told her that Erin is now resting comfortably at the hospital thanks to fluids, pain medication, and oxygen.

   After that, I let her know that our beloved beagle, Sally, was also in the hospital. Sally began acting strangely on Wednesday night. She wouldn't get up and her body trembled. She needed to be carried outside to go potty. We kept watch over her and called the local emergency vet on Thanksgiving morning. After being informed that they were busy and it would take hours for Sally even to be assessed, we decided to keep her at home and make her comfortable until we could get her to our doctor this morning. Spending hours in the parking lot waiting for her to be seen and then adding assessment and treatment time to that just wasn't an option with the other things going on in our family. She has been diagnosed with pancreatitis, resulting in a hospital stay of her own. She is almost 12. We are very concerned.

Once I filled Lisa in on both Erin and Sally, I told her exactly what I would like 2020 to do. I will spare you the actual words; I'm sure you have the idea. Her answer to me was that there were some good things in 2020, which she then listed. My reply was that I know that; I'm just having a really rough time today. Rather than scold me for my self-indulgence and pity, she shared some of the truest words and most honest, compassionate advice I've heard in quite some time.

She started out by acknowledging how hard it is to be thankful this year and how sometimes God seems absent in the worst times. She went on to say that I'll be thankful when things work out or grateful for God and faith if they don't.

She ended our conversation by telling me she loves me and is always thankful that I love her back. The tears flowed at all of the above realizations, and I told her that.

After we talked, the realization that God is not absent hit me afresh. 2020 has been challenging, frustrating, confusing, and downright scary at times. However, the truth remains. He's just taking us a different route to get us where He wants us to be. Another gratitude point for today - He's taking us; we are not wandering aimlessly on our own. We are not forsaken.

So, today I am thankful for my childhood friend, cohort in crime, and adult friend as well as cheerleader, encourager, and honesty giver. I am so grateful for you, Lisa. I have been more than blessed by God bringing you into my life and the love and friendship you so generously give. And yes, I love you back always.

"As iron sharpens iron, so a friend sharpens a friend."
(Proverbs 27:17)

"So be strong and courageous! Do not be afraid and do not panic before them. For the LORD your God will personally go ahead of you. He will neither fail you nor abandon you."
(Deuteronomy 31:6 NLT)

Thankful, Day 28

I am thankful for words. I am thankful for the words I am given to write; they are truly a gift. I am thankful for words of encouragement, love, kindness, and compassion; they rain upon my spirit like rays of sunshine upon flowers, which causes them to blossom. I am thankful even for words of derision, insult, and meanness; they reveal much about their speakers to me that I need to know to rid my life of toxicity as well as offer forgiveness for those words. Foremost, I am thankful for The Word. The Father's love letter to us has all we need to build an abundant life, both here in this world and in heaven. I am truly grateful for words but most grateful for The Word.

"These words I speak to you are not incidental additions to your life, homeowner improvements to your standard of living. They are foundational words, words to build a life on. If you work these words into your life, you are like a smart carpenter who built his house on solid rock. Rain poured down, the river flooded, a tornado hit—but nothing moved that house. It was fixed to the rock. But if you just use my words in Bible studies and don't work them into your life, you are like a stupid carpenter who built his house on the sandy beach. When a storm rolled in and the waves came up, it collapsed like a house of cards."
(Matthew 7:24-27 The Message)

Thankful, Day 29

     Today I am thankful for marriage. 45 years ago, I married my high school sweetheart. We were young. We were starry-eyed. We were in love. We had no clue what was to come. We had no idea how much hard work marriage really required. Both our sets of parents made it seem easy. The example they put before us was one of love and commitment. We didn't see the sweat equity they gave underneath all of that.

     There is nothing in this marriage I wouldn't go through again - not even the toughest of times. There were times we turned our backs on each other in stupidity and anger. There were moments when we didn't know if our relationship would survive. God had other plans. Through all of it, He was teaching us just what commitment was. He was showing us just what loving each other truly meant. He was molding us for His purpose. The first thing marriage means is putting Him at the center and then each other next. Everything else falls into place after that. Each of those exceedingly difficult moments has brought us here - to 45 years, and we pray for many more after this one. Yes, it's still hard work to maintain the standard He has taught us, but it's joyous work.

     I am blessed by the man God has placed in my heart and life. He is generous to a fault (if there is such a thing as fault in generosity). He is loving, kind, and always compassionate. He is my best friend and a best friend to many others, even those he doesn't know. He is a man of integrity. Thank you, Michael, for putting up with my quirks, my flaws, and my propensity to be stubborn. Thank you for laughing with me and at me. I love you beyond words, beyond measure, beyond time and space. This may not be the anniversary we had planned under the circumstances (it's certainly not Disney as it was five years ago), but we will celebrate it as we have done everything else - our way.

Today I am thankful for marriage - both my marriage and the Marriage of Christ and His church. All of us have that Best Friend and are loved beyond comprehension. One day we will celebrate at a feast to beat all feasts. Thank you, Father God!

"For this reason a man shall leave his father and mother and be joined to his wife, and the two shall become one flesh. So they are no longer two, but one flesh. Therefore what God has joined together, let no man put asunder."
(Matthew 19:5-6 Modern English Version)

"Then I heard again what sounded like the shout of a vast crowd or the roar of mighty ocean waves or the crash of loud thunder: 'Praise the Lord! For the Lord our God, the Almighty, reigns. Let us be glad and rejoice, and let us give honor to him. For the time has come for the wedding feast of the Lamb, and his bride has prepared herself. She has been given the finest of pure white linen to wear.' For the fine linen represents the good deeds of God's holy people."
(Revelation 19:6-8 NLT)

Thankful, Day 30

On Day 30, I am thankful that God fights for me - for all of us. The battles raging around us, both corporately and individually, have seemed so insurmountable this year. In human terms, many of them are. In God's terms, no mountain is too high, no river too wide, no valley too low (you get the idea... is that song going through your head now?) - no battle is too tough for Him. We are rescued before our lips utter prayers for help. He sends His angels in assistance at our first cry. Our earthly attempts to fight our battles are often misguided and unsuccessful. Thank God that He fight for us, all battles belong to Him, and the victory is always His.

"Now while I was speaking, praying, and confessing my sin and the sin of my people Israel, and presenting my supplication before the Lord my God for the holy mountain of my God, yes, while I was speaking in prayer, the man Gabriel, whom I had seen in the vision at the beginning, being caused to fly swiftly, reached me about the time of the evening offering. And he informed me, and talked with me, and said, 'O Daniel, I have now come forth to give you skill to understand. At the beginning of your supplications the command went out, and I have come to tell you, for you are greatly beloved...'"
(Daniel 9:20-23 NKJV)

"Lift up your heads, you gates; be lifted up, you ancient doors, that the King of glory may come in. Who is this King of glory? The Lord strong and mighty, the Lord mighty in battle. Lift up your heads, you gates; lift them up, you ancient doors, that the King of glory may come in. Who is he, this King of glory? The Lord Almighty—he is the King of glory."
(Psalm 24:7-10 NIV)

Unceasing Gratitude

As I said at the beginning of this season's section, Thanksgiving should be every day. I wasn't feeling very grateful by the time the day of my thirtieth entry ended. Michael's condition was deteriorating, and I was scared. His fever would spike and then recede. His appetite had left him, and those who know him well know that is a *big deal.* Add to that the fact that I was beginning to notice a scratchy throat and you have what appears to be the perfect storm of despair.

Writing this now, I have the advantage of hindsight. Yes, it was still a perfect storm, but God is always faithful through the waves, winds, and torrential downpours. My blindness, which was self-imposed by my fear, just kept me from remembering that. By the following morning, Erin was being released from the hospital and was well on the road to recovery. Jason's test results had come back positive for the virus, but he never attained any level of severity. It just seemed like he had a bad head cold. Both of these things were something for which to be thankful.

The week wore on, and I continued with symptoms that came to include minor body aches, low grade fever, and fatigue. Michael's condition continued to worsen. Thankfully, I was able to be on my feet and take care of the dogs and my husband while taking care of myself. That sounds like another moment of gratitude. Good friends and family members checking in on us and willing to do porch drop-offs for much-needed items added more moments of grateful time.

God may not have spared us from the virus, but He certainly was making sure there was nothing we lacked in this time of need.

By the end of that week, my symptoms had subsided. I was still tired and had an occasional cough, but that would be the extent of it for the next two weeks. I was more capable of doing what needed to be done around the house and cook nourishing meals for Michael, although he wasn't able to eat much. At the beginning of the first full week of December, we couldn't ignore the gravity of the situation any longer. He was still spiking a fever and began having some breathing difficulty. He was extremely weak and had to be hospitalized. The perfect storm of despair became the dangerous eddying of a dark sea threatening to drag me under its depths. After watching the ambulance pull away, I made the necessary phone calls. Then I cried out to the only One I knew could help us. Thankfully, He answered - as if there was ever any doubt – but yes, I had doubts.

He sent help in the form of meals from a dear friend of Jason's and ours and dropped off by her daughter, who we had long ago "adopted" as our granddaughter. Seeing Helena's smiling face and feeling her love as she threw me a kiss through the window lifted my weary soul. My sisters-in-law messaged me frequently to see what I needed or wanted. My friends called. Sue talked to me that first night until I was ready for some sleep. Lisa offered her expertise as far as medical treatments to ask the doctors about, and Michael was able to call me at least once a day. These were all answers to the cries on that first morning - answers for which I was very grateful.

Amid the anxiety and fear, the blessings poured over us. Michael did not need to be placed in the ICU. He was given steroids and Remdesivir. The turnaround was remarkable. He was home after three days, although he would be out of work for the rest of the month. My heart overflowed and still overflows as we continue to recover. We have become thankful for the smallest measure of health - a block or two added to our walks, being able to breathe a little more deeply, a day without the feeling of fatigue that calls for a short nap, and the ability for him to be back at work and me to be able to care for my dad once again. These are things we once took for granted before but not anymore.

I learned during this time just how easy it is to say something and then how hard it is to do it. On the 24th day of Thanksgiving, I wrote that I was thankful for trials and difficulties and went on to explain why all of us should be. Then the waves and winds crashed into our lives. I completely forgot my own advice and encouragement. I balked at the words God had given me for that day. *"Grateful for this? You've got to be kidding me!"* That was the only thought bouncing around my mind in my worst moments.

I learned just how true the words of our Lord were on the night before His crucifixion – *"...The spirit is willing, but the flesh is weak."* My spirit wanted to acknowledge the gifts God showered upon us during this time. Yet my flesh was wont to cry out in fear and accusation that God didn't care. I am sorrowful to

269

confess that my flesh won the battle more than not. I cannot begin to tell you just how humbling that was and is.

Blessings continue no matter how stormy life becomes. If only we would overcome the fear for just a moment and ask God to open our eyes, they are there for us to marvel and receive. They are there for us to realize how much we are loved. Realizing how much we are loved places our focus on Him and not the stormy depths that threaten. When we focus on Him, we can walk across the water that is violently churning beneath us, *and even if we lose that focus and our footing for a moment, He will keep us from being pulled under.* What more do we need to bring forth thanksgiving from our hearts? What more do we need to sing our gratitude before our feet hit the floor every day?

"After he had sent the crowds away, Jesus went up the mountain by himself to pray. When evening came he was there by himself. The boat had already gone some distance from the shore and was being smashed around by the waves, since the wind was against it. At the very dead of night he came towards them, walking on the water. The disciples saw him walking on the sea and panicked. 'It's a ghost!' they said, and they screamed in terror. But Jesus at once spoke to them. 'Cheer up,' he said, 'it's me! Don't be frightened!' 'If it's really you, Master,' said Peter in reply, 'give me the word to come to you on the water.' 'Come along, then,' said Jesus. Peter got out of the boat and walked on the water and came towards Jesus. But when he saw the strong wind he was afraid, and began to sink. 'Master,'

he yelled, 'rescue me!' Jesus at once reached out his hand and caught him. 'A fine lot of faith you've got!' he said. 'Why did you doubt?'"

(Matthew 14:23-31 New Testament for Everyone)

The Season of Anticipation, Joy, Giving, and Renewal

The Little Things

As children we always went for the biggest gift under the tree. We couldn't wait to see what was in that big box! I suppose it is simply childhood nature to believe bigger is better, or is that simply adult nature? It doesn't matter. The fact is it's not true. Gifts come in all sizes. All of them are wonderful. The small ones, however, are the ones we must purposefully notice or we might miss them.

The rainbow in a raindrop, the peeping sound of baby birds, the slight smile on the lips of a sleeping infant - all these little things are tiny miracles that bring much joy to life. This year of 2020 has been a time when we need that joy. The well of problems has run deep in our world. It's run deep in our communities and in our families. Stay-at-home orders, shutdowns, and restrictions have been the necessary rule of the day in an effort to keep the population safe, or as safe as humans can possibly try to be with an invisible enemy running rampant. Divisive disagreements and fear have been abundant, allowing our other invisible enemy to run rampant as well.

Yet the gifts were many. We have taken more notice of people who were just shadows in the background before. They're getting some recognition that they've long deserved. We've become closer to our families - both those we live with and those who are in other households. We've sympathized, empathized, and loved more deeply. We've had more constant contact with friends via Zoom, phone, and social media than in person, and it's given us a deeper appreciation for them. We sit at dinner tables *together* with the rest of our household because activities have been drastically scaled back. Family conversation once again has become the daily norm. These fretful times have brought renewal. How sad, however, that it took a pandemic that has killed so many to bring these things back to the forefront.

As I write this final section introduction, I am reminded of the everyday gifts that I love and am now missing. My husband and I both are battling this virus at the moment. Sleeping and spending our time in separate spaces, only seeing each other for a second or perhaps a minute in passing in the hallway for hours on end - these are difficult things. It's the little things...

We miss lying next to each other as we fall asleep each night, a simple good morning, see you later or good night kiss, sitting on the sofa and watching our favorite shows while holding hands - it's the little things.

Every single thing is a gift. Every single thing should be approached with anticipation. Every gift we receive should be regifted - given to someone else in an effort to bring joy. Every gift should be appreciated for the worth it has, even if we don't yet know what that worth is. We must simply *know* that the worth is there.

We must remember, even after this current danger is past, that the little and unnoticed things are often those that have great worth. We must remember to look for them and acknowledge their worth in times of blessing as well as in this time of trepidation.

We must also remember that division is never a good thing. We can differ in our opinions, but we must never let them divide us as things have this year. We must renew our minds to accept the little things upon which we differ so that we can expound on the little things that make us the same and join us as one.

In the Season of Anticipation, Joy, Giving, and Renewal, it's the little things - like the tiny baby that would save the world.

"For God so loved the world, that he gave his only begotten Son, that whosoever believeth in him should not perish, but have everlasting life."
(John 3:16-17 KJV)

The Anticipation of Joy

One of my favorite songs in my early teens was written and performed by Carly Simon. "Anticipation" spoke of thinking about the future and not knowing what is to come. It spoke to how we wait for those things. Finally, it spoke of living in the moment. Of course, it was written in the context of romance, and that went to the core of my teenage heart. What young girl doesn't long for her true love?

Now that I am well into adulthood, I find that I still anticipate the future. The words of that song still ring through my mind sometimes, not so much in the context of romance but more in the context of the truth of some of its lyrics. We cannot predict what will happen to us on this earth in the future. We cannot hurry it along or plan it down to the minute. We cannot know what tomorrow will bring, and we cannot wish away the things we don't want to happen. However, we can anticipate the joy that every day will certainly bring because *there is joy in every day.*

So many in biblical history did not know what the future would hold for them, yet they held an expectant hope rather than trepidation in the days to come. God had made promises to them - promises they held in their hearts along with the belief that they were true. Some of them waited days, some months, and some years to see their hope realized. Many others would not live to see the promises come to fruition, but they held on to the anticipation of the joy to come anyway. *They fully believed God would do what He said*

He would do, even if it was to happen after their journey to their true home.

Abraham realized the promise of Isaac yet did not see the word of the Lord fulfilled regarding his descendants becoming as numerous as the stars in the sky (Genesis 22:17). David anticipated God's promise to establish his line in Israel forever with great joy but didn't see the ultimate King born to sit on the throne in the form of Jesus Christ (2 Samuel 7:16). There were countless prophets who foretold the birth of the Messiah, clinging to the promise with incomparable joy, and yet they did not witness the birth that came years and years later. And yet there were those who waited their entire lives and were blessed to see the promise of salvation realized for Israel. Simeon and Anna had looked forward to the birth of Jesus with prayer and hope for most of their lives. When Jesus was taken to the temple to be presented to God, their joy was made complete. They saw the Messiah they had been waiting for and knew God had granted His salvation to all who would believe (Luke 2:25-38). And there were so many others who lived with the anticipation of joy as they traveled God's path for them.

I think we have lost the ability, or at least the desire, to be content with what is in front of us and the anticipation of the joy to come. I also think that we have become miserable in our day-to-day lives because we lack that desire and ability. The world today has such a tendency toward instant gratification and entitlement. We need to return to that childlike state of rutsching-in-our-seat excitement (yes, my Pennsylvania Dutch is coming out) for each day the way we used to do for

279

Christmas morning or birthdays. There is so much joy to be had in the present! There is so much joy to anticipate in the future - whether that future be earthbound or heavenward!

We need to remember the words of our Lord in Luke 18. *"Truly I tell you, anyone who will not receive the kingdom of God like a little child will never enter it."* Let your inner child shine.

God has promised us many things. Some have come to fruition, and some have not yet been realized. Either way, we should be giving thanks. Either way, we should be elated and eager to face each new morning with the anticipation of joy. Father God has granted our desires, blessed us, and given us life just as He did David. We want for no good thing. Let your anticipation be seen. Let your joy be heard.

"You have granted him his heart's desire and have not withheld the request of his lips. You came to greet him with rich blessings and placed a crown of pure gold on his head. He asked you for life, and you gave it to him—length of days, for ever and ever. Through the victories you gave, his glory is great; you have bestowed on him splendor and majesty. Surely you have granted him unending blessings and made him glad with the joy of your presence. For the king trusts in the LORD; through the unfailing love of the Most High he will not be shaken."
(Psalm 21:2-7 NIV)

*Anticipation, written by Carly Simon, and performed on her album of the same name, 1971

New Fallen Snow

Each year there are those who eagerly await the beauty of a freshly fallen covering of glimmering white snow. If it falls in its season - and for me, that season is Christmas and only Christmas - it is even more welcomed. However, sometimes what we anticipate is actually needed sooner than we'd like.

While it was not wanted or welcomed by most, it is clear that God decided it was time to blanket our area in a fresh, clean coating of white yesterday, November 14th - and not just a coating but a thick, fluffy covering that reached depths of up to eight inches of early snow. He saw a need, and He fulfilled that need.

The white stuff definitely made for some tricky and patience-trying travel for those of us who needed to go to work or drive to accomplish necessary tasks. Schools let out early as did some workplaces, roads with hills were shut down because they were impassable, commuters were stranded for hours on highways due to accidents, and others, like myself, crawled at 15 miles per hour to make it home safely at the end of the workday.

There were, as there always are, those who felt the need to fly by those of us who were traveling at a slow but safe pace. There were those who felt the need to blare their horns in their impatience or yell out their windows at traffic that just didn't seem to be getting anywhere. Unplowed and untreated roadways brought out the worst as we mumbled insults about those whose job it is to clear a path. Things were out of our control, and we weren't happy about it. We like to be in control.

Yet amid all of the struggle to get where we were going, there was also the quiet that the falling snow brings and the beauty of a changed landscape that went from dried and dusty leaves to a beautiful vision that looked like a bride dressed in her best wedding white.

This morning, the pines behind my home are dusted in flakes, standing tall like a groom waiting at the altar. The silver maple next to them shimmers as the sun's rays touch its ice-coated branches. The blue skies above them radiate with early morning light as puffy, fair weather clouds float by in a lazy trip from west to east. The cardinals, bright in their winter red, are flitting from tree to feeder and back again, their music filling the quiet with song. Indeed, the beauty is breathtaking, even though we griped and complained just 12 hours ago at the mess nature was forcing upon us.

This is the story of life - the arrival of trials and the relinquishing of control so that something better is able to replace them. Then comes the marriage of struggles and beauty that creates an incredible vision of grace and light, followed by the blanket of mercy that makes this disheveled, stained world whiter than snow. Finally, on the heels of mercy rises the song of gratitude with which overflowing hearts burst because to contain it is impossible.

All of us need that fresh covering at some point. It seems yesterday was the day to notice it, receive it, and find the beauty that lay beneath the tainted surface of our sight.

"Behold, you delight in truth in the inward being, and you teach me wisdom in the secret heart. Purge me with hyssop, and I shall be clean; wash me, and I shall be whiter than snow."
(Psalm 51:6-7 ESV)

Perpetual Joy

What exactly is joy, anyway? We hear a lot of talk about it. From an earthly standpoint, we equate it with happiness. Yet that's not quite it. Happiness is fleeting. It's an emotion of the moment - here and gone when the next trial comes. Joy is something different.

I don't believe fully that joy is an emotion. To me, joy is more of a lifestyle. It runs in the same category as worship. Worship is not a verb for me. Worship is the way I strive to live. The two are definitely intertwined. Both come from the realization that Jesus died for me, Jesus rose for me, and Jesus lives for me today. It is because of all of those things that I want - I *need* worship to be a lifestyle and not just something I do when the mood strikes me. It is because of all of those things that I can live in joy no matter what the world or the evil one throws at me on any given day. It is because I am alive *in* Christ that I have full confidence that nothing thrown at me will stick and I will conquer. Joy is my life's response to the gift of Jesus just as worship is...or should be; I am after all only human and will falter at times. And just like the gift of Jesus, joy will never be stolen from me.

When I am happy because things are going well or because I am realizing the desires of my earthly life, it's a feeling of elation that I know will soon pass. Happiness is temporal. Let's face it, the world is an imperfect place and things will go wrong from time to time. Sometimes things will go wrong more than they seem to go right. Of course, from God's point of view,

284

nothing is truly going wrong. Things are just settling into place for the purpose of His plan. He is using all of it to set us up for the ultimate success - His success. If we set our mind on that particular truth, we will be able to live in the joy of the Lord. Joy will become what it is supposed to be, which is an everyday attitude of life that inhabits our hearts and footsteps. That means when happiness goes out the door as sadness or even frustration comes in the window, our feet will still be dancing in time with His joy.

Thinking about joy immediately brings thoughts of David to mind. David did not live a charmed life. He spent much of his young life in the fields watching over his father's flocks. It's a lonely life - so lonely, in fact, that he wasn't even invited to the meal with Samuel during which Israel's next king was to be anointed. Yet God had other plans. While David might have been lamenting that his brothers were present at such an occasion and he was not, Samuel would not continue until David was brought home to join them as per God's plan. God made what was going wrong turn to right.

Even after being chosen as king, David's life took many twists and turns. He was beckoned to work for his predecessor. Saul suffered from a form of mental illness. The only thing that seemed to calm him was David's harp playing. Of course, even that had its limits. David ended up having to dodge a spear aimed at him by Saul even while doing his job. It certainly didn't end there. David spent many, many nights hiding in caves and remote areas while Saul attempted to hunt him and take his life. Does this sound like happiness to you?

Does it sound like things were going right and everything was coming up roses for David?

By our standards, his life was certainly tough at best and void of happiness. We would be hard-pressed to find a reason why he shouldn't be whining and angry. Yet as you read the Psalms, you will find a continuous attitude of joy even in the midst of David's searching for the answer to the question, "Why?" While he might start a Psalm asking why God has allowed wicked people to hunt him, set traps for him, and besiege his name, he always ended telling himself to not be downcast and would sing the Lord's praises. His success came in his steadfastness in faith and worship of the God of all creation. Is it any wonder that the Father called him "a man after God's own heart?"

That, my friend, is perpetual joy. No matter the circumstances, David knew there was a bigger and more perfect plan. He knew he was a part of that plan. He realized how blessed he was that God wanted to use him, a lowly shepherd boy, to accomplish that plan and was filled with joy.

Let the truth of joy sink into the depths of your spirit. Know that you are never without it. You have been placed where you are and subjected to the experiences you have to complete your part in God's glorious plan. Walk in His joy through it all and know that you are blessed.

"O Lord, Your loving-kindness goes to the heavens. You are as faithful as the sky is high. You are as right and good as mountains are big. You are as fair when You judge as a sea is deep. O Lord, You keep safe

both man and animal. Of what great worth is Your loving-kindness, O God! The children of men come and are safe in the shadow of Your wings. They are filled with the riches of Your house. And You give them a drink from Your river of joy. All life came from You. In Your light we see light."
(Psalm 36:5-9 New Life Version)

Laugh!

We've all heard it said that laughter is the best medicine. It turns out that studies have proven this to be true. Patients who laughed more frequently and longer healed more quickly from debilitating illnesses and injuries than those who didn't. Laughter is both physically and mentally/emotionally healing. While it doesn't eradicate difficult circumstances in life, it can make them easier to walk through and tolerate.

Laughter's healing properties seem to be boundless. Laughter keeps you young both inside and out, at least in my opinion. On the outside, I feel that laugh lines are much more attractive than frown lines, and just the slightest uptilt of the corners of the mouth generates a response of wanting to know what's under that smile. We are simply more drawn to the pleasant appearance of a smile and the sound of laughter. It's youthful. It's uplifting. It's engaging. It's joyous and hopeful!

Laughter lifts and strengthens the spirit within us. It brings joy into any moment. My mom's family was, in my (slightly biased) opinion, a perfect example of this fact. She and her sisters were well known among friends and family for their tendency to laugh out loud for long periods of time when they were together, and her brothers often joined in the mirth. They smiled and laughed at memories, current circumstances, and themselves. The sound of their joy was a staple of my childhood and early adult years. While they now laugh together in heaven instead of on this earth, I can still hear them if I listen closely enough. It is a sound that is unforgettable, encouraging, familiar, comforting, and very dear to my heart. The remembrance and reality of their joy never ceases to pull me out of any dark place into which my spirit has settled. It lifts me and enables me to smile and laugh on my own. One of my fondest memories of this, although it may seem odd to some, was the service for my grandmother's passing when I was nine years old. The funeral home was not quiet and somber during the viewing/visitation hours or afterward at the post-funeral gathering. It was filled with the voices of beloved family and the sound of their laughter. There were some who questioned what seemed to be an impropriety, yet it was not an impropriety at all. It was the realization that Grandmom had lived an extraordinary life that filled us with love, joy, and wonderful memories that we needed to share among ourselves and with others because it was the balm that healed our grief and loss. We knew she had gone to a perfect place and was continuing to live that extraordinary life, and we celebrated her with laughter. I am blessed to say that my cousins and I continue that family tradition of joy and laughter whenever we get together. We lift each other with hope while honoring the memory of those who taught us so well.

My dad's family is much the same way. He and my uncle in particular proudly own that contagious laughter that permeates their time together. I've always said that if you put the two of them into a stadium filled with people, I would be able to find them simply based on the sound of their joyous and raucous laughing! No one within earshot of that sound can let it pass unnoticed. They all want to know where that joy comes from and what the reasoning is behind it.

We all have times that our tears fall, our hearts and spirits hurt, and we simply cannot imagine that there are smiles and laughter in the midst or on the other side of them. The fact is, whether we feel like it or not, all we need to do is put on a smile, even if it's pretend. That one simple act opens the door for a true smile and even laughter to follow. I firmly believe this is why we all have at least one person in our lives who always says something that seems completely inappropriate or laughs out loud in the middle of a dire situation. Those people have been placed in our paths for that exact moment when we are at our lowest point because, whether we want to admit it or not, their words or actions will cause us to forget our own trouble in that second and bring a smile to our lips and heart, allowing healing to begin. I am blessed to have a few friends who are able to do just that when I am feeling down and beaten. And yes, I say, "blessed." Never chastise people like that in your life. As I said, they have been placed in front of you in all their perceived obnoxiousness to lift you out of the mire of your circumstances. They have been placed in your path to bring back the smiles and laughter you are missing.

Another familiar phrase is this: "If I didn't laugh, I would cry." This is a simple truth throughout our lives. There are many, many times that it is simply a choice of one or the other. Find the laughable. Laughter will promote more laughter, and tears will promote more tears. The choice is always ours to make. Laughter really is the best medicine. It is a panacea for the world's ills and for ours. Just ask my mom and my aunts - and those of us who remember just how they cured their ills and solved their problems. I can hear their laughter ringing through the heavens now, and it really does bring joy to my spirit.

The simple lesson is this: let the laughter commence! Spread that stuff wherever you go.   And then let the healing begin.

"We were filled with laughter, and we sang for joy. And the other nations said, 'What amazing things the LORD has done for them.' Yes, the LORD has done amazing things for us! What joy!"
(Psalm 126:2-3 NLT)

The Presents of Friendship

The use of "presents" above rather than "presence" is intentional. After all, what true friend is not a present?

Ralph Waldo Emerson said, "A friend may well be reckoned the masterpiece of nature."

Friends come in all types. There are online friends and lifelong friends. There are friends that are more acquaintances and those that are like sisters and brothers. There are friends that stick closely by no matter the circumstances, and those who, for whatever reason, drift apart. Each one is a unique blessing that cannot be measured against another, for it would be like comparing apples to oranges.

Friendship is to be treasured whether its time has come and gone, it lives in the present moment, or it has come, gone, and returned once again. It is much like love. It doesn't ask more than it is willing to give, it always believes in the ties that bind, and it doesn't become jealous or boastful. It is understanding, generous, and kind even in the midst of disagreement. It revels in the fact that it is one of a kind and floats on the waves of change while remaining what it was born to be - a relationship based on these mutual characteristics: give and take, need and desire, gratitude, and being a support as well as being supported.

I had lunch today with a lifelong friend. We grew up together from grade school on. We had times of togetherness and times of separation. Life took us to opposite sides of the country, but once we reconnected it was as if our hearts never skipped a beat. No, our friendship was not always perfect. What is? Yet here we are in our imperfection. It is the grace we have been given that allows us to be gracious to one another. It is the love we have been shown that allows us to love each other. Even our separate journeys seem to have paralleled in some connected way, and that only deepens the affection we have for each other.

What brought us together today was far from a happy occasion. She recently lost her mother. That loss along with the loss of my mom is a tie that binds us together and allows joy (yes, joy) in the midst of grief. The wondrous thing for me is that our moms knew one another long before they married their husbands and gave birth to us, and we ended up in school together not knowing the connection. That alone makes me smile.

As we prayed before our meal, I thanked God that we knew they were (at least in my heart's eyes) sitting together and watching us, wondering why in the world we were so sad. I could hear them both saying, "We're fine! Be glad!"

We talked of children and siblings and of my grandson. We shared stories that made us smile and some that brought tears. Friendship is like that. It can move from one emotion to the other without a thought, knowing it is perfectly safe to do so because there will be no judgment in any circumstance.

I suppose the key is to be truly grateful for the people who have come into our lives as well as for those who had to leave. Friendship will allow wings to fly when needed, even if the wings carry a friend away from you. Who doesn't want to see someone grow and reach for the stars and catch one by the tail?

I was blessed to have this girl in my life so many years ago. I am doubly blessed to have this woman in my life as a dear sister now. And in between? I thought of her with a smile, prayed her life was one of happiness, and cheered on the successes I hoped she would have. Hopefully, she has always known these things. If not, she knows them now.

Life is always good with a friend, even during the saddest of times. It's even better when the two of you share the ultimate Friend. And therein lies the true blessing of our friendship.

"You are better off to have a friend than to be all alone, because then you will get more enjoyment out of what you earn. If you fall, your friend can help you up. But if you fall without having a friend nearby, you are really in trouble. If you sleep alone, you won't have anyone to keep you warm on a cold night. Someone might be able to beat up one of you, but not both of you. As the saying goes, 'A rope made from three strands of cord is hard to break.'"
(Ecclesiastes 4:9-12 CEV)

Receiving the Gift of Silence

The blessed quiet. It is in the moments when a blanket of silence surrounds us that we are most able to hear - not only with our ears but with our hearts, souls, and spirits. Yet we seem to think we need to fill those very moments with something, anything. We don't seem to understand that what we seek - what we desperately need - is in the silence. It is in the hush that we can be contemplative and honest within the deepest recesses of our being. It is in those moments that we can most effectively wait on the wisdom we need, the peace we desire, and the strength we must gather to go forward. It is during this time that we can cast off the burdens we harbor and be renewed and refreshed.

Our first impulse is to turn on the television, open the Pandora or I Heart Radio app, boot up the laptop, dial, or text. We simply cannot seem to recognize that the muting of the world around us is a gift and a much needed one. Yes, the quiet is a divinely gracious and timely gift.

We can choose to accept and embrace it gratefully or fight against it by filling it with noise that will never fill us and never give us what we so desperately need.

Choosing to accept and embrace with gratitude doesn't mean we have to like something. It doesn't mean we have to understand it. Medicine for the body or spirit is seldom pleasant to endure, and spiritual medicine is seldom, if ever, logical. Accepting with gratitude simply means that we realize the silence truly is a gift and that fighting against it will only deplete our already strained reserves of wisdom and strength while eroding the little peace we possess into dust. No wonder we are exhausted and drained to the point of dryness of spirit! We spend what little we have left inside of us resolving and attempting to fill the silence with empty calories that will never nourish the soul. Better to take in the nourishment our languishing and desperate bodies, minds, and hearts need to be able to put one foot in front of the other and face each moment equipped for whatever it may hold and require.

A soldier does not go into battle without preparation. Jesus did not go to the Cross without sitting in a multitude of hushed moments where he was filled with the wisdom, direction, strength, and peace of the Father. We cannot face life unprepared and empty because we choose to fill the quiet with worldly noise and sustenance. It won't end well for us. The only way to infuse our parched spirits, troubled minds, and weak bodies with what is needed is to sit in the silence and wait for what is given to satisfy our thirst before moving on to the next thing before us. Dry bones and breathless hearts cannot truly live and thrive, only exist. Sit in the quiet, taste, and see!

"The hand of the Lord was on me, and he brought me out by the Spirit of the Lord and set me in the middle of a valley; it was full of bones. He led me back and forth among them, and I saw a great many bones on the floor of the valley, bones that were very dry. He asked me, 'Son of man, can these bones live?' I said, 'Sovereign Lord, you alone know.' Then he said to

me, 'Prophesy to these bones and say to them, 'Dry bones, hear the word of the Lord! This is what the Sovereign Lord says to these bones: I will make breath enter you, and you will come to life.'"
(Ezekiel 37:1-5 NIV)

Are You Willing To Give?

The three small tents were hidden far back in a wooded area. We almost missed them. There had been others in that same area that were more noticeable, but they are now gone. Only these three remain. Upon arrival, we called out and asked if anyone was home, telling them we had provisions to help them for a time. There was no answer. We returned to the car to grab three bags of supplies, three blankets and some heavy, lined hoodies. We decided to leave them at the camp for when the occupants returned.

Returning to the camp, we noticed movement. We knew immediately they had been there when we called to them but were fearful of why we had come. The young couple spoke very little English and didn't understand at first what we might want. As we handed the bags, blankets, and coats to them, their faces turned from concern to understanding and then gratitude, even tinged with a bit of joy. The food won't feed them for long but it was very much welcomed. We left them with a smile and told them we would return again, hoping they understood by our actions and expressions, if not our words, that we only wanted to help and meant no harm. It is not unusual for a couple with or without children to set up camp rather than enter a shelter. They don't want to be separated from each other during the night as is the practice of most shelters.

It was a simple five minutes that left an indelible mark on our hearts. We both felt heavy in spirit because we had noticed the stroller at the campsite. Tears filling our eyes, we prayed that there was not a small child with them but that the stroller might be simply for hauling supplies back to the camp when they needed to do so. Two adults, three tents, one stroller... our fervent prayers continue.

On to the next camp that had been in another area for quite some time. We walked the wooded path to find it had been deserted. Tents no longer lined the path, and not much was left behind other than that which is no longer useful. This was a camp that had contained several tents and occupants. We had been here many times before to help those who called this small wooded area home. More wondering, more praying, more concern - where have they gone? Hopefully, on to a new circumstance that includes warmth, a roof, and employment. More fervent prayers for their safety and circumstances joined the first.

A young man sat on the curbing with his small backpack beside him and an obvious look of desperate need. His clothing is full of holes, and he's obviously cold. We sat beside him to ask how he's doing. His answer takes us aback slightly just because of the honesty and, yes, hope behind it. "Pretty good today, but not as good as I wanted. How are you?"

The next question we asked is why he is not as good as he wanted. A seemingly stupid question because of the apparent answer, but you need to ask the questions to get the story and know how or if you'll be able to help. And here's the key - you can't just ask the questions without letting them know you truly care and really are listening. You can't just say, "Hi," hand them a bag, and turn away, and still let them know that they, indeed, matter in this world.

Jay came to Reading from another county because he had found some work. He has a wife and two young children that he left behind in a shelter in the hopes of the work providing enough to get them back on their feet after losing their jobs and home. The work turned out to be temporary, and so his hopes faded quickly. He continues to work day labor when it's available and had been living in a tent until the weather conditions made it impossible. His statement of being "pretty good today" comes from the fact that one person had compassion for him, and he is now staying in a barn. It's still cold and damp, but it provides a roof over his head and shelter from the elements. He is determined to find permanent work that will allow him to put a roof over the heads of his wife and children and support them in a stable environment. He doesn't ask for anything from us and seems unsure of taking the food, blanket, and coat we offer. After more conversation, he accepts the provisions.

This last young man's situation hits my husband particularly hard. He can't imagine leaving his family behind to find work to provide them with a better life - not because he wouldn't want to provide us with a better life but because he wouldn't want to leave us under any circumstances. He can't fathom the love and determination that drives this young man to continue looking, continue hoping, and continue taking whatever day labor in the meantime until he can reach that seemingly far-off goal of providing for a wife and children he loves so deeply. We cannot gain the depth of understanding to comprehend how he could answer our first question with, "Pretty good today," when to us there seems nothing good about being in such dire straits. We will be visiting Jay again in the near future. He told us that while he spends his week doing what he needs to do to further his goal, he does sit in this spot each Sunday, relying on the kindness of strangers, even though he wishes he didn't have to do it. We pray we added more of something pretty good to his day and that there will be more pretty good days and even much better days ahead for him.

Yes, we pray for each person we meet on the streets and even those we have not yet met. Prayer is of utmost importance in our lives and, we feel, in all lives. Yet we cannot just pray. God will answer those prayers, but many times He answers with these questions: What are you willing to do to help? Are you willing to work beside Me? Are you willing to give what I have given you to reach out and give a hand up to the least of these? Are you willing to give what I haven't yet given you but have promised?

Our answer is, "Yes, Lord." It is with the deepest of convictions that we feel we cannot just utter the words and then stand by to watch what happens or what others will do. These people, these lives matter as much as we and ours do.

"'Which of these three, do you think, was a neighbor to the man who fell into the hands of the robbers?' He said, 'The one who showed him mercy.' Jesus said to him, 'Go and do likewise.'"
(Luke 10:36-37 NRSV)

"Jesus told him, 'If you want to be perfect, go and sell all your possessions and give the money to the poor, and you will have treasure in heaven. Then come, follow me.'"
(Matthew 19:21 NLT)

The Gift of Family at Christmas
(written December 2016)

At this time of year, I am reminded of just how many wonderful people have blessed my life. Even more, I am reminded of family members who are no longer with us, and that makes me even more grateful for those who are. This is to honor those who are gone and also those who remain.

Christmas was always a time of loved ones gathering in our family. As a child, I remember going to spend time with grandparents, aunts, uncles, and cousins. It started with Christmas Eve church services, where my Uncle Miller (who was visiting for the holidays from Massachusetts), Uncle George, Aunt June, Daddy, and sometimes Momma, and Aunt Toots sang in the choir. Even as a little girl, their voices would ring out loudly and clearly amid the others, singing praises and Christmas anthems to the Newborn King. Daddy and Momma are still with us, and I catch them singing from time to time to the same carols on the radio. As for my wonderful aunts and uncles, I can still hear their voices clearly in my heart.

I also remember my Uncle Fritz spending the holidays at my Grandma's and Pop-pop's home, and my Aunt Jean, who it seemed was ALWAYS in the kitchen. Whenever we would visit there, the smells wafting from the kitchen through the house were so good you could taste them. And when you finally got one of those treats into your mouth, it was downright heavenly.

Uncle Connie would patiently wait for whatever was to come out of the oven. He loved my aunt with a love that was obvious in his eyes and on his face, and he loved to tease us and make us laugh. Uncle Art, it seemed, preferred to be in the background, yet to me was no less noticeable. He had this quiet, gentle way of just being there. You knew that if you needed him, there he was. That's what I love most about my memory of him.

Then there are my cousins, who it seems I miss more and more each year. My childhood memories of spending hours on Christmas day at Uncle George's and Aunt June's bring many smiles to my face but also tears to my eyes. Roland, Bobby, and Ted, although older than me, were always there. I remember their smiles and the long, deep discussions that were inevitable between my Dad and (particularly) Bob and/or Ted. What I wouldn't give to see those smiles and hear one of those discussions today, especially now that I'm grown up enough to understand them! We girls would play at doing "shows." I particularly remember acting out scenes from The Sound of Music - the ones where the children sang. The entire family would gather, eat, and talk, and it seemed no one wanted to leave. It was always that way when Momma's side of the family would get together.

Daddy's side of the family lived further away, some north of here in the coal regions and others on the western side of the state. However, the love was just as tangible from a distance as it was when we would all get together. Spaghetti dinners at Aunt Peggy's and Uncle Chinky's house were infamous. A long table with all of us gathered, talking, and laughing loudly. I always said you could pick out the Bowman laughter even if they were scattered in a football stadium full of fans. I'm sure Uncle Chinky is serving that fabulous dinner to the angels in heaven even as I write this. He loved feeding his family.

Aunt Florence's and Uncle Clyde's home was just as full of love and just as loud when we would gather there. The fact that they had five children probably had a lot to do with the volume level. I loved staying overnight with my cousins when I was little. And as I got older, I loved spending time with my aunt and uncle as well. I learned to appreciate how hard they worked, how much they sacrificed, and how much they loved, even if I didn't understand their methods as a child.

My husband's family was filled with many of the same traditions. Large family gatherings were the norm, and love and laughter prevailed. The Sunday nights before Christmas day were spent with his Dad's side of the family. Nana Wert was a wonderful woman who dearly loved her children and grandchildren. I remember her holding Jason when he was little and seeing the twinkle in her eye. Poppy was the same way. I have a picture of him holding my grandson, Thayer (his great-great-grandson), and I see that same twinkle in his eye in the photograph. They were all about family.

Christmas day was spent at the home of my mother- and father-in-law. Her parents, Nana and Poppy Miller, were always present. It was another day when no one wanted to leave, and the joy of close family would abound.

There are many who have left us over the years from Michael's family as well. His grandparents, Aunt Doris, Uncle Cliff and Aunt Dot, and cousin Debbie are all celebrating Christmas with the angels this year... as, for the first time, is his Dad.

The Wert Christmas celebration didn't seem the same this year without the family patriarch playing Santa. While the family was gathered and there were gifts under the tree, Dad, wearing his Santa hat and handing out the gifts, was missing. Yet we all felt him there and, in our hearts and our own way, wished him a Merry Christmas and told him we loved him. And we know he was smiling at those two new great-grandsons having their first Christmas with the family. It especially brought a tear to my eye when Michael, now the oldest male in the family, took over the Santa duties albeit minus the Santa hat.

There have been many Christmas gifts already given to us this year and not the kind that money can buy. As I've already said, there are two new members of the Wert family - Carter and Charlie, who are coming up on four months old. There is also our son, Jason, who is recovering after a car accident back in October, and we are so blessed and happy to have him with us despite the seriousness of the accident. Michael's Mom is home after quite a bit of time in the hospital undergoing surgeries for cancer and then much time in rehab. We are so thankful to have this wonderful woman back home and in the midst of her family. Lastly, I am blessed to say that my parents are still with us and doing well. Who needs presents under the tree when you have them with you every day?

For all of those family members that I am still blessed to have in my life, my brother John, my nieces and nephews, Aunt Francie and Uncle Sonny, Aunt Deb and Uncle Dick, Aunt Betty and Uncle John, cousins galore on both sides of my family, as well as all those in Michael's family... you have all impacted my life in a blessed way that you can never imagine. I wish you all the same blessing, multiplied one hundred times over.

For my husband, Michael, my son, Jason, my grandson, Thayer, and Momma and Daddy, words cannot express the love I hold for you in my heart and the thankfulness that goes with it. You are the lights of my life and a blessing I could never have imagined.

And finally, for you, my dear readers, I wish for you the blessings and traditions of the season, along with all the love I've experienced over the years from these blessed members of the Bowman/Ulle and Wert/Miller families. Treasure every moment and save the memories in your heart. That way, you won't miss a second of life with those you love or a single moment of the enduring gift of the Father's love.

*"I pray that out of his glorious riches he may strengthen you with power through his Spirit in your inner being, so that Christ may dwell in your hearts through faith. And I pray that you, being rooted and established in love, may have power, together with all the Lord's holy people, to grasp how wide and long and high and deep is the love of Christ." **(Ephesians 3:16-18 NIV)***

The Best Gifts

Sometimes, the best gifts come at unexpected times and in unexpected places. Late last evening, well after the household had settled in to bed and was asleep (those who know me know we retire early around here), we were awoken by the doorbell ringing and the sound of the UPS truck pulling away from the curb. Once I was finished grumbling at the delivery driver for waking us (do they really need to deliver well after 9:00 p.m.?), Michael got up to bring the package inside. It was for me. He told me it was from Chewy, a pet supply website. Odd, because I hadn't ordered anything. In my half-asleep state, I decided to wait until the morning to open it.

In the morning, I looked at the box. It surely said "Chewy" in big, blue letters. A closer inspection revealed that it was from a Facebook friend, Sandy, who lives in Texas. I opened the box to find a beautiful deep dish pie plate with an inscription of the recipe for an amazing woman. I smiled broadly, and that was followed by tears springing to my eyes. This was the most recent in a long line of unexpected gifts from this wonderful woman and her husband, and it came at a time when my heart was torn with the grief of missing Momma this first Christmas season without her.

Sandy was the first unexpected gift I received some months ago. She was a mutual friend on Facebook with a longtime friend of mine. She and her husband were engaged in a long battle with cancer that had invaded his body. They were undergoing treatments, side effects, and doctor appointments. They were on an emotional roller coaster that can rival any manmade contraption at any amusement park. I completely understood their situation after having been through it in my own family with both Momma and my in-laws. I knew the stress, the exhaustion, and the ups and downs of the journey. And so, I sent Sandy a card with what I hoped was some encouragement and included a gift card for a local eatery. Time for cooking is not in the schedule when battling the monster that is cancer.

The second unexpected gift I received was the encouragement given in return by their journey. The strength, grace, and passion with which they pursued their enemy and the hope with which they greeted each day was amazing. No matter the twists and turns, they put on their boxing gloves and fought through any and every obstacle. Each round they came out swinging, and each round they ended standing on their feet even if bruised and battered. What a blessing of example as to how to live in the face of great adversity!

The next gift to unwrap was the news that Tim's surgeries and treatments were successful. The cancer had been stopped in its tracks. I include this among unexpected gifts because, while we always hope with all of our hearts that the outcome will be what we long and pray for, there are so many times the outcome is not what we wish. Cancer is a big deal. It is truly a formidable foe. Yet there are times when the big deal becomes small and the formidable becomes conquerable. Keep pulling at those knotted ribbons! They are quite capable of opening to the unexpected and beautiful within!

In this season of gifts, I could go on for pages and pages about the unexpected, but I won't tax your eyes or patience by doing so. Instead, I will end the list with the provision of these examples.

People who are truly angels walking this earth are unexpected gifts. Sandy from Texas is one of those.

Encouragement can be found in the most unlikely places, even on social media where the order of the day seems to be arguments over politics and political memes, criticism of 50 (or more) year old seasonal traditions, and endless discussion of who is right or wrong. It is found and given by those traveling an extremely difficult journey even more than it is found in those walking the easy path. It was certainly found in a beautiful pie plate this morning.

Beauty is an unexpected gift found at the bottom of the box filled with chaos, sadness, and all that life can throw at us. Persistence is the key. There may be many layers of wrapping to get to the box and many items to examine and toss aside, but the beauty is in there and you will find it.

Lastly, there is the greatest gift of all without which these other gifts would not be possible. This gift arrived in the middle of the night under a starry sky and rested in a manger amid the sounds of cattle and sheep. He brings unending love, joy, and beauty to the spirit of all who gaze upon Him. He was and is truly an unexpected gift in an unexpected place given to a waiting and hurting world.

"Whatever is good and perfect is a gift coming down to us from God our Father, who created all the lights in the heavens. He never changes or casts a shifting shadow."
(James 1:17 NLT)

Unwrapped Gifts

I recently wrote a single line in my journal. "The best gifts don't have wrapping or ribbons." This year, 2020, has made that fact even more real to us in the Wert family. The first gift was that of being on the road to recovery from this virus for Michael, myself, Jason, and Erin. The second gift was that my dad never contracted the virus despite us caring for some of his needs. As we've been recovering, more presents have been opened in our lives, although they didn't come in boxes, paper, and bows. The care, love, and compassion of friends has been just the beginning.

This past week has been a week of recovering, getting restless, and yearning for some kind of normalcy after almost four weeks in the house. We started trying to attain that normalcy with holiday activities like baking. Any other year during our 45-year marriage, the cookie baking was my task. It's really not a task, chore, or job; I love doing it. This year was a bit different because my strength level was just not at its best. It seemed cookies just would not happen this year. The other difference was that I was blessed to have Michael home with me instead of at work, where he would have become exhausted dealing with the extra busyness and sometimes irate customers during the holiday season. I have often told people that I don't have a husband between Thanksgiving and New Year. It's pretty much true. Long days and multiple consecutive days without time off have been the norm in our marriage until this year.

Hence, the next gift of Christmas 2020 - a husband who was by my side (minus the 3-day hospital stay) for the entire Christmas season. Isn't it funny how a blessing and gift come on the heels of and out of a curse like Covid? With both of us trying to regain strength, we decided to bake cookies together - him measuring, me mixing; me filling trays, him manning the oven. We didn't bake as many as I normally do, and it was over the course of days instead of in one day, but we (and Daddy) have Christmas cookies.

We had our first date night in a couple of months last Tuesday. We dressed warmly, got into the truck, and drove to a church in the western part of the county to watch a Christmas light show set to music. At a time when we normally would have been in bed because of rising early the next morning, we went for a drive, holding hands and talking about different things along the way. When we arrived at the church, we stood outside the truck together and held each other to keep warm while watching a beautiful light display for about fifteen minutes. The cool (not cold) air was good for our breathing, and the short time of enjoyment and focusing on the truth of the season was just what the doctor ordered for us. You can't buy that type of time together or the realization that the simple existence of Christmas testifies to how deeply you are loved.

After a few more days of rest and staying indoors, which was necessitated by a nine-inch snowfall, we were restless once again. During a doctor appointment on Friday, we were cleared and told we were no longer contagious, couldn't transmit the virus, and were immune for the relatively short period of time of about three months. Michael is able to return to work with some restrictions on December 23rd. Complete recovery could take three more months or so, but this declaration from the doctor was huge. This was the biggest gift of the season, comparable to that big box you would find under the tree when you were a child - the box you had hoped for all year long that was filled with nothing but good things. This was priceless. It brought us to our knees in gratitude and praise. This meant we could see those we love, safely and in small family units, and deliver the gifts we had purchased online and had shipped to our home. It meant we would be able to have Daddy in our home for Christmas! Joy overflows!

With that joy still spilling out of our hearts, we loaded the car on Saturday morning with our gifts. Our first stop was at my brother's home. We visited outdoors with John and Allison for a bit. The bonus gift at this stop was that Allison was on her feet with the help of crutches just 24 hours after having knee surgery. She told us that she had some discomfort, but it was nothing like the pain she had been experiencing prior to surgery. What an added blessing to already being blessed by just being able to visit!

Our next stop was Jason's. This visit was particularly heart-filling for us. Jason and Erin had begun to battle the virus just a week before we did due to her contracting it at work. They, too, have been cleared and able to return to work and some sense of a normal life. To be able to sit down with them in their living room and spend time with them was emotional and lifted all of our spirits. I'm not sure any of us had smiled like that in some time.

The second to last present of the day was with our grandson, Thayer. It had been quite a while since we were able to see him. Phone calls and texts are nice, but nothing beats being able to see your grandchild, hold him close, and hug him. I am still carrying that hug and cherishing his smile as I write this.

Our last stop was a wonderful gift to open. We hadn't seen Robin and Jeff in quite some time. What is said about real friendship is true: time and distance don't stop it or allow it to fade. The love and camaraderie remain in spite of all things. You pick up where you left off and keep on going. The visit was filled with catching up, laughter, the sharing of memories and burdens, and perhaps a few tears. Mostly, it was filled with love.

We ended the day tired but happy. We needed a good night's sleep before heading into Sunday and a very important tradition for us, even if it would happen a bit differently from our normal practice during the holidays.

Sunday afternoon we headed into downtown Reading with a box of warm hats we had purchased to meet with other supporters and the founders of an organization named Providing Hope. The founders, Paul and Sandra, were introduced to us by a mutual friend at what can be considered nothing short of a predestined time about two years ago. We had been unable to make our normal trips into the city to help the needy due to family responsibilities. We also had to admit that we were getting older and walking the camps while carrying supplies was becoming more difficult for us. Enter Paul and Sandra, who are younger and share that same fiery passion for helping those in need and sharing the ultimate love with other people.

We met on Court Street at 3:00. There were probably about twenty volunteers in all. We unloaded vehicles, organized food items, clothing, winter gear, and toiletries, and began serving our friends who had gathered. Much like prior years when the Carpenter's House would set up to help, the supplies were exhausted quickly. The need is still great, perhaps even greater in this tumultuous year of 2020. Yet Michael and I still are touched deeply by the demeanor of all of these people. The volunteers are caring, loving, and always sharing a smile. Those we served were patient in their waiting, respectful, gracious, and grateful. Yes, we saw some familiar faces, which reached deep into our core with sadness. The many new faces also touched us with sadness. Again, our thoughts turned to a wish to be able to solve this problem - to provide homes, to provide for daily needs, to provide mentorship to help them return to societal living in safety and to prosper there. The greatest gift of this weekend was the gift of being able to serve. It is a gift we will keep and ponder in our hearts always.

The biggest box under the tree certainly was huge. It did not disappoint. As we opened it with joy, we were humbled by all of the gifts that spilled from it. A clean bill of health, visiting John and his family as well as Jason and Erin, Thayer, and Robin and Jeff, Providing Hope with Paul, Sandra, and all the volunteers and clients, and the gift that will arrive on the 25th of Daddy being able to spend Christmas with us - our gratitude and praise know no bounds. We will hold these moments that came without paper and bows close in our hearts and think on them often withgreat love.

As you celebrate this season, think about the true gifts you are given, and think about the greatest gift of all - a little baby laid in a manger who was and is our King. His name is Jesus. He is our gift every moment of every day here on earth, into eternity, and beyond. Ponder all of the gifts you are given with love and humility. Then sing of God's glory with the angels above.

"And, lo, the angel of the Lord came upon them, and the glory of the Lord shone round about them: and they were sore afraid. And the angel said unto them, Fear not: for, behold, I bring you good tidings of great joy, which shall be to all people. For unto you is born this day in the city of David a Saviour, which is Christ the Lord. And this shall be a sign unto you; Ye shall find the babe wrapped in swaddling clothes, lying in a manger. And suddenly there was with the angel a multitude of the heavenly host praising God, and saying, Glory to God in the highest, and on earth peace, good will toward men. And it came to pass, as the angels were gone away from them into heaven, the shepherds said one to another, Let us now go even unto Bethlehem, and see this thing which is come to pass, which the Lord hath made known unto us. And they came with haste, and found Mary, and Joseph, and the babe lying in a manger. And when they had seen it, they made known abroad the saying which was told them concerning this

child. And all they that heard it wondered at those things which were told them by the shepherds. But Mary kept all these things, and pondered them in her heart."
(Luke 2:9-19 KJV)

The Christmas Light

Even when the clouds seem to threaten, the light shines. As the clouds gathered on this morning before Christmas, they could not banish the light that shone through them. They were not quick enough to erode the perfectly painted, deep blue of the winter sky. They couldn't contain the beautiful strokes of salmon pink tones at earth's horizon or the bright outlines of the sun's rays (just one more reason I love residing in the midst of farm country - the beauty is never ending, even on the dreariest of days).

We should all be more like that light. We are too often darkened by the burdens we bear and the wearying of the world pressing in from all sides. The light is never extinguished, although it would appear so to those who witness our clouded state. It is simply hidden - pressed down, covered up, and only smoldering when it should be burning brightly.

There is always someone whose burdens are heavier than ours, whose darkness looms a bit closer, whose pressure is greater and more suffocating than that which we are under. It is those whose lights are in danger of flickering and dying. It is those to whose sides we need to draw close, sharing the light we have hidden and covered to a mere smoldering spark.

This became more than apparent this past Saturday evening when Michael and I visited with a very sweet couple in an attempt to bring them a bit of Christmas joy. Their year has been more than difficult. He suffered a stroke while at his place of employment.

The ensuing damage to his brain has left him paralyzed on his right side, unable to work or completely care for himself. His wife has now also assumed the role of caregiver, a difficult role at best. They have lost their income and their insurance. Waiting for disability benefits to be approved is a full-time job in itself and could take months. She is unable to work because he needs care at home, and even if she did find employment, her paycheck would all go to paying professional caregivers to come into their home. It's a vicious circle that one would think is closing in on them and stifling whatever joy and peace they once had.

What we found was that the total opposite is true. Their light has not flickered nor has it been extinguished. It is not even in danger of doing so. It dances in their eyes and warms their home. The time we spent with them was full of smiles that reached the depths of their eyes, and their hearts are full of gratitude for what they do have - each other, a loving family both here and abroad, and a true sense of peace that everything will work out for their good at the perfect time.

What we found was that we wanted to be light and joy for them, but they were light and joy for us.

Let your light burn brightly. Tomorrow is a new day - indeed, it is Christmas Day. It is the day the gift of Light was given to us. It should also be the day we give the gift of our light to others - even if we feel we have no light to give.

"I am the light of the world. Whoever follows me will not walk in darkness, but will have the light of life."

(John 8:12 NIV)

After Christmas

The wrapping and ribbons are gone. The leftovers have taken over my fridge and, as usual, I baked more than enough cookies. Michael says we'll have them until Valentine's Day. Somehow, knowing him, I doubt that.

So, what happens next? The trees and decorations will be put away until next year, and gifts will be worn, used, and gazed upon with smiles. It seems so sad to see it all end, but does Christmas ever really end? I suppose in some ways it does, but in others it definitely shouldn't.

I tried to sit here and write some of this yesterday, but I couldn't get past the lump in my throat and the tears that threatened to leak from my eyes. Someone (I think it was Daddy) once said that we Ulle girls suffer from "leaky eye syndrome." I suppose that has become even more true of me now that I am missing Momma and my in-laws. Things just aren't the same.

I had two very vivid memories visit me yesterday morning. The first came as the Disney Christmas parade was broadcast. Santa and Mrs. Claus rode down Main Street in the sleigh, smiling and waving. The Santa hat caught my eye as a picture filled my mind of my father-in-law wearing the same hat while handing out gifts to his children, grandchildren, and great-grandchild with my mother-in-law smiling proudly and bursting with love as she looked at each one. It was a yearly tradition at the Wert family

Christmas celebration. So many gifts were given, but the most obvious gift was love. Michael now has taken the reins of playing Santa, although he doesn't wear the hat because "the kids aren't little anymore." No matter how I try to convince him, he just won't do it. I think it's more that things just aren't the same.

The second memory came as music filled the room during another program. The melody and voices lifted softly in a rendition of "O Little Town of Bethlehem." It was Momma's favorite Christmas carol. My heart and mind could very clearly hear her beautiful voice singing the words as she had so many times during Christmas Sunday and Christmas Eve services over the years. I could also see the tears that she gently dabbed away from her eyes as she sang - not tears of sadness but tears of joy for what this song meant to her. "Yet in Thy dark streets shineth the everlasting light; the hopes and fears of all the years are met in Thee tonight."* Oh, how she loved that light - the light of Jesus! I remember the Sunday before her last Christmas with us. She was unable to attend services, but her favorite music show was on that morning. The organist played this carol, and while she didn't sing, I could hear her humming along and watched her dab those tears away even as she smiled. Again, things are no longer the same. My tears when I hear that song now are mingled joy and sadness.

So, back to the original question. What happens next? Yes, surely the decorations and tree will come down until the next season, and the cookies and leftovers will definitely be eaten. However, I am determined that the spirit of Christmas will not end, as we should all be.

We may not wear Santa hats all year long or even at all, but the giving of gifts has to continue each and every day, especially the gift of love. My in-laws certainly didn't only give it once a year on Christmas; they gave it generously every day.

We may not sing "O Little Town of Bethlehem" every day, but shining His light in the darkened areas of our lives and the lives of others we meet has to continue each and every day. How else will the "hopes and fears of all the years"* be met?

Keep giving gifts. Shine light and be generous with your heart and treasure as others cross your path. Raise your voice in songs of joy and praise. Christmas isn't just a day or a season; it's a way of living.

No, things are not the same. There are those we miss terribly - but they haven't gone far. Their light still shines, and their love still envelops us.

"If you give to others, you will be given a full amount in return. It will be packed down, shaken together, and spilling over into your lap. The way you treat others is the way you will be treated."
(Luke 6:38 CEV)

*O Little Town of Bethlehem, Phillips Brooks, 1868

The Story of Christmas 2020

It's the day after Christmas, and there are still gifts to be realized. In a year when many complained about the problems that plagued us all, there are things for which thanks must be given. There are things that transcend our problems. There are those who are without homes and food. There are those who have lost loved ones, many of whom tragically had to die alone. There are those who have loved ones in the hospital, not knowing how things will progress or not progress from here. There are children who are going without breakfast this morning and perhaps dinner tonight. There are those without love, light, peace, and hope. The list could go on. For those of us not included in those numbers, it is time to silence our complaints no matter what those complaints might be. It is time to strive to bring love, light, hope, and peace as well as provision to those who are lacking. It is time to be grateful that we are only inconvenienced and not sitting and sobbing in tragedy. It's time for a new perspective.

The quote below is from a post I read early this morning. It speaks to the reality of where our hearts should be. It speaks of true gifts - gifts that we can pass on to others, if we are willing. It speaks of love and hope. I hope it touches your heart and brings tears to your eyes the way it did mine.

"So, here's my late Christmas post. This has obviously been a rough year for everyone, our family has definitely had its share of struggles. Months of lost work due to shutdowns, not seeing family and friends, our battle with Covid, watching E leave in an ambulance on Thanksgiving only to have my Dad make the same trip days later, and then Christmas. Christmas was not going to be the same, I'm sure everyone was stressing about that. Well, nothing was traditional this year, we didn't see 2 of our 3 boys, we didn't see our grandson for his first Christmas, we didn't see my Mom and Dad, or Poppop, and although E & T got to spend a little time with them while taking them dinner, I didn't see my in-laws. Dinner was not traditional either, although still pretty damn good. *Still, it was a wonderful holiday. Even though we weren't all in the same room, we still talked, we still loved, we were still blessed, because even when we're not in the same room we are still together. We are always with one another. Whether we are thousands of miles apart, or separated by heaven & earth, we are always together, as a family we are one, always. Love knows no boundaries, I am blessed every moment by the unbreakable bond of my family.* I love you all, Merry Christmas." (Italics emphasis mine)*

He said, "We were still blessed." And there, my dear readers, is the key. We are *always blessed.* I truly believe we need to be reminded of that from time to time, for it is only when we realize just how blessed we are that we can be a blessing to others instead of a stumbling block in our complaints.

"Consider it pure joy, my brothers and sisters, whenever you face trials of many kinds, because you know that the testing of your faith produces perseverance. Let perseverance finish its work so that you may be mature and complete, not lacking anything.

Blessed is the one who perseveres under trial because, having stood the test, that person will receive the crown of life that the Lord has promised to those who love him. Do not merely listen to the word, and so deceive yourselves. Do what it says. Anyone who listens to the word but does not do what it says is like someone who looks at his face in a mirror and, after looking at himself, goes away and immediately forgets what he looks like. But whoever looks intently into the perfect law that gives freedom, and continues in it—not forgetting what they have heard, but doing it—they will be blessed in what they do. Those who consider themselves religious and yet do not keep a tight rein on their tongues deceive themselves, and their religion is worthless. Religion that God our Father accepts as pure and faultless is this: to look after orphans and widows in their distress and to keep oneself from being polluted by the world."
(James 1:2-4, 12, 22-27 NIV)

*Shared with the permission of the post's author

My Fervent Prayer

I pray that all who need homes would find them, that all who are hungry would have food on their tables, that all who are cold would have warmth, and that there would be abundance where there is lack.

I pray that those, like myself, who grieve and miss dearly loved family members and friends would find comfort in the joys of Christmases as well as ordinary days past. May we all find peace in the knowledge that those who are out of sight are still looking upon us from heaven and feeling all the love we still have to give them.

I pray that addictions and anxieties would be healed along with all catastrophic diseases that cause children to lose their parents and parents to lose their children.

I pray that children would never know the fear of violence and abuse but instead the security of loving, nurturing parents and the protection of a caring society that allows them the childhood they deserve.

I pray that peace would envelope the soul of everyone on earth, erasing the craving for power, the need for offence, greed, hatred, and the resulting insult and injury all of these incur.

I pray that we would all begin to care for the earth we've been given rather than carelessly using and abusing its provision and beauty.

I pray that hearts that are hardened would be softened, eyes and ears that are closed would be opened, and hands and feet that are stagnant would be moved - all with compassion, kindness, love, and selflessness.

I pray that all people would find the goodness in each other, speak words that are encouraging instead of derogatory, take time to listen and not just reply, extend arms to embrace rather than push away, and march to aid as opposed to destroy.

I pray that hearts would be touched by the unconditional love of Jesus Christ, that God's grace would not just flow but be received, and that all mankind would realize the incredible gift of life given by our Creator.

Amen.

Call me a dreamer, but I believe it can be accomplished. All it takes is a willingness to live in light, a little Christmas magic, and a spirit willing to give a lot of love. Be the change the world needs to thrive and not just exist. A single candle can banish the darkness of an entire room. Think what the light of one person can do in the world. That's what Christmas is about.

"The people that walked in darkness have seen a great light: they that dwelt in the land of the shadow of death, upon them hath the light shined. Thou hast multiplied the nation, thou hast increased their joy: they joy before thee according to the joy in harvest, as men rejoice when they divide the spoil."
(Isaiah 9:2 ASV)

To Resolve or Not to Resolve

I don't believe in making New Year's resolutions. Yes, I've made them in the past. Perhaps that's the reason I no longer believe in the practice. They usually end up being nothing more than the result of being caught up in the moments just before and after midnight. They are also usually forgotten as the weeks of the new year quickly pass into months. Sure, my intentions were good. I truly believed I could follow through on them. If only my spirit was as resolute as those fleeting emotions of the moment. Sadly, they ended up not only forgotten but utterly and intentionally cast aside as other feelings of other moments overwhelmed them.

This year my goals are not really resolutions at all. They are simple steps forward that we all take each day. (At least I'm hoping I take steps forward and not backward.) I will get up each morning. I will continue to strive for kindness, compassion, love, and empathy in all things and with all people I meet. I will go through my days continuing to do my very best at the tasks at hand and remember to get back up again should I fall. And when I do fall, should I not be able to get up on my own, I will reach out for the hand that will help me. I will continue to look at an inability to do something not as failure but as success in making the attempt. I will try again. I will learn from the mistakes, grow from the difficult circumstances, and press on in the face of obstacles.

I will repeatedly remind myself that I don't know it all. In fact, I don't even come close to that kind of wisdom. And as I remind myself and realize the deep truth of that fact, I will rely on the One who does know everything and is sovereign over everything. I will continue to learn from those I meet - even those with whom I disagree - for I know they are placed in my path for that very reason. I will continue to be disciplined and educated by a loving Father God because I need that discipline and education. Will I always accept those things? Probably not. Thankfully, His patience is abundant with this wayward child.

I will (again) try not to ask why things I don't like happen to me, but instead seek the reasons behind the circumstances - whether they be consequences for some error in my judgment, opportunities for personal growth and enlargement of my faith, or the simple reasoning of allowing me to go through them so that I may help others who face them. I will help others with whatever resources I am given - even when it seems I have no resources. I am not destitute. There is always something I can give.

I will love and treasure those in my family even more this year than last. My heart is enlarged moment by moment in its capability to sustain love because I have been taught how to love by Someone who first loved me. I will be thankful for all of those blessings that have been given to my life - my dad, my husband, my son, my grandson, and countless other family members, extended family members, and friends. I will not fail to show them how much I care, how much I love, how much I need and want them in my life. I will continue to be thankful for all those loved ones who have made the journey heavenward. Their impact on my life continues to steady my feet and provoke a response of love from deep within my heart.

I am resolute in these small, day by day, step by step, attainable goals. These are the everyday goals that are not so easily forgotten and not so easily cast aside. They are a constant presence and deserve my complete attention.

Yes, I am resolute in these things. Perhaps I do believe in resolutions after all - just not the emotion of the moment ones that hold little importance in the grand scheme of things. Love, kindness, compassion, and the like - these are the resolutions that count. Will you make them with me? It's really quite simple: take the first step, and the next, and the next.

"But when the Holy Spirit controls our lives he will produce this kind of fruit in us: love, joy, peace, patience, kindness, goodness, faithfulness, gentleness and self-control; and here there is no conflict with Jewish laws."
(Galatians 5:22-23 Living Bible)

Let the Healing Begin!

It's December 31st. It's time to let the healing power of the coming new year begin.

Don't forget the past, but reflect on it for its lessons and joy and not the mistakes you feel you have made. Mistakes are nothing more than lessons in humility and stepping stones to the next thing on your journey. Reflection is not for the what-ifs or the what-could-have-been but for the purpose of letting go of that which causes shame, pain, and bitterness. Those things are not ours to hold. We will find that they are gone as soon as we open our hands to release them, even as our hands are filled with encouragement for what lies ahead.

Don't focus too much on today, thereby lacking anticipation for the future. Today should simply hold your efforts to become better and your steadfast hope for tomorrow. At the same time, be sure to treasure the truly important people and things that may be here today but not tomorrow.

Don't rely on tomorrow, for it is not promised. This doesn't mean we shouldn't prepare for it, since preparation shows the hope that lives in us as well as a serious taking of our responsibility. Above all, we should always be preparing for the tomorrow that is everlasting - the tomorrow where our true hope lies.

This new year is just like any other new year and yet completely different. We will pass from one year into the next, whether or not we feel we're ready just as we have in the past. However, the year will hold new opportunities, new twists and turns in our journey, and new people that are placed in our lives to help us grow, give, love, be kind, and live in humility. The experiences may be similar to those of the past but will not be exactly the same. Never enter a new year saying, "Oh, I've been here before." You haven't. It's a new chance, a new beginning, and a new chapter to write. You hold the power of the pen. The outcome is within your scope of control when it comes to spending your time and treasure and your responses to whatever comes your way. Be sure to seek wisdom for the trip.

Determine that this will be your year of "more" - more of the things that really matter and more of the things that make you who you are. Don't wear a mask or pretend at life. Live it honestly and abundantly as it has been given to you as a gift. Pass on all the gifts you are given to others. Make someone smile. Make someone comfortable. Make someone feel needed, accepted, and loved. Live a life full of praise and generosity.

I wish each one of you, my dear readers, a New Year filled with such abundance of healing, love, joy, and hope that you cannot possibly hold it all and have no choice but to give it to others. And I thank you with a heart full of love and gratitude for your love and support each day.

Let's bring in this new year with full hearts, open hands and a shout of praise!

"Praise the Lord! Praise God in His holy place! Praise Him in the heavens of His power! Praise Him for

His great works! Praise Him for all His greatness! Praise Him with the sound of a horn. Praise Him with harps. Praise Him with timbrels and dancing. Praise Him with strings and horns. Praise Him with loud sounds. Praise Him with loud and clear sounds. Let everything that has breath praise the Lord. Praise the Lord!"
(Psalm 150 New Life Version)

Surrender

I woke with my mind whirling this morning. My first thought was that it's January 8th. One year ago today, we made the trek through heavy snow falling to Indiantown Gap National Cemetery to commit Momma's ashes to the loving care of the military caretakers at the cemetery. It was a beautiful (but very cold) ceremony attended by family members, both those by blood and those given us by God's grace and mercy.

My second thought was of the light coating of ice and snow that had fallen last night. Daddy is insistent that he will be going to breakfast with his American Legion friends this morning. I cannot deter him. My prayers immediately went up for his safety both in walking and driving as well as a good time of fellowship between these wonderful men.

Next were grateful thoughts for the slowly quieting environment here after a month of holiday preparations and celebrations at home and the close of year-end accounting at work. I've been praying for a sense of normalcy to return (whatever that is; around here it's just a setting on the dryer!) after all of that. It seems so difficult sometimes for us to quiet our busy minds and hands during what should be a season of reflection and deep gratitude, doesn't it?

Over and above all of this was the thought of my great need for Jesus. The word "surrender" keeps bouncing through the cobwebs.

The past week here has been filled with memories of last year and the last four days that I spent away from home and with Momma and Daddy as I helped care for their needs. At any given point, I relived every moment, ran through every conversation, and cried over the fresh grief of relinquishing her into the arms of Jesus once again. Relinquish... just another word for surrender. There it is again.

It occurs to me that I cannot surrender anything without God's help. I can try, but my efforts are useless without His mercy flowing over me to ease the difficulty of letting go and His grace filling me to replace the seeming loss of surrender with joy.

Some things are easier to surrender than others. Difficulties and trials are easily given over to His hand (most of the time), while joys and pleasures are held firmly grasped in a tight fist. Yes, I still need His help (and seek it) to release my cares, concerns, and troubles. However, my need of His urging, understanding, and patience to release all He has given into my life is so much greater. I'm selfish. I want to hold onto those good things for myself, relish the feeling they give, turn them over and under while gazing upon them with a smile, and put them into "storage" for when I may need them most. I want to feel good all the time, and when I don't, I want to be able to have that boost of happiness the good things bring to my life. Why would I surrender that?

Because Jesus surrendered all for me, down to His last drop of blood and His last breath, that's why.

Because the Father will always provide the joy

needed in my life (as well as everything else), that's why.

Because the sacrifice of praise and thanksgiving means surrendering *all of it*, that's why.

Because I claim to love God, Jesus, and the Holy Spirit with my whole heart, that's why.

"But seek first His kingdom and His righteousness, and all these things will be added to you," that's why.

I seek, but in seeking I must surrender as well. The two go hand in hand. Just because I have a hard time remembering that in the good times doesn't negate the truth of it.

And so, in this moment when the season of celebrating Your birth has just passed and the season of renewal is at hand, Jesus, I need You. I need You to remind me, encourage me, and help me to open my tightly closed fists and surrender all. I need You to help me understand that the joy of letting go is even greater than the joy of holding on. After all, it's not mine to begin with, is it?

"I surrender all; I surrender all. All to Thee, my blessed Savior, I surrender all."*

"The earth is the Lord's, and everything in it, the world, and all who live in it; for He founded it on the seas and established it on the waters."
(Psalm 24:1-2 NIV)

* I Surrender All written by Judson W. Van DeVenter, put to music by Winfield S. Weeden, and first published in "Gospel Songs of Grace and Glory", 1896

Reborn Through Water

My husband and I live a life that is incredibly hectic and taxing at times. This is not because we want life to be this way but simply by necessity. In other words, our schedules are not of our choosing and are not filled with frivolous and unneeded or unwarranted activity. Instead, they are filled with activities required by the commitments of love and compassion. It is a sometimes difficult but always rewarding life. It can, however, be an overwhelming life as well.

Being overwhelmed requires refreshment and renewal. For us, that means spending time by the water. I'm not talking about a vacation, although being near the ocean is preferable when we get the rare opportunity to get away. I'm talking about a few stolen moments or hours sitting or walking by the water's edge and letting its calm, cleansing ambience infuse us to the depths of our spirits. It doesn't really matter what the body of water is. Our go-to place is a lake about twenty minutes from our home. We have been there in all seasons and the result is always the same. We marvel at the beauty, the sounds, the way the sunshine creates a thousand diamonds on the water's surface, and the wildlife. We sit, stand, or walk silently as the undemanding surroundings bring peace to our inmost being. It's truly a gift from God.

It is the same whether we walk by a lake, pond, creek, river, or ocean. All water is cleansing and restorative for us. Our time by the water takes what is mucky, dingy, exhausted, and overburdened in us and recharges our spirits, giving them stainless, shiny, invigorated, and liberated life once again. It is almost like this is what our Father intended when He created the bodies of water on the earth. Judging by our experience, I am quite sure this is at least one of the things He intended.

The Jordan River was a flurry of activity in the days of John the Baptist. As he proclaimed that the Kingdom of Heaven was near, many came to be baptized in the Jordan's waters as they confessed their sin. They wanted to be cleansed. They wanted to be unburdened. They wanted to be renewed in the waters. *They no longer wanted to be dead in their sin but desired God to grant them new life.* Even Jesus came to the Jordan to be baptized in its waters, and while John questioned this because he knew who Jesus really was, he did it to fulfill the law.

The disciples of Christ continued the practice of baptism after John's purpose had been fulfilled. Many more were made clean by the symbolic depths of the Jordan and other bodies of water in Israel. Today, baptism continues as a symbol of our faith in and commitment to Jesus. We are made new in Him as we rise from the water. We receive the promise of rebirth and eternal life as the Holy Spirit enters in and baptizes our spirits with guidance, wisdom, and power.

Follow the urging of the Holy Spirit in you. This earthly life will become tiring and overwhelming at times, whether by necessity or your own making. The world will leave its dirt and dinge on you. That's when your Father will beckon you to be recharged. That's when He will call you to the water where you can experience renewal. That's when the death that is hounding your spirit can be banished, and you can brought back to life.

"Or have you forgotten that all of us who were immersed into union with Jesus, the Anointed One, were immersed into union with his death? Sharing in his death by our baptism means that we were co-buried and entombed with him, so that when the Father's glory raised Christ from the dead, we were also raised with him. We have been co-resurrected with him so that we could be empowered to walk in the freshness of new life. For since we are permanently grafted into him to experience a death like his, then we are permanently grafted into him to experience a resurrection like his and the new life that it imparts. Could it be any clearer that our former identity is now and forever deprived of its power? For we were co-crucified with him to dismantle the stronghold of sin within us, so that we would not continue to live one moment longer submitted to sin's power."
(Romans 6:3-6 The Passion Translation)

The Life of Faith

A Life, Not Just a Season

Faith can never be just a season. Faith is the entirety of life. All the seasons in this book - Lessons Learned, Grace, Thanksgiving, and Anticipation, Giving, Joy and Renewal - are purposefully and intricately woven together to create a life of faith. Each one builds upon the one before. Each one depends on the others for existence. Each one is fortified on the foundation of Jesus Christ. God gives each one of us a measure of faith that is just enough. It's never too small or too big. It is always exactly what we need and tailored to exactly what we are facing.

I look at times in my life and can see where faith seemed to waver but was actually being grown. I can see that my faith was never unfounded. I admit there were times I questioned things and not just the reasoning behind any given situation. I questioned why I should bother having faith. The trial I was facing at that moment seemed impossible and heartbreaking. The answer was always the same. I should have faith because in circumstances prior to the terrifying one I was now facing, God had never failed me. He always came through. Sometimes the answer and solution came immediately. Sometimes it took a bit longer. Sometimes the wait seemed eternal. *However, God always came through with the best possible outcome at the perfect time, and I realized I had the perfect amount of faith to see it through.*

The faithful life is not an easy one. There are moments when the waiting will get the better of you.

There are seconds that will seem like hours and days that will seem like months. I remember one particular answer to prayer that was years in coming to fruition. It didn't just seem like years; it was actually years. I fully believe that God was waiting. He was waiting to see if I would give up the fight. He was waiting to see if I would release it to Him without taking it back again. He was waiting to see if I trusted Him. He was growing and stretching my faith into the right size for the moment at hand. Oh, how wonderful it was when the answer came! I could not have imagined such joy. So, when that time seems to stretch into oblivion, don't give up and don't stop believing. Your joy *will* be complete. Your hope *will* be realized. Your faith will be grown, and just like every time before that moment, God will come through for you in the way that is best for you and everyone involved.

Faith is standing in the face of the darkness and declaring that there is light *even as you struggle to see*. Faith is knowing we never walk through anything alone. Faith is the surety that God is right there even though we can't see Him. Faith is an abiding hope that will never disappoint us.

A life of faith is an imperfect and beautiful life well lived that shines as a bright ray of light for others and draws them to the Savior who loves them beyond all comprehension.

"The apostles said to the Lord, 'Increase our faith!' He replied, 'If you have faith as small as a mustard seed, you can say to this mulberry tree, 'Be uprooted and planted in the sea,' and it will obey you.'" **(Luke 17:5-6 NIV)**

What Came First?

No, I'm not referring to the chicken or the egg, although that question has been batted about humorously almost since time began. What I'm referring to is gratitude and faith. It's a deep and difficult question. In the context of this book, I listed thanksgiving as a season that, when added to all the others, creates a life of faith. Yet I'm not so sure that faith doesn't enable thankfulness. I'm thinking as I write this that it doesn't matter. Much like the chicken and the egg, you need both to make a life complete and fruitful.

It doesn't matter what point of your life you're facing, where your journey has landed you, or what your desired destination may be. You will need faith to take the first step and all steps afterward. You will need faith to navigate the pitfalls, twists, turns, and darkened spaces. You will also need to be thankful - not just for the moments the sun shines and you get through the coagulated jungle of circumstances but for the problems and circumstances themselves. An attitude that stands firmly yet humbly, trusts God with all that is in you, *and* is thankful for every moment, good and bad, is necessary to reaching the goal that is intended for you. Again, you might ask which is more important and which should come first. The truth is that you cannot have faith without gratitude for all things, knowing they are orchestrated by the Father, and you cannot have gratitude for all things without faith that your heavenly

Father is walking with you and will see you to the other side of them.

A life of faith doesn't just happen. It is enabled by the grace of God planting that mustard seed in your heart and spirit. Even that is not the entirety of gaining and maintaining faith. You must do your part as God continues to do His. He can give you all the ability He desires, but if you don't access it and use it, its fruit will not blossom in your life. Scripture tells us that the mustard seed you have been given can move mountains. Imagine what more it can do if you nurture it and allow it to grow!

Father God will bring about opportunities to stretch and grow the faith you have been given. It is your choice whether you allow that growth to take place or curl up in a corner somewhere and let the waves carry you without actively participating in the process. You will get to the shore either way. The difference in participating or not comes in the next wave that will overtake you - and be sure of this: there will be a next wave, and a next, and a next because we live in a broken world. The difference will show in how you respond to each circumstance as it arrives. If your faith is nurtured, growing, and fruitful, you will ride those waves and arrive on the shore in triumph, if a little bit battered by the wind with sand in your hair as well as in between your toes. If not, you might be tossed upon them in your fear. If you ride them in triumph, you will be an example for others who are searching for that joy and peace you've been given as a result of that mustard seed. If not, they may be left questioning where God is in all of this. The choice is yours; the choice is mine.

I suppose the importance of which came first depends on our outlook. It doesn't really matter which came first. God has given us all of these things so that we might have abundant life and the tools we need to live that life. We simply need to remember these things:

Stand firmly but humbly.
Trust God.
Walk in the path He provides.
Be thankful for *everything*.
Allow Him to work in and through you.
Keep your eyes on the goal He has purposed.

"Therefore, just as you received Christ Jesus as Lord, continue to live your lives in him, rooted and built up in him and firm in your faith just as you were taught, and overflowing with thankfulness."
(Colossians 2:6-7 New English Translation)

Do You Believe?

As I write this, it is Monday - the day after Easter. Holidays over the past few years are very bittersweet for us. Many times it doesn't hit me how bittersweet until after the holidays have passed. Usually, life gets so caught up in the preparation for the grand event, I don't have time to think about the downside of loved ones no longer being with us until after the fact. Easter Sunday was no exception in some ways but a huge exception in others.

Michael decided he wanted to give me a break this year and take Daddy and me out to dinner. He made reservations at a local country hotel for the three of us. There was no time of preparation for the huge family meal that I am accustomed to cooking. Instead, there was just the relaxation and time to reflect on what this Sunday was all about. That also left me way too much time to think about the people I missed. It seemed the two things were exclusive in my mind when, indeed, they are intertwined.

After church, we made the trip with Daddy to the Indiantown Gap National Cemetery to take an Easter lily and daffodils to place on Momma's grave. The skies that were grey when we left brightened considerably by the time we arrived at our destination an hour later. We spent some time looking at her marker, each consumed with our own thoughts and making small talk while looking at the area a short distance behind her that was being cleared to make room for more markers when they were needed.

350

Once back in the car, we left for our next destination - Salem Berne Church, where Michael's parents are buried. The more we traveled the interstate towards that cemetery and home, the more the sun began to fade behind clouds once again.

I mentioned that fact to Michael. He replied that he noticed the same thing. "Momma brought the sunshine for us," I said. He smiled. Then I added, "I'd rather have her." The tears I'd been holding back quietly fell.

The remainder of the drive was mostly silent. That is, it was silent until I asked him to hurry by a truck he was in the process of passing because I wanted to take a picture. With that loving look he always gives me when he thinks I'm a bit crazy, he complied.

Arriving at Salem Berne, we took the laced-edged pink tulips from the car we'd brought for Mom and Dad. We placed them in front of the gravestone and manipulated the pot into the ground so it wouldn't blow over in the wind. We then visited Michael's grandparents, great-grandparents, aunt and uncle, and cousin.

As we walked back to the car, the memories poured forth. The tears followed. This day was so difficult and seemed so filled with loss.

It was time to leave so we would return in time for dinner. We arrived just in time for our reservations. The sense of loss retreated as gratitude for Daddy and Michael and our time together pushed to the forefront. After a delicious family-style meal and short drive home, our long trip came to an end.

Upon arriving home, Daddy decided to rest, and Michael went out to cut the grass and work off some of the three plates from dinner. He's always been able to eat like that and never gain even an ounce (a small and longstanding bone of teasing contention between us).

That left me to my own thoughts. The sense of loss inevitably followed. I looked at the picture I had taken on the way home. The structure of the clouds had caught my attention because of the prominence of one, causing me to reach for my phone.

There was an almost perfectly circular cloud against a bank of others. Looking at it again, I realized it quite resembled a large stone. You know, the type that the angel rolled away from the tomb. A light of joy broke through the darkness of my loss.

You see, the stone was not just rolled away from the tomb in which Jesus laid. It was rolled away from every tomb of every person we were missing today because they believed in Him with abiding, deep faith. And so, why was I looking for the living among the dead?

Yes, we had suffered loss, but the loss was not permanent by any means. They are alive and well in Christ. I was focusing on the ground instead of looking up. But when I raised my eyes, oh, what joy awaited there!

We will miss them until the moment our own stones are rolled away and we see them again, but I need not let the sadness overtake the joy that is rooted so deeply in the faith modeled for all of us by Momma, my mother-in-law, and father-in-law. I need only look to the heavens and see what God has to show me instead of concentrating my gaze on the ground on which I stand.

None of us needs to remain in the overwhelming presence of sadness. All of us can have the joy that is purposed for our lives. We all need only to look up as I did. God has something to show us. For me, it was a simple circular cloud resembling the stone at the tomb. For you, it may be something completely different. The point is that it's there. All we need to do is open our eyes and let our hearts see. All we need to do is live in His grace through faith.

"Jesus said, 'Your brother will be raised up.' Martha replied, 'I know that he will be raised up in the resurrection at the end of time.' 'You don't have to wait for the End. I am, right now, Resurrection and Life. The one who believes in me, even though he or she dies, will live. And everyone who lives believing in me does not ultimately die at all. Do you believe this?'"
(John 11:23-26 The Message)

Worry or Well-Being?

      I'm writing this to myself as much as for anyone else this morning. "New year, new me" - not so much. I woke with that familiar and unwelcome feeling of a salad shaker causing tumult on my insides this morning. Worry over things that could but haven't happened wound its way into the recesses of my mind like an octopus' tentacles. I can almost feel the little suction cups trying to latch on and wipe out anything good that is worthy to ponder while trying to leave behind worst-case scenarios that fluster and frustrate me and make me fearful. Did I mention that I absolutely hate octopuses? Even a picture of one grosses me out and raises the tiny hairs on the back of my neck.

      Worry is the single most harmful and useless thing that can ruin a day and threaten days going forward, particularly worry about things that are beyond our control. And even if things are within the scope of our control, worry won't change them. As a matter of fact, worry will simply sap our strength and mental capability to do what needs to be done to change things.

      Worry is a choice we make that overrides choices we should and want to make. Worry won't resolve a problem, but it could create new ones. We cannot worry away a financial problem, an illness, a relationship chasm, or the behavior of others. We can, however, worry away our physical, emotional, and spiritual well-being.

So, if we - if I - know all these things, why do we allow ourselves to do it? Why don't we stop ourselves and concentrate on that which is positive, worthy, wise, and beautiful?

Because we make the wrong choice. Yes, that's a simple and blunt answer, but it's the honest answer.

We allow our minds to go where they shouldn't instead of turning left or right at the first sign, and then we're entangled in the tentacles from which it's extremely difficult to free ourselves. And so we just give up and give in to the self-imposed pain. I call that self-implosion. I'm quite familiar with it.

The right choice is to be practical. Ask yourself the following questions about worry: Is it worth it? Will it help me control this? Will it help me change this? The answer is no to all three.

Once the answer of no is determined, it's time to move on to better things, starting with clearing our minds and hearts of this harmful enemy called "worry."

Worship starts with the same three letters as worry but ends quite differently, both in spelling and results. It will still wind its way around your mind and heart, but not in strangulation the way worry's tentacles will. It will fill you on the inside, but not in salad shaker style. And I'm quite certain that worship doesn't look anything like that octopus that makes me go, "Ew!"

While worship may not directly solve whatever situation your mind has conjured, it will gently release the hold of those suction cups and leave calm and clear thinking in its wake. It will light up those recesses and keep you from stumbling in the darkness of a spirit collapsed by self-implosion. It will remind you of the all-encompassing power of the One in Whom you have placed your faith. That faith is not unfounded and is well placed. It will lead you into your day focusing on the worthiness of a God Who can change, control, and cure whatever is threatening you or those you love. He is going to do that *or* He is going to walk you safely through it for your good. From there, you will know what you should or shouldn't and can or cannot do. From there, you might even find some joy in the journey.

"Are not two sparrows sold for a penny? Yet not one of them will fall to the ground outside your Father's care. And even the very hairs of your head are all numbered. So don't be afraid; you are worth more than many sparrows."
(Matthew 10:29-31 NIV)

356

But I Can't See It

"I'll believe it when I see it." How many times have we said or thought those words? We want evidence of what we're supposed to believe. We want tangible proof that something exists. We want to know that our trust is well founded in something or someone that won't let us down. I have some not-so-hot news for all of us: everything and everyone on this earth will let us down at some point. Yes, *everything and everyone.* It's basic human nature. It's the nature of a broken world and an earth flawed not by its Creator but by its residents.

There was a time when earth was perfect. The Garden of Eden was created in perfection for its inhabitants. The earth and everything in it, created by Father God, was *very good.* Then someone got it into their heads to reach beyond their grasp, disobey the rules, and trust in a snake in the grass. Trust turned to doubt. Perfection was marred. We were banned from the garden with our "we know better" attitudes and our arrogance, and angels were placed to guard the entrance to paradise and keep humankind from entering.

The good news is that God had already planned for such things. He knew in giving us free will that we would make the wrong choices. He was hoping we would make the right ones and respond to His love for us with love and obedience in return, but He knew we would need saving at some point. He knew He would have to redeem us. Praise the Lord; He knew and acted accordingly!

The bad news is that we haven't changed. We still think we know better. We still live by what we can see. We still hear the voice of the snake in the grass and listen to it. We have seen the results of wrong choices, not trusting in Him, and going our own way, yet we still question. Even those of us who are "seasoned" believers have our moments. We have to cast those moments to the wind and let them be blown away from us.

But how do we know, *with certainty,* that God is there? How do we know He is with us in any given moment, good or bad circumstance, right or wrong choice, or day-to-day routine? We know because He has said so. He promises to "watch over your life" and "your coming and going now and forevermore" (Psalm 121).   And here's the great news: God cannot break a promise. Breaking a promise would be lying, and God, by His very nature, cannot lie.

I know that the temptation is to say, "But I can't see Him." The only answer I have is something I was told as a child. You can't see the wind, can you? Yet you know it exists. You can see what it does - leaves flying, trees bending, rain going sideways - the evidence of the wind is endless. You can't see the air, but you know it exists because you are breathing and it keeps you alive. For me, sometimes the simplest explanations are the best. You can't refute those things. Food for thought: can you refute the evidence of God's hand in your life? I know that I can't. Its nature is too vivid to be blinded to it.

I am not saying that I never doubt. I certainly (and sadly) do. Yet even in my doubt I always believe, because even in my darkest moments I am able to dimly remember the moments of light that came before this. I *know* He is real. I *know* He is with me. I *know* He is there even if I can't see Him or feel Him right now. Why? Because He's always been there before!

In today's world, we no longer have the mantra "I'll believe it when I see it" as much as we once did. Technology has caused us to trust in many things without seeing them first. Online shopping, social media, and the like have created an environment where we buy and accept things without seeing them in person. Some may think this is a good thing. For me, the jury is still out on that since we live in a broken society. The point is this: if we can be so quick to trust selecting an item, paying for it, and having it delivered without seeing evidence of it (other than on a screen), then why can we not trust in the Creator of the universe, the Redeemer of our souls, the Author and Finisher of our faith, and the One to Whom we shall return? If we have faith in technology and all it offers, why would our faith waver in the One who knows us best, has our best interests in His heart, and loves us more than anyone ever could?

The things and people of this earth will surely disappoint. Our Father in heaven will not. We need to be sure that we don't misplace our faith. There is only one thing that will not pass away - the Word of the Father and all He has ordained in it. God will never change.

Human trust is a leap from the mountaintop, hoping you will float to the ground and land with ease, uninjured and on your feet. Faith is a spiritual leap from the same mountaintop, knowing you will reach the ground and, even if broken in some way on the descent, be lifted up into the arms of Father God as He lovingly heals you and prepares you for what comes next, expanding that faith, and moving you towards purpose.

Yes, we need to have the human characteristic of trust to some degree. However, we need to have faith to the furthest degree. In the end, faith is what will lead us home and be counted as righteousness to us.

"This is what the Scripture says: 'The word is near you; it is in your mouth and in your heart.' That is the teaching of faith that we are telling. If you declare with your mouth, 'Jesus is Lord,' and if you believe in your heart that God raised Jesus from the dead, you will be saved. We believe with our hearts, and so we are made right with God. And we declare with our mouths that we believe, and so we are saved. As the Scripture says, 'Anyone who trusts in him will never be disappointed.'"
(Romans 10:8-11 NCV)

"The fundamental fact of existence is that this trust in God, this faith, is the firm foundation under everything that makes life worth living. It's our handle on what we can't see. The act of faith is what distinguished our ancestors, set them above the crowd. By faith, we see the world called into existence by God's

word, what we see created by what we don't see."
(Hebrews 11:1-3 The Message)

Where or Who Is Your Source?

We are all seeking provision. We need strength to continue on our paths, the ability to cope with whatever each day holds, rest when we feel we just can't close our eyes, funds to enable us to pay bills and put food on our tables, solutions to problems we encounter, and simply the provision of another breath, followed by another and another.

There are times when it seems provision for our needs is far in the distance. There are just as many times when we don't know if we'll make it through to the other side of any given need. I suppose it depends on the sources to which we look to satisfy our needs. I know it depends upon where we place our faith.

In 2005, Michael and I made the choice for me to not work other than an early morning paper route since my mom was diagnosed with breast cancer. In actuality, there really was no choice. We wanted and needed to care for the wonderful woman who had cared for us for so many years. It would be a year-long journey.

The numbers didn't add up in any sense of the word. Least of all was the financial strain to our budget. Every time we sat down to run through the payment amounts for monthly bills and daily physical needs, it seemed the end result was in the negative. The other and more important totals that didn't seem to fall in our favor were those of time, strength, and mental and emotional coping capabilities. It was a scary time, and that's an understatement.

Yet here's the thing: each month the bills were paid on time and in full. There may have been only a few dollars left in our account afterward, but they were paid. Every time exhaustion set in with the myriad of treatments, doctor visits, hospital stays, and the routine day-to-day care Momma required, rest and renewal came just when we thought we couldn't take another step. Emotional and mental breakdowns threatened on what seemed like a daily basis from the crushing weight of it all, but time and again were quelled by one or the other of us listening, calming, and holding on to the other so that the first priority of caring for the needs of my parents could continue. The biggest provision of all was that of her healing.

The provision seemed far away and lacking, but it wasn't. It was always there - on time, never early and never late.

The same proved itself true during the first nine months of 2012 when she faced several other health crises after knee replacement surgery. Falls and repeated rehab visits, medication errors, infections, and chronic muscular weakness leading to more rehab visits gave us circumstances that seemed insurmountable. They weren't. We just needed to look in the right direction. The greatest provision was at the end of that nine months when I watched her walk up the street for the first time using her walker and with her therapist at her side.

Again in 2016, when our son was in a serious auto accident requiring surgery to repair a badly broken leg as well as months of therapy to be able to walk again and a total recovery time of nine months at home, it seemed the weight of the burden would crush each one of us. Financially it meant Michael and I trying to support our own household as well as helping our son so that he wouldn't lose his home. Disability just couldn't cover everything. We don't know how the accounting worked out, but it did. Emotionally and mentally, it meant coping with the fact that we had almost lost our only child and now had to watch him struggle to regain his strength, ability to walk, and deal with the ensuing anxiety and PTSD that set in after the accident. We were lost. There wasn't much we could do to help him heal. It was frustrating and heartbreaking. Our tears could have filled the world's oceans. What do you do when it seems all you can do is hold the hand of your child and tell him you love him? What do you do when you don't feel like that is enough?

You look beyond the circumstance. You look purposefully for provision. *You wait for it to come because you know it has always come in the past.* You trust the source even as you fret, cry, and sometimes scream for help.

Provision came. Jason's body healed, and so did his mind. Today my son can hike the trails and riverbed at Hawk Mountain and does so frequently.

We are all looking for provision, no matter the depth and seriousness of the circumstance. While it seems a simple solution (or maybe not), the only thing we can do is trust. Trusting means falling to our knees, looking up, crying out, and waiting. It means placing our faith in the only One who has our backs and loves us fully. Our Source will not be late in answering. Whether it be funding, rest, peace, healing, patience, or sustenance, the provision will arrive just at the right moment.

"So then, forsake your worries! Why would you say, 'What will we eat?' or 'What will we drink?' or 'What will we wear?' For that is what the unbelievers chase after. Doesn't your heavenly Father already know the things your bodies require? So above all, constantly chase after the realm of God's kingdom and the righteousness that proceeds from him. Then all these less important things will be given to you abundantly. Refuse to worry about tomorrow, but deal with each challenge that comes your way, one day at a time. Tomorrow will take care of itself."
(Matthew 6:31-34 The Passion Translation)

You May Not Be Where You Belong!

Did you ever feel like you're not where you're supposed to be? Chances are that's because it's the truth. We seldom like to see that kind of truth. We like to stay where we're comfortable and where we're around people and things we like. Or perhaps we like where we are because changing course takes effort we don't want to expend. I suppose that is a matter of comfort as well. Either way, to stay in that place where we're not supposed to be is misguided. As a matter of fact, it's downright disobedient.

We tend to ignore the subtle promptings of that still, small voice when it's time to get up and move. We put them down to imagination, or too little sleep the night before, or that we were surely mistaken, because we are convinced this is certainly where we should be. We push them aside, no matter how often they try to get our attention, because *we* know what's best, and this (whatever this is) is best for us. The stars haven't aligned perfectly enough just yet to facilitate the ideal move. Meanwhile, the little things get tougher, our tempers (yes, we have them) get shorter, and our sleeplessness and restlessness grow because of - yes, I'm going to say it - our laziness. Oh no, she didn't! Yes, I did. When we're comfortable we become lazy. Many times, when we choose not to move, it suddenly becomes apparent that comfortable won't be as comfortable anymore *because we chose to disobey.*

Imagine what a different world this might be if people stayed where they were simply for convenience and comfort. Children would never leave home. As a parent, I find this unimaginable. Don't get me wrong; I love my son with my whole being. However, once he reached adulthood with his own opinions and ways of doing things, I breathed a sigh of relief when he moved into his own place. (I love you, Jas!)

But seriously, let's take someone like Abraham. God said, "Go to the land I will show you." It wasn't a request. Yes, Abraham had free will just as we do, but I don't think he would have flourished had he been disobedient, not to mention the fact that the nation of Israel as we know it would be a different people. The genealogy would be completely different, and the name Abraham not even known as someone of importance in history.

Moving on to Moses, the same concept applies. He could have declined. As a matter of fact, he tried to with many excuses. Don't we all? "We're not special enough," "We aren't well spoken or well written," "We're clumsy," "We're unskilled," or the ever-childish whining attempt, "But God! I don't want to!" The list goes on and on. Had Moses decided to be disobedient, who knows how much longer the Israelites would have been enslaved in Egypt?

We all know what happened to Jonah when he didn't move as directed. Instead of going to Nineveh, he tried running away. He moved, just not in the way he was supposed to move. He ended up in the belly of a large fish for three days before being vomited onto the shore. How comfortable does that sound?

Fear, comfort, laziness, and the like should never stop us from listening to that prodding that tells us to move. There's so much we miss out on by standing still. We need to be more like David was as a boy - motivated, faithful, and courageous. Grab that sling and those stones to conquer the giants and move. Put one foot in front of the other and leave the place in which you don't belong for the place you do.

Will God continue with His plans if you disobey? Of course He will. He relented to allow Aaron to accompany Moses as spokesman since Moses felt he was slow of speech. He fulfilled the promise to give Abraham descendants as numerous as the grains of sand through the child of His promise, Isaac, even though Abraham and Sarah tried to help things along by him having Ishmael with Hagar. He can and will use whatever choice you make to further His purpose and His Kingdom. Should you choose disobedience, He is quite capable of moving on to the next person who is willing to be obedient, or taking the long way around with you until His purpose is fulfilled. He might even let you stay in your comfortable world to let you figure out for yourself that you're missing out on the blessing of being used by Him.

Or He might see that you end up in the belly of a huge fish and later vomited onto the shore to help you understand that you needed to do what He asked of you. Now that doesn't sound comfortable at all; it just sounds disgusting.

Of course, there's always the "wandering around in the wilderness for 40 years" option. That doesn't sound too comfortable to me either.

While moving when told without explanation might be difficult, we must step forward while relying on a few things. The first is faith. We may not know where we're moving, but God does. The second is humility. We only think we know what is best. The truth is that we don't, but our Father does. The third is a willingness to obey. God will use whatever choice we make and still accomplish His will. Don't we want to be a part of that?

Even better, rely on this simple statement of fact: obedience is truly and simply a matter of love. It is also a matter of faith.

"Jesus replied, 'All who love me will do what I say. My Father will love them, and we will come and make our home with each of them. Anyone who doesn't love me will not obey me. And remember, my words are not my own. What I am telling you is from the Father who sent me.'"
(John 14:23-24 NLT)

"These people all died having faith in God. They did not receive what God had promised to them. But they could see far ahead to all the things God promised and they were glad for them. They knew they were strangers here. This earth was not their home. People who say these things show they are looking for a country of their own. They did not think about the country they had come from. If they had, they might have gone back. But they wanted a better country. And so God is not ashamed to be called their God. He has made a city for them."
(Hebrews 11:13-16 New Life Version)

It Will Be Accomplished

Have faith! Whatever the Father wishes to be accomplished will be done. Whether it's a task you feel needs to be completed, words you feel need to be said to benefit and encourage someone, or anything else, His purpose will be served - even when it may not seem so.

This comes from a simple realization that has washed over me recently. It seems that Facebook has changed the way it handles pages they consider business pages, which is what they consider my author page. When I first started this page several years ago, my posts appeared in the newsfeed whenever I wrote them. The "reach" (number of people who saw my posts) ranged from 150 to 200 or so and rose from there depending on the number of people who shared these posts. As stock in the company became more popular and the need to keep stockholders happy rose, there was a direct correlation to the "reach" of my posts dropping.

After speaking to others who have specific pages (some authors, some churches, and some small businesses), I learned that in order to consistently reach more of the people who have liked my page and perhaps some outside of the page's likes through the newsfeed, I would need to spend money. Paying Facebook for newsfeed presence would extend my reach according to their "encouragement" to do so. This does, after all, make sense since they are a business who must maintain certain financial numbers to satisfy their supporters. For me, however, spending money to have my posts show up in everyone's newsfeed is not something I am willing to do. My writing is more of a hobby, for lack of a better word, than a business, even if it is inspired by and a gift to me from God. I suppose it is a business - God's business. I work solely for Him. And so, if people want to see everything I write for this page, they would have to visit the page daily to see if there is anything new.

This is where the faith part enters the picture. I have never made it a secret as to why I write and share publicly. It started as a desire to honor my parents by telling their story in "Grace - A View From the Mountaintop." I honestly thought that was the end of it. However, God always has ideas and thoughts that are much different from ours. He "graduated" me to public awareness in the form of stories about the homeless community. And finally, He entrusted me with the task of putting out the words He gave me in the form of inspirational writings - some of those writings being ones that actually came into being 15 years before being published.

I am grateful. I am humbled. I am overwhelmed by His trust in me to do what He has willed.

Faith has taught me that I am not everyone's cup of tea, but that's okay. It has taught me that whether 200 or 2 see any given thing I write, whether published or posted, they are exactly the people He has desired to reach in some way. It has also taught me that my heart's desires can be achieved (as in the desire to honor my mom and dad) without notoriety, popularity, or reaching the New York Times Best Seller list.

I know my faith is well placed. There have been those who have come to me to let me know they read something on my page or in one of my books that they really needed deep in their soul on that particular day.

Again, I am humbled. All glory to Him who sits on the Throne yet has chosen to use me for something special. Amen!

Have faith! You won't be disappointed.

"As the rain and the snow come down from heaven, and do not return to it without watering the earth and making it bud and flourish, so that it yields seed for the sower and bread for the eater, so is my word that goes out from My mouth: It will not return to me empty, but will accomplish what I desire and achieve the purpose for which I sent it."
(Isaiah 55:10-11 NIV)

Absolute and Unwavering

There comes a time in the life of faith that belief graduates from an intensity of rare to occasional, occasional to most of the time, and finally, from most of the time to absolute. I don't know if the change in intensity is the result of age, experience, necessity, or a combination of all of those. I do know that it happens. Scripture is filled with references to absolute belief - the unwavering faith of people who had come to a crossroads of some sort in their lives. There are records in the Bible of people who would do anything to gain the attention of Jesus, and if they couldn't gain His attention because of the enormous crowds around them, they would fight their way through those crowds or yell to Him from the side of the road with one simple hope - to touch the hem of His robe or have Him touch them in healing intent. What did they think a simple touch of fabric was going to do, or even the simple touch of His hand? They didn't think it would do anything; they *knew.* They knew that simple touch would bring healing (Mark 5:21-43, Matthew 20:29-34). In other cases, they simply asked for a life-altering word to be spoken. They made it clear that they knew His time was valuable and they didn't deserve the consideration of Him traveling to make a house call. They simply asked for a word from His mouth. What did they think a word would do? They didn't think it would do anything; again, they *knew.* They knew the words from the mouth of the Son of God would bring restoration and life (Matthew 8: 13). These people possessed absolute and unwavering faith in Jesus Christ.

I fully believe my mother had that absolute and unwavering faith in her life. The first time I was truly aware of it (although I'm sure I witnessed it before then) was in 2000 when my dad had to undergo a lengthy and complicated surgery for an abdominal aortic aneurysm. It had been discovered a year prior during testing for something completely unrelated and was relatively small when it was discovered. For whatever the medical reasons are, surgery is not performed until the aneurysm reaches a certain size. They kept an eye on it, and by October of 2000, it had reached the proportions where intervention was necessary. They scheduled the surgery for December 10th.

Early that morning, my dad, mom, brother, and I got into the car and drove to the hospital. Surgery was scheduled for 6:00 a.m. It would be a lengthy surgery. I believe the estimate was about six to seven hours. We gave our hugs, said our "I love you," and watched as they wheeled Daddy down the hallway towards the operating room. My brother and I were full of jitters, which is severely understating how we felt. Momma was calm. She suggested breakfast in the snack shop.

We spent the rest of the day in the surgical waiting room. It was much different than it is now. Surgeries were not scheduled so closely together or so many at one time. There were very few of us waiting. As the day wore on, we became the only people remaining. As time passed the six and then the seven-hour mark, John and I began to have intense feelings of panic but at least tried to seem calm for Momma's sake. She was still quiet and calm. There had been times all day when she would have her eyes closed in prayer in between reading parts of the book she had brought with her. I never saw her shake or waver in the total belief that this would all work out perfectly.

Somewhere around nine and a half hours after surgery began, the doctor walked through the waiting room entrance. John and I stood while Momma remained seated - another testimony to how calm she was. The doctor sat down to talk to us. Tears started to fall from my eyes. If he was sitting down this couldn't be good, right? He started out by saying that Daddy was in recovery. Then he told us that there was no medical reason Daddy should still be here. When they made the incision to begin the aneurysm repair, they discovered it had grown beyond the bursting point. The large majority of people would not have survived the surgery. Due to the delicate nature of the repair necessitated by the size of the aneurysm, surgery had taken much longer than expected. The doctor had no logical explanation for its success. Momma knew the reason, and so did we. It was successful only by the grace of God and the healing touch of Jesus through the hands of this skilled surgeon. Momma thanked the doctor with a smile. She then suggested we all go downstairs to eat dinner until we could see Daddy. I didn't see a single tear escape her eyes to fall upon her cheeks. She knew everything was going to be fine. She knew she would be seeing Daddy awake and on the road to recovery once he was back in his room. She *knew.* She had absolute faith.

That absolute faith continued as Daddy recovered first in the ICU, then in a regular room, and back to the ICU again. The incision from the surgery was huge. I will spare you the details of it. In order to repair the aneurysm, they had to remove one of his kidneys from his body and then return it once the repair was made. The kidney did not want to function once it was returned to his body. He ended up in kidney failure, which would require dialysis.

They returned him to the ICU, and the following day sent him to the kidney center for dialysis. Shortly after beginning, he had a Type A reaction to the dialysis. Type A reactions are severe and can lead to cardiac arrest or worse. Dialysis was no longer an option. Instead, he was returned to his room and stabilized. He would begin to receive blood transfusions to help raise his red cell count. This treatment for his kidney failure would take time, patience, and - you got it - absolute and unwavering faith.

Thankfully, Momma had an abundance and plenty for all of us. Daddy returned home to recuperate after his lengthy hospital stay. I am very happy to say that, 21 years later, he is still with us.

The absolute and unwavering faith of our mother would be evident many more times between then and now. Momma, now residing in heaven, still shares her absolute and unwavering faith with us every day. The light of example she set before us lives in each of us.

I long for the day I have reached the maturity of absolute and unwavering faith. I'm not quite there yet - not even close in my opinion - but thankfully I am further along that path than I used to be. I do believe that much of that maturity comes from seeing God work in impossible situations, making all of them possible. In my life I have seen healing of physical, mental, and emotional illnesses among those I love, restoration of treasured relationships once thought beyond broken, the life of my son spared from critical circumstances, and the seemingly improbable reconciliation of my marriage after five years of separation in the early 1990s. These things, along with much more inconsequential ones, have stretched, grown, and bolstered my faith in Father God who loves us and has a plan for each of us.

I pray that everyone has examples of great faith in their lives. If for some reason you cannot recall a person who exhibited this kind of faith for you, please take the time to study those in biblical times who relied on faith to move through life, and please remember my family's story. Most of all, look back in your own life to the most tumultuous of times and see what God has done. Let faith inspire you to great things.

"(A Hymn of Faith) Though the fig tree does not blossom, nor fruit be on the vines; though the yield of the olive fails, and the fields produce no food; though the flocks are cut off from the fold, and there be no herd in the stalls— yet I will rejoice in the LORD; I will exult in the God of my salvation. The LORD God is my strength; He will make my feet like hinds' feet, and He will make me walk on my high places."
(Habakkuk 3:17-19 Modern English Version)

Finding Your Roots

I had a really bad day the day before yesterday. No, seriously - *a really bad day.*

It started out as a combination of a practical errand and a few much-needed hours of time to administer some self-care. I was meeting a friend I hadn't seen in over a year, thanks to Covid, at a local park for a walk, some catching up time, and for her to take some photos of me for a book cover.

We ended up spending about three hours together. There was a lot of love and laughter. Our conversation proved we had both needed the break from the pressures of real life. We were both very happy to be able to provide that for each other.

Our time together came to an end and I made the drive home. I felt happy and at peace. I felt revitalized. I felt all of that until I walked in the door.

Real life has an annoying way of saying, "Hello! I'm still here!" It does this whether we want it to or not. Phone calls, interruptions, demands - they will all wind their way back into the peace you thought you had established.

This particular day it was too much. It had been an overwhelmingly stressful several months. The fragile peace I had built by spending a few hours away and out in nature with Kristin was shattered amid the onslaught. The result was a tearful, sobbing meltdown of epic proportions. I questioned my abilities. I questioned my strength. I questioned my worth. *I questioned my very existence.* By the time my head hit the pillow for the night, my eyes were swollen and burning and my head was thumping.

The next morning wasn't much better. My eyes were gritty and my brain still hurt. I did, however, realize one thing as I ran through the day before in my mind: I had questioned everything about myself except for one thing. *I never questioned my faith.*

Holding on to that one small beacon, I pulled myself together enough to tearfully crawl onto my heavenly Father's lap while desperately clutching my belief like a worn, threadbare security blanket. As I did so, I returned to the roots of my faith in a simple hymn of worship that has been a favorite since childhood. "Holy, holy, holy, there is none beside thee, perfect in power, in love and purity."*

Those childhood roots wrapped around me like loving arms. I could hear the whisper of the One holding me as He soothed my spirit with the answers to my questions.

"You are able because I will help you." (Psalm 46:1)

"You are strong because I will transform your weakness by My strength." (2 Corinthians 12:9)

"You are worthy because I have clothed you in righteousness." (1 Corinthians 1:30)

"You are here because I knit you together in your mother's womb - fearfully and wonderfully." (Psalm 139:13-14)

"You are my child - a beloved daughter of God." (1 John 3:1)

As the calm realization of His love washed over me, a valuable lesson of remembrance was instilled in me. Twenty-four hours had passed since the onslaught. The faith my mom held so dear - the faith that amazed me every day - is my faith as well. Nothing that is trying to block my path, whisper lies in my ear, or unseat me and cause upheaval can shake me *as long as I remember to unplug and return to my roots and as long as I remember who I am.*

It is the same for you, my friends.

"And now, just as you accepted Christ Jesus as your Lord, you must continue to follow him. Let your roots grow down into him, and let your lives be built on him. Then your faith will grow strong in the truth you were taught, and you will overflow with thankfulness." **(Colossians 2:6-7 NLT)**

*Holy, Holy, Holy, words by Reginald Heber and music by John Bacchus Dykes, first published posthumously in *A Selection of Psalms and Hymns for the Parish Church of Banbury* (Third Edition, 1826)

The Unexpected

       Thursdays are Michael's early days at work. He gets up at 4:30 a.m. each Thursday morning as compared to the other days when the alarm is set for 5:30. An hour may not seem like much, but it can really throw off your body rhythm. I've found that I'm more sluggish and my eyes are more heavy- lidded on those days. If I sit too long in one spot, I might just end up taking a catnap.

       This morning's rising was even earlier. For some reason the dogs became restless earlier than normal. They always seem to have us awake before the alarm does its job, but this was way before. We decided to try to ignore them until closer to 4:30, but we were unable to go back to sleep. I decided to get up and head for the bathroom. When I did, I immediately noticed the house had a bit of an icy feeling. Upon examination of the thermostat, we discovered it was a mere sixty degrees. Just a bit, indeed.

       Michael headed for the basement to check the furnace. He tried the reset button. The unit kicked on and ran for some time, and we heard the water rush through the baseboard pipes (a bit louder than usual). The result, however, was not what was expected. The temperature in the house really didn't warm much. Thank goodness for our electric fireplaces because it was too early to call the service technician. They wouldn't heat the entire house, but our bedroom and the living room would at least be warmer.

The service technician arrived in the late morning. He checked the furnace and the baseboards. He didn't find anything out of the ordinary with the exception that it seemed the igniter was slightly delayed when the system started. Phone calls were made, support weighed in, and the decision was made to replace the igniter and nozzle. Thankfully, this was all covered under our service contract.

He then discovered two other problems that were unrelated to the furnace itself. First, one of our expansion tanks had a leak. It was only dripping every so often, which is not a huge problem in and of itself. However, it would eventually start to spray, and that wouldn't be good. Secondly, the system needed to be purged because there was too much air in the baseboard pipes. These were water-related repairs and are not covered by the service contract. Ah, the unexpected! You're going along just fine when all of a sudden something jumps out from behind the nearest door, tree, or rock and yells, "Surprise!" If you're not careful, it could knock you off your center and you would end up on your behind.

Life is full of the unexpected. From breakdowns like our heating system to accidents that destroy your car to unforeseen illness, there is always something for which you aren't completely prepared. I certainly was not prepared, nor did I want to have to bundle up inside my house this morning. Even the dogs were burrowed under their sheepskin beds for a while. The fact was that prepared and wanted or not didn't matter. Unexpected will do what unexpected wants to do. It's up to us to see the unexpected, greet the unexpected, and do what we are equipped to do to settle the unexpected back into its place, *but first we have to remember that the unexpected was not unexpected by God.*

As a matter of fact, God will allow the unexpected to happen to perfect our response to it. Our response should always be one of faith - faith to know that He expected it and has prepared us for it, even if we're unaware that He has. Nothing happens outside of His sight and reach, even simple heating system failures. I fully believe this happened so that we didn't wake up one morning to water spraying from the expansion tank all over our basement. God knew it needed replacing. He knew it could cause a bigger problem. He decided to see that it was addressed and corrected before it did.

The same principle applies to every unexpected moment of life. You may not be able to see it at the time, but once you allow His presence to calm your reactions, mind, and heart and allow Him to point out what needs correcting, your eyes will see and your mind will comprehend why the unexpected happened. The process could take minutes, hours, days, or even longer, but you will be able to see why His hand moved as it did in your life.

When the unexpected decides to burst through the door at the most surprising or inopportune moment, remember this: *it's not really unexpected at all. It's God moving us towards His purpose and reminding us that our faith in Him is warranted and will help us all get to there at just the right time.*

Speaking of time, it's time for me to write the check to the heating company. I really don't mind so much. I'm just grateful that the unexpected happening helped solve what could have been a much bigger problem. Thank You, Father God.

"You know when I leave and when I get back; I'm never out of your sight. You know everything I'm going to say before I start the first sentence. I look behind me and you're there, then up ahead and you're there, too—your reassuring presence, coming and going. This is too much, too wonderful—I can't take it all in!"
(Psalm 139:3-6 The Message)

"I myself will prepare your way, leveling mountains and hills. I will break down bronze gates and smash their iron bars. I will give you treasures from dark, secret places; then you will know that I am the LORD and that the God of Israel has called you by name."
(Isaiah 45:2-3 Good News Translation)

Faith in the Seasons

It's difficult on these cold winter mornings to find motivation. With a temperature of 19 degrees and a feels-like temperature of 16, grey skies that almost completely blend into the snow-covered landscape, and more snow in the forecast, I have the most urgent need to crawl back under the covers and place the pillow over my head. While I once looked forward to the occasional snowfall and colder temps, I am no longer a winter person. I spend most of my days between the first of December and the end of March longing for spring, with its little green buds becoming prominent on the trees and daffodils poking through the ground with the promise of bright yellow blooms to come.

Winter for me is just another season to muddle through until the good stuff arrives. That goes for the drearier seasons of life as well. I get the same urge during life's grey days as I do with nature's - under the blankets, cover my head, wake me when the beautiful brightness gets here - but as I sit here in my home office looking out the window at the finches, chickadees, tufted titmice, nuthatches, and cardinals vying for a spot at my feeders this morning, I wonder just how many bright spots of color I miss in both nature and life while covering my head and trying to avoid the dinge.

Although I try desperately to avoid the cold and grey, I know it's needed for the next season to be successful. The deep blanket of snow that now covers the ground is also insulating what's underneath and will water it to prepare it for spring and summer's successful blossoms. It is the same in life. The seemingly cold season we may be living in right now is the same season that will bring nurturing, beauty, and maturity to the next. We might not see it that way while in its midst, but that doesn't negate the truth. For this reason alone, we should be greeting it with eyes opened widely and hearts that are expectant of the flashes of color that are sure to present themselves amid the dingy landscape.

Let's remember to allow ourselves to grow and thrive in our grey seasons just as the daffodil shoots grow beneath snow's blanket. Just as they do, we will be reaching for the warmth of the sun before very long. Let's not hide from the dinge but welcome it, knowing a fresh covering of snow will send it packing as it melts into us and leads to spring. We will emerge stronger in body, mind, and spirit. Our faith will have sprouted new growth. And one more piece of the artwork that is our lives will present its beauty.

No more hiding under the covers and pillows - just standing firm in the open field of life with faces and arms raised toward the Son we know is there.

"Sing out with songs of thanksgiving to the Lord! Let's sing our praises with melodies overflowing! He fills the sky with clouds, sending showers to water the earth so that the grass springs up on the mountain fields and the earth produces food for man. All the birds and beasts who cry with hunger to him are fed from his hands. He blankets the earth with glistening snow, painting the landscape with frost. Sleet and hail fall from the sky, causing waters to freeze before winter's

386

icy blast. Then he speaks his word and it all melts away; as the warm spring winds blow, the streams begin to flow."
(Psalm 147:7-9, 16-18 The Passion Translation)

A Beacon of Faith

I love lighthouses. Part of that comes from replicas being scattered throughout our home when I was growing up; my mom's collection was a sizeable one. The other part of that love stems from the simple beauty of those cylindrical structures towering over rocky coastlines as waves crash below them. Their practical purpose as a beacon of safe passage for ships also bears an aura of the romantic, and at heart I am a hopeless romantic. The light shining into the darkness of night, the thickening fog rising from the waters, or the low-hanging clouds of impending storms touches some part of me deep inside. It brings pictures to mind of wives and children running to the docks to greet husbands and fathers as boats come to shore - the warmth of loving embraces, radiance of smiling faces and hearts filled with gratitude casting almost as much light as the beacon above them.

We have that same kind of light guiding us throughout life. We know how treacherous the seas of our lives can be when darkness pervades and storms threaten. We know how lost we would be without a beacon to see us through the ebony depths as well as the rocky shallows. We grasp the faith that shows us the Light in the black, murky waters and hold on for dear life. How thankful I am for the grace that gives me faith! Oh, the gratitude that fills my heart for Jesus Christ, the Lighthouse that keeps me from being dashed upon the rocks!

Our world is living in so much darkness today. So many lack faith, and its existence is threatened in those who possess it but whose grasp on it is fragile. The craggy coast is hungry for ships gone astray in the storms. The very lives of humanity are at stake.

We can help. We can be lighthouses for those who have lost their way. We can point them to the Beacon of our faith where they can be brought safely to shore and find refuge. Jesus was hung on a cross to be Life and Light for the world below. He was raised to life again to shine brightly so that all could find their way to Him. We have been raised to life through Him to point others to His light and grace.

The hopeless romantic in me is stirred once again. I remember falling in love with Jesus the first time. I remember feeling found instead of lost, held instead of aimlessly floating, safe instead of threatened, and loved - oh, so loved. Do you remember those feelings? I want others to feel all of that. I want to see them have safe passage to the shore of God's gracious and merciful heart. And I want to help them in some way.

Father, mold us in the image of Jesus. Shape our hearts to spread His love. Use us as lighthouses here on earth to point everyone to the perfect Lighthouse. Help us help others to see Jesus. Amen.

"We have seen and heard everything He did in the land of the Jews and in Jerusalem. And yet they killed Him by nailing Him to a cross. God raised Him to life on the third day and made Him to be seen." **(Acts 10:39-40 New Life Version)**

Faith in Action

We all know that faith is the hope for things not seen. We also know that even a tiny amount of faith can do great things. Faith is a gift to us from God because of His gracious nature. He will give us exactly the measure we need at any given time, allowing circumstances to come into our lives to strengthen and build on His initial gift to us.

We cannot earn His grace. Nothing we can do, no matter how good it is in the eyes of the world, no matter how kind, loving, or generous, can buy our way into His good favor. Yet faith must be acted upon to keep it thriving. No one wants to carry around dead faith. We might not feel like doing anything, even though we know we should. It might not be a good moment, day, week, month, or year for us. We might be tired. We might be depressed. We might be _____. Fill in the blank. It doesn't matter. The opportunity to show our faith through our actions is going to arise no matter how we feel, where we are, or what we're going through at the time.

A family friend who had just lost a loved one called me recently. She had some clothing and toiletries to be donated for the homeless. This act of working out her faith astounded me. Her loss was still fresh. Her mourning had just begun. Yet she pushed all of that aside to reach out to others in the love of Christ and share her faith.

As I helped her pack the items into a bin, tears welled up in her eyes multiple times. I gently explained that we didn't need to do this at this exact moment. There was plenty of time on another day when she was feeling less stressed and had had time to process her emotions. That way she could be sure there weren't items she wanted to keep rather than donate. I assured her that it would be okay to do so.

Her reply floored me.

"I don't want to be selfish."

Selfish? If anyone had a right to a little selfishness right now, it was her. I answered her with a shaky voice and my own tears threatening.

"You're not being selfish. There are things here that hold loving memories for you."

Again, her words struck deep within me.

"There are so many who need these things much, much more."

Faith in action. Even in the depths of her grief she knew God would provide whatever she lacked, be it peace, joy, or comfort to be found in some memorable item.

My heart broke and swelled at the same time. This woman who was suffering loss was still thinking about the losses and needs of others. She was loving with a whole heart even though her heart had been shattered. She was allowing God to shine through her current darkness to bring His light to others.

Shouldn't we all be doing the same - no matter where we are in our lives?

Shouldn't we all be examples of faith in action?

It is my prayer that we all answer those questions with a resounding, "Yes!"

"Share your food with everyone who is hungry; share your home with the poor and homeless. Give clothes to those in need; don't turn away your relatives. Then your light will shine like the dawning sun, and you will quickly be healed. Your honesty will protect you as you advance, and the glory of the Lord will defend you from behind."
(Isaiah 58:7-8 CEV)

In Conclusion:
Musings on 2020 and Life in General

We went into this year with hopes, dreams, plans, and expectations. As we all know now, hopes and dreams changed, plans were foregone, and expectations didn't even come close to being exceeded. That might sound like a complaint, and perhaps it is. As I write this, however, I am simply looking at it as a statement of fact. Within that statement of fact is this simple truth: hope does not disappoint no matter how appearances seem to indicate differently.

"There's more to come: We continue to shout our praise even when we're hemmed in with troubles, because we know how troubles can develop passionate patience in us, and how that patience in turn forges the tempered steel of virtue, keeping us alert for whatever God will do next. In alert expectancy such as this, we're never left feeling shortchanged. Quite the contrary—we can't round up enough containers to hold everything God generously pours into our lives through the Holy Spirit!"
(Romans 5:3-5 The Message)

I believe with my whole heart that God decided we needed to adjust our focus, our goals, and our attitudes. All of us, in one way or another, had become so single mindedly intent on living life on our terms, focusing solely on our desires, and dreaming only for our betterment and not that of others. As we planned our goals and blindly set out to pursue them, we became oblivious to the love and grace poured out into our lives that we were supposed to pour into the lives of others. God saw this path we had meandered upon outside of His will, and knowing we needed a time of redirection, stopped us in our tracks. He wanted us to think about what we were doing. He wanted us to focus our eyes, hearts, and thoughts heavenward. He wanted us to remember what was important.

"Therefore, since we are surrounded by such a great cloud of witnesses, let us throw off everything that hinders and the sin that so easily entangles. And let us run with perseverance the race marked out for us, fixing our eyes on Jesus, the pioneer and perfecter of faith. For the joy set before him he endured the cross, scorning its shame, and sat down at the right hand of the throne of God. Consider him who endured such opposition from sinners, so that you will not grow weary and lose heart." **(Hebrews 12:1-3 NIV)**

What have we learned from all of this? What wisdom have we gleaned and put to good use? What redeeming qualities have we gained or regained that we will carry forward? While some answers may be the same for all of us, some answers also will be different. Some of those answers we might not like. Being made aware of our errors is uncomfortable. Admitting them is humbling. Correcting them is difficult - if we try to correct them on our own. In particular, trading self-serving hopes, dreams, plans, and goals for the good of human kind, or at least the human kind in our circles, and for the purpose of almighty God creates a paroxysm of utter despair in our hearts. It's not that we want to be selfish. It's our basic human nature. Okay, yes, it's that we want to be selfish. We want to scream, "What about me?" We want to throw that tantrum, kick, scream, and cry. Some of us have.

"If we say we have no sin, we are deceiving ourselves and the truth is not in us. If we confess our sins, He is faithful and righteous to forgive our sins and purify us from all unrighteousness."
(1 John 1:8-9 Tree of Life)

Another lesson learned has been the lesson of contentment. We had to rethink where and how we spent our time. Stay-at-home orders and business shutdowns meant we were within our own walls with our families. We didn't run out for dinner with friends or a shopping trip just for fun when we didn't really need anything. Those with children balanced working from home and schooling from home as well as the need to see that children had activities to keep them occupied during times where they would normally be at a playdate or running at the local playground with friends. We traded our going-out clothes for our staying-in clothes. For those used to dining out several times a week, home cooking became a new thing. A change of scenery meant moving to a different room or going outdoors for a walk or to play with the kids and/or dogs in the yard. For some like me, we learned to be content with our concern and the practical steps we could take while our spouses worked as essential workers with the public. We learned, as the Apostle Paul wrote, to be "content in every situation," whether that meant being content to be out of work and at home with family, home with family instead of out with friends, donning a mask when running necessary errands, attending worship services online, or catching up with those we love via telephone, Zoom, or social media instead of in person. We learned contentment, even when it meant not kissing our loved one hello as they came in the door, making sure they didn't touch anything, and almost running for a hot shower to wash away any contaminants - while we carried the can of Lysol™ spray behind them, disinfecting in their wake. Those who couldn't or wouldn't learn the lesson of contentment found even more difficulty in dealing with day-to-day life during a public health crisis.

"Not that I was ever in need, for I have learned how to be content with whatever I have. I know how to live on almost nothing or with everything. I have learned the secret of living in every situation, whether it is with a full stomach or empty, with plenty or little. For I can do everything through Christ, who gives me strength." **(Philippians 4:11:13 NLT)**

We learned to hold our tongues. It was harder for some of us than others. I admit there have been times I have not been able to hold mine. Reading articles and social media posts from those who were convinced this was a hoax of some sort and those who simply refused to respect the health of others got under my skin, especially since Michael was out in the world every day making sure fresh food was stocked and available for purchase at the risk of himself and his family. Having relatives who work in hospitals - one as a chaplain whose job it has been to hold the hands of those who were dying without family members allowed to be present - and then go home to their spouses and children worried about taking this illness home with them has put me on edge with those who treat this illness with such a cavalier attitude. Seeing friends go through the death of a loved one has been especially heartbreaking. Watching this virus ravage my own family loosened my tongue further than I ever though it could be loosened. The first lesson for me was to vent my anger and fear to Jesus instead of the public. The second lesson has been to realize that I cannot change people, but I can remove myself from their lives for my own physical, mental, and emotional health if it needs to be done.

"Conduct yourselves wisely toward outsiders, making the most of the time. Let your speech always be gracious, seasoned with salt, so that you may know how you ought to answer everyone."
(Colossians 4:5-6 RSV)

We learned to communicate our love for each other. I've always tried to make sure that those I care about know how much I love them. This year has brought those three words - "I love you" - even more to the forefront. While I already said them frequently, I say them even more now. Besides the words, I show it even more now. I send cards, emails, and private and text messages. I make phone calls. I find out if anyone is in need of any help that I might be able to give. I keep in touch because I need the people I love to know how I feel and that I'm close by should they need me, even if it's through a window or as a porch drop-off.

"A new commandment I give to you, that you love one another; as I have loved you, that you also love one another. By this all will know that you are My disciples, if you have love for one another."
(John 13:34-35 NKJV)

We learned that we cannot do any of this alone. In cliches - no man (or woman) is an island; it takes a village; I get by with a little help from my friends. Mostly, we cannot do this without the sovereign God of all creation pouring His grace, mercy, love, and healing upon us each and every day, or without relying on the strength only He can give. I learned that He will not leave nor forsake me. He will provide for all of my needs and those of my family and friends. He has a plan, even if I don't understand what it is. He will walk beside me, uphold me in His mighty right hand, and set me in a firm place. After our family battles with the virus in November and the beginning of December, I am surer of all of this than ever. Two of us battled Covid at home while two others were rushed to the hospital. Prayers were lifted, needed items dropped off, calls made offering help and asking for updates, financial help offered, and long-distance hand holding, shoulder and ear lending, hug giving, and love proclaiming ensued.

"God is our safe place and our strength. He is always our help when we are in trouble. So we will not be afraid, even if the earth is shaken and the mountains fall into the center of the sea, and even if its waters go wild with storm and the mountains shake with its action. There is a river whose waters make glad the city of God, the holy place where the Most High lives. God is in the center of her. She will not be moved. God will help her when the morning comes."
(Psalm 46:1-5 New Life Version)

We learned to be thankful because we are *always* blessed - even when it doesn't seem so. We have been blessed by God's ever-present hand in our lives. We have been blessed by His healing. We have been blessed by His provision. We have been blessed by each loving friend He has made known to us during this time and by His wisdom, discernment, and direction. We have been blessed by my dad's health and safety throughout this year. We have been blessed by family - the best family we could ever ask to have in our lives - and the addition of a new family member back in April in the form of a great-grandson. Even without these things, we are blessed. Every day is a blessing no matter what it holds. *Every day is blessed simply because it is.* And so, we are thankful for all of it. Nothing happens without God's allowance and orchestration, and He knows what He's doing; trust me. Even more, trust Him.

"'For My thoughts are not your thoughts, nor are your ways My ways,' declares the LORD. 'For as the heavens are higher than the earth, so are My ways higher than your ways and My thoughts than your thoughts. For as the rain and the snow come down from heaven, and do not return there without watering the earth and making it produce and sprout, and providing seed to the sower and bread to the eater; so will My word be which goes out of My mouth; it will not return to Me empty, without accomplishing what I desire, and without succeeding in the purpose for which I sent it.'"
(Isaiah 55:8-11 NASB)

All of these things apply even in years that are not like 2020. Our hopes, dreams, expectations, and goals should never be just for ourselves. We should always seek God's purpose and be humble enough to consider others before and then along with ourselves. We need to be sure our focus is heavenward and not earthbound. Keeping our eyes on Jesus will tell us what we need to do and how we need to do it. We need to have the obedience to stop and change our paths and trust that God knows what is best. We need to be content with what we have, where we are, and what we're able to do until God says it's time to move forward, gain more, and do more. We need to remember what's important - God, loving *all* others, faith, family, and extended family including those not by blood but chosen. We need to measure our words, season our speech with love and kindness, and remove harmful influences from our lives unless our Father tells us to keep them there for a reason, in which case He will protect us from the harmful influence. We need to remember to communicate our love to others in many ways. We need to accept help and wisdom when we need it rather than set out alone into dangerous territory where pitfalls await us - remember pride always goes before a fall. We need to be thankful in all things: the good, the not-so-good, and the in-between. God doesn't orchestrate things for our convenience but for our benefit (there's a difference). He orchestrates them for heavenly purpose. *We* have been put here for heavenly purpose. *We are blessed.*

"Shout praises to the LORD, everyone on this earth. Be joyful and sing as you come in to worship the LORD! You know the LORD is God! He created us, and we belong to him; we are his people, the sheep in his pasture. Be thankful and praise the LORD as you enter his temple. The LORD is good! His love and faithfulness will last forever."
(Psalm 100 CEV)

As 2021 (or any new year) approaches, it is my prayer that I will remember the lessons of 2020 and that I will look at each moment and each experience as something to be treasured, whether it is something that thrilled me, tugged at my heartstrings, wrapped me in love, broke me and tossed me into God's arms, or taught me a valuable lesson. I pray that I will look at all things through the eyes of faith - a faith that has been stretched, grown, and strengthened in the past year -

for without faith there is no abundant life. My prayer for all of you is the same.

"Celebrate joyfully in the Lord, all the time. I'll say it again: celebrate! Let everybody know how gentle and gracious you are. The Lord is near. Don't worry about anything. Rather, in every area of life let God know what you want, as you pray and make requests, and give thanks as well. And God's peace, which is greater than we can ever understand, will keep guard over your hearts and minds in King Jesus."
(Philippians 4:4-7 New Testament for Everyone)

About the Author

Carol Wert lives in Kutztown, Pennsylvania with her husband of 45-1/2 years, Michael. They have learned much in their time together about just what love, hope, trust, and faith can do in what seem like helpless and hopeless circumstances. They've also learned that sometimes things don't go as planned or according to convention. When that happens, they do things "their way," as they term it, which really means they just wing it by stepping out in faith, knowing they don't know everything but trusting God to discipline them and correct their mistakes for His glory. That principle seems to have worked thus far for them. They say this with a smile on their faces and joy in their hearts knowing that, "Anything that happens is by heavenly design. God is in complete control of all things."

This is Carol's fourth book. She considers each one a gift from above. "I never expected to write for anyone else to read," she says. "God obviously had other ideas. I am beyond thankful He did."

Other Titles from Carol Wert

- Grace – A View from the Mountaintop (2014)
- Faces With Names (2017)
- Growing in the Garden of Faith (2018)

All titles are available on Amazon.com.

Made in the USA
Middletown, DE
25 April 2021